Poems and Prose

of

Mihai Eminescu

Mihai Eminescu (1850-1889)

Poems and Prose

of

Mihai Eminescu

Edited by Kurt W. Treptow

With Original Illustrations by A. Bordenache

The Center for Romanian Studies
Iaşi ♦ Oxford ♦ Portland
2000

Published in Romania by

THE CENTER FOR ROMANIAN STUDIES
The Foundation for Romanian Culture and Studies
Oficiul Poştal I, Căsuţa Poştală 108
Str. Poligon nr. 11a
6600 Iaşi, Romania
www.romanianstudies.ro

Published in Great Britain by

THE CENTER FOR ROMANIAN STUDIES
c/o Drake International Services
Market House
Market Place
Deddington
Oxford OX15 0SE
Great Britain

Published in the United States of America by

THE CENTER FOR ROMANIAN STUDIES
c/o International Specialized Book Services
5804 N.E. Hassalo St.
Portland, Oregon 97213, USA
www.isbs.com

Original illustrations by A. Bordenache from the collection of Dumitru I. Grumăzescu

National Library of Romania Cataloging-in-Publication Data

EMINESCU, MIHAI.
Poems and Prose of Mihai Eminescu / Mihai Eminescu. Edited by Kurt W.
Treptow, Iaşi, Oxford, Portland: The Center for Romanian Studies, 2000.
240 pp., 22 cm.
Illus.
ISBN 973-9432-10-7

1. Treptow, Kurt W. (ed.)

821.135.1-1=111
821.135.1-32=111

ISBN 973-9432-10-7

Contents

Poems

Prose

Introduction

The one hundred and fiftieth anniversary of the birth of Mihai Eminescu, Romania's national poet and one of the key cultural figures who gave shape to modern Romania in the nineteenth century, marks an appropriate moment for the publication of a new collection of English language versions of poems and prose by this great writer. Seventy years have passed since the first edition of poems by the Romanian national poet Mihai Eminescu appeared in English. In his introduction to that volume, the great Romanian historian Nicolae Iorga pointed out the book's purpose: "To translate the works of Eminescu is to render a valuable contribution to the task of introducing the soul of a people, as yet scarcely known in English-speaking countries." That edition, translated by Sylvia Pankhurst and I.O. Stefanovici, also contained a short preface by the well-known English writer George Bernard Shaw in the form of a letter to Sylvia Pankhurst. Having read Eminescu in translation, Shaw referred to the Romanian poet as, "the Moldavian who raised the XVIII-XIX fin de siècle from its grave." Yet Eminescu is much more than an imitation of Romanticism; he is, in fact, as Iorga pointed out, a symbol of the Romanian spirit. It is fair to say that in order to have an appreciation of Romanian culture one must be acquainted with the works of Mihai Eminescu. This is the motivation behind the present edition of his poems and prose.

The leading cultural figure of nineteenth century Romania, Eminescu was not only a poet, but also a philosopher, prose writer, translator, and journalist. He is best seen as a man who embodied the national culture and, therefore, through his work, helped to give it shape. In this respect Eminescu played a role for the Romanians similar to that of Vuk Stefanovic Karadzic among the Serbs, or Naim and Sami Frashëri among the Albanians, to name only a few. Still, it would be wrong to merely categorize him as a national figure. As Queen Marie of Romania, the granddaughter of Queen Victoria of England, aptly observed, Eminescu was "this bard of the Romanian people whose soul embodied suffering, nature, and beauty and gathered together all that is human." Like the Romantic poets of the early nineteenth century, Eminescu strove to understand the human spirit and human nature, giving his work, together with its specific national characteristics, a universal element.

Romania's national poet was born Mihai Eminovici on 15 January 1850 at Botosani in the northern part of the Romanian province of Moldavia. He was born into a family of small boyars whose moderate wealth and social position opened up many possibilities for the young boy. In 1856, the Eminovici family, which included eleven children, moved to Ipotesti, a small village, not far from Botosani. When he was eight years old, young Mihai was sent away to school in Cernauti, then part of the Austrian Empire, where he proved himself to be a talented student, with an adventurous nature, running away with a theater company for a time in 1864. At school in Cernauti, the young boy demonstrated a wide range of interests, assiduously reading from the Romanian library of his teacher Aron Pumnul.

Pumnul was an important cultural figure among the Romanians of Bucovina. Born in Transylvania, at that time also under Austrian rule, he studied in Vienna before becoming a teacher at the Romanian high school in Blaj. For his role in fighting for the national rights of the Romanians during the 1848 Revolution in Transylvania, Pumnul was condemned to death by the Hungarian authorities. He managed to escape and fled to Bucharest and Iasi, before settling in Cernauti at the end of 1848, where he became a teacher. Until his death in 1866, Pumnul influenced a generation of young Romanians and help them discover their national culture; the most important among them was Mihai Eminovici.

The budding poet dedicated his first published poem, *On the Death of Aron Pumnul*, to his beloved teacher. The poem appeared in the influential journal *Familia* in Oradea, whose editor, Iosif Vulcan, changed the name of the poet from Eminovici to the more Romanian sounding Eminescu, a change that the sixteen year old boy readily adopted.

After the death of Pumnul, Eminescu travelled throughout the Romanian principalities of Wallachia and Moldavia, which had united to form Romania in 1859 following the election of Alexandru Ioan Cuza as prince of both countries that year. He also travelled throughout Transylvania, then in the Hungarian part of the newly-established dual monarchy known as the Austro-Hungarian Empire. During these years, he demonstrated the keen interest in the Romanian language and culture that had been encouraged by his teacher, and began to write some of his earliest poems.

In 1869, he left the Romanian lands to study at the University of Vienna. He became deeply interested in philosophy, enthusiastically devouring the works of such great thinkers as Descartes, Spinoza, and Kant. He also took part in the rich cultural life of the Imperial capital, together with other Romanian students, such as the future prose writer Ioan Slavici. It was during this time that he wrote *Prince Charming — The Tear-Begotten*, a fantastic story containing elements of the Orphic myth, demonstrating the author's desire to integrate Romanian myths into Western culture generally.

He returned to Romania briefly in 1872 and became involved in the Junimea Literary Society in Iasi, of which Titu Maiorescu (1840-1917) was a leading member. Maiorescu, professor of logic and the history of philosophy at the universities of Iasi and Bucharest was the leading literary critic of his generation and played a major role in shaping Romanian culture in the late nineteenth century. He took a strong personal interest in the career of the young poet. From this time on, Eminescu published much of his literary work in the society's journal *Convorbiri literare*.

After leaving his native land again in 1872, this time to study at the University of Berlin, Maiorescu urged Eminescu to earn his doctorate so that he could return to Iasi as professor of philosophy at the University. In Berlin, as before, Eminescu displayed a wide range of interests, encompassing not only philosophy, but also mythology, the history of religions, law, history, and even the Sanskrit language of ancient India. During this time he also translated Kant's *Critique of Pure Reason* into Romanian. Kant's philosophy, together with that of Schopenhauer, would have a profound impact on Eminescu's literary work. Despite this, he lacked the discipline or desire to finish his doctorate.

Eminescu returned to Romania in 1874 and Maiorescu arranged for him to become director of the Central Library of the University of Iasi. He also began to take part in the activities of the Junimea Society. This literary group, with its challenging motto, "Enter who wishes, Remain who can," sought to promote excellence in Romanian culture and society, a goal which

Eminescu wholeheartedly shared. Junimea decried mediocrity and superficial imitations of western society, seeking to create a healthy basis for the development of Romanian society. They also opposed excessive Latinizing tendencies in the development of written Romanian, advocating basing it on the spoken language.

It was also during this time that Eminescu met and fell in love with Veronica Micle (1850-1889), a beautiful young poet who, at times, served as Eminescu's muse. Micle, however, was married to a university professor and even after her husband's death in 1879, circumstances prevented the two lovers from having a permanent relationship. After losing his position as director of the university library because of a change of governments, Eminescu became a school inspector. While on an inspection in Iasi in 1874, he met Ion Creanga (1837-1889) and the two struck up a friendship that would last the remainder of their lives. Born to a peasant family in Humulesti, near Targu Neamt, Creanga had a gift for story-telling. Eminescu encouraged him to write down the tales that he frequently recounted orally and, as a result of the latter's influence, Creanga, the peasant sage, became one of the leading figures in Romanian literature.

Eminescu's next job was as editor of the newspaper *Curierul de Iasi;* it was here that he published his romantic love story *Caesara.* After the Junimea Society joined the Conservative Party in 1877, Maiorescu arranged for Eminescu to become editor of the party's newspaper, *Timpul,* in Bucharest. Thus, in 1877, the year Romania declared its independence from the Ottoman Empire, Eminescu left Iasi, leaving behind both his love, Veronica Micle, and his friend, Ion Creanga. His work at *Timpul* gained him fame and a reputation as an insightful journalist. He shared with his mentor Titu Maiorescu the belief that Romanian society suffered from having adopted the forms of Western democratic societies without developing the foundations to support these forms, expressed in the Junimist formula "forms without foundation."

In Bucharest, Eminescu also continued to write and publish poetry. His work culminated in his poetic masterpiece *Lucifer* published in 1883. In the spring of that fateful year, Eminescu returned to his beloved Iasi for the unveiling of a statue of the famous Moldavian prince Stephen the Great in front of the Palace of Culture. Though unable to attend the unveiling, he read one of his finest poetic works, *Doina,* a bitter, nationalistic poem he had written especially for the occasion, at a meeting of the Junimea Society.

The bell tower at Eminescu's home at Ipotesti

A. Bordenache

Shortly after this, Eminescu's health deteriorated and he began to suffer from periodic fits of madness. When Maiorescu, who published the first collection of Eminescu's poems in late 1883, presented him with a copy of the book during a visit to the sanitarium where Eminescu was confined, the poet reacted with indifference. He spent the last six years of his life, before his death in Bucharest on 15 June 1889, in and out of various sanitariums in Romania and abroad.

Eminescu was a complex personality; at once a philosopher, politician, journalist, and prose writer, but above all a poet. The range of subjects and emotions displayed in his writings cannot be reduced to a simple formula. His prose works encompass philosophy, fantastic stories, variants on popular traditions and myths, translations of foreign writers, history, and politics. The themes expressed in his poetry are likewise vast, ranging from love poems, such as *Whenever* or *The Lake,* to verses concerning politics, history, and social problems, such as in *Emperor and Proletarian* and *Satire III.* The expanse of Eminescu's work must speak for itself. Sylvia Pankhurst, who first introduced Eminescu to the English-speaking world, rightly declared, "Eminescu's works are for all time. Every line of his verse and prose is a polished jewel. His themes, clothed with masterly art in the picturesque trappings of this or that time or story, are the fundamental problems of human existence which never grow old, illuminated by a powerful and original intellect with arresting thoughts."

In the over one hundred and ten years since his death, Eminescu has retained his status as the leading personality of Romanian culture and continues to be revered in his native land. As a result, the poet has been transformed into an icon. Nevertheless, it must not be forgotten that he was a man of his time. It would be wrong to think of him as a Romanian Shakespeare, for his work will never be assimilated into world culture in the same manner as that of the British bard. It is better to refer to him, as Nicolae Iorga did, as "one of those rare spirits in whom one seems to hear, not the individual, but the people itself, united and embodied in him." Eminescu is "an expression of the Romanian soul." This is the secret of his undying greatness that has transcended time and makes him Romania's leading cultural figure.

. . .

The poems presented in this edition include some of Eminescu's best known verses, together with some lesser known, but important and interesting ones. In the English version of *Eve on the Hill* the translator, Petre Grimm, chose to leave out the third stanza of the poem, as well as six stanzas from *Lucifer.* In addition, in his translation of Eminescu's masterpiece *Lucifer* he uses the name "Lucifer" with its Latin meaning "Morning Star," or "Hyperion." One of the translations, *Emperor and Proletarian,* is from the Pankhurst-Stefanovici edition of 1930, the publication of which, as we have previously mentioned, marked the first attempt at making Eminescu's poetry known in the English-speaking world.

This edition of poems and prose of Mihai Eminescu is dedicated to the memory of Irina Andone (1968-1998), a talented, young poet from Iasi and my co-translator on several of the English versions of Eminescu's poems presented in this collection. Also included are several translations by Petre Grimm (1888-1944), the founder and head of the English Department at the University of Cluj, and one of the finest translators ever of Eminescu's poems into English. In his book of translations of Eminescu's poetry published in 1938, he stated, "Eminescu's poems are in Romanian perfect symphonies owing to the poet's masterly handing of all the musical possibilities of his language. Very much of this is lost in the translations, though we kept as close to the original text as possible and especially respected throughout the original form." His words hold true for the translations presented in this volume as well.

Kurt W. Treptow

Poems

Mihai Eminescu

A. Bordenache

Doina

From Tisa to Dniester's tide
All Romanians to me cried,
That they could no longer dwell
Amidst the foreign swell.
From Hotin until the sea
Rides Muscovite cavalry,
On the way they're always seen
From the seashore to Hotin,
And from Dorna to Boian
Plague is spreading on and on.
The foreigner is everywhere
Like you were no longer there;
Up to mountains, down to valley
Enemies on horses rally,
From Sacele to Satmar
They as flooding waters are.
Oh, the poor Romanians all
Like the crab they backwards crawl;
A cruel fate to them begotten
Autumn is no longer autumn,
No more summer in their hand
Now all strangers in their land.
From Dorohoi to Turnu
Enemies in steady strew
All, together, overcome you,
As they arrive by railway
All our songs they drive away,
All the birds fly out of sight
From the wretched foreign plight.
Over shadows of a thorn

Doina

A. Bordenache

Are the poor Christians born,
Ravaged is the country's face,
Forests — our refuge place —
Bending, their axe abide,
Even pure springs are dried,
Poor in poor countryside.
He who loves the foes about
May his heart the dogs rip out,
May desert his home efface
May his sons live in disgrace!

Rise O' Stephen, mighty prince,
From sacred Putna come hence,
Let the holy Prelacy
Guard alone the monastery,
Let the saints and their deeds
In the trust of pious priests,
Let them ring the bell with might
All the day and all the night,
And may mercy grant thee Lord
Redeem thy people from the horde.
Rise, O' Stephen, from the ground
So I may hear your horn sound
And gather all Moldavia 'round.
If you blow your horn one blare
All Moldavia will be there,
If you sound a second time
All the woods will fall in line,
If your horn is blown again
All our enemies will be slain
And our borders we'll regain,
That the crows may hear their cry
Above the gallow trees so high.

Translated by Kurt W. Treptow and Irina Andone

Eve on the Hill

Dreary the horn sounds in the eve on the hill,
  Sheep flocks return, stars on their way twinkle still,
  Water springs weep murmuring clear, and I see
Under a tree, love, thou art waiting for me.

Holy and pure passes the moon on the sky,
Moist seem the stars born from the vault clear and high,
Longing thine eyes look from afar to divine,
Heaving thy breast, pensive thy head doth recline.

. . .

Tired with their toil, peasants come back from the field,
From the old church, laborer's comfort and shield,
Voices of bells thrill the whole sky high above;
Struck is my heart, trembling and burning with love.

Ah! very soon quietness steals over all,
Ah! very soon hasten shall I to thy call,
Under the tree, there I shall sit the whole night,
Telling thee, love, thou art my only delight.

Cheek press'd to cheek, there in sweet ecstasy we,
Falling asleep under the old locust-tree,
Smiling in dream, seem in a heaven to live,
For such a night who his whole life would not give?

Translated by Petre Grimm

Ode (In Ancient Meter)

 never believed I'd ever learn to die,
Forever young, wrapped in my gown,
My dreamy eyes I've often lifted to the star
       Of solitude.

When at once you rose in my way,
You, suffering, painfully sweet,
To the bottom I drank the great delight of death
       Unmerciful.

In woe I burn alive, tortured like Nessus
Or like Hercules poisoned by his cloth,
My fire I cannot extinguish, with all
       Waters of the Sea.

Of my own dream consumed, I moan,
On my own pyre in flames, I perish,
Can I rise again brightly out of it
       Like the Phoenix?

May the tempting eyes vanish from the way,
Come back to my heart sorrowful indifference,
That I can die peacefully, to me
       Restore myself!

Translated by Irina Andone and Kurt W. Treptow

Ode (In Ancient Meter)

A. Bordenache

Whenever

Whenever branches tap the pane
    And poplars quivering sigh,
    It brings forth thoughts of you again
  And slowly draws you nigh.

Whenever stars glare on the lake
    Its depths illuminating,
It brings comfort to my heartache,
    My mind begins unclouding.

Whenever thick clouds clear away
    So the moon is shining through,
It brings to mind from faraway
    My incessant thoughts of you.

Translated by Kurt W. Treptow

The Lake

In the lake of forests, blue,
  Yellow lilies are afloat.
    The lake stirring ripples white
Gently sways a rowing boat.

And I pass along the shores,
Seem to listen, seem to rest,
Wait for her rise from the reeds,
Softly fall upon my chest;

Then step into the little bark,
Echoed by the water's tide
And I'll let slip the rudder
And slide the oars aside;

Floating along enchanted,
Under glow of the mild moon,
May wind rustle through the reeds,
May shivering waters croon.

But she's not coming... solitude.
In vain I sigh and moan
Beside the lake so blue
By lilies overgrown.

Translated by Kurt W. Treptow and Irina Andone

A Dacian's Prayer

When Death was not, and nothing immortal had been wrought,
Nor light's divinest kernel the world its life had brought,
When yesterday, tomorrow, today had yet no name,
When one was all, wherever, and all was one, the same;
When earth, and air, and heavens, the whole world that is seen
Were in the deep abysm like things that have not been —
Thou wast alone, and anxious myself I'm asking now:
Who is the God, to whom we, with hearts most humble, bow?

Sole God he was, when others were not, and in the dark
Unfathomable ocean gave force to light's first spark,
He is mankind's great savior and source of happiness,
To gods gives soul and power and everything doth bless:
Cheer up your hearts! Adore him and praise in sacred hymn,
For life and resurrection from death all come through him!

He gave me eyes most happy that they may see the light,
He filled my heart with pity, with light, divine delight,
How through the world he paces in roaring winds I heard,
I heard in songs most holy his sweetest voice, his word,
And still one thing I ask him from inmost bosom's core:
That he may now allow me to rest for evermore!

To curse all those who pity will show for me, to bless
All those who make me suffer and ruthlessly oppress,
To those who spurning mock me to listen, and believe,
And to the arm that kills me the utmost force to give,
And he among all others as first may praisèd be
Who e'en my stony pillow will steal away from me.

Pursued by all and hunted shall pass away my years
Till they will have exhausted the fountain of my tears,
Till I shall feel that each man for me is but a foe,
Till my own self thus hated by all I shall not know,
Till endless pain and anguish my heart have so oppressed
That I may curse my mother whom I, of all, loved best —
When utmost cruel hatred like love seems to my eye,
My suffering forgetting, perhaps I might then die.

And if, by all accursèd, I die a stranger, they
Upon the street my body to dogs shall throw away,
And him who sets them on me, that they may tear my heart,
O him, my gracious Father, the highest crown impart,
And him who stones will on me with hatred throw, O give,
My Lord, that he in glory eternally may live!

Thus only can I, Father, sing praises thanking Thee,
That graciously Thou gavest this earthly boon to me.
I do not bend my forehead for other gifts, Thy ire,
Thy curses, and Thy hatred are all that I desire,
To feel how disappearing my breath by Thine is quelled,
And in the night eternal I traceless am dispelled.

Translated by Petre Grimm

A Dacian's Prayer

A. Bordenache

Lucifer

In olden times, long, long ago,
    As in old tales it's said,
    From kingly parents born, once lived
A fair, most lovely maid.

So beautiful and with no peer,
Her parents' only child,
As is the moon among the stars,
'Mong saints the virgin mild.

She 'neath the palace's high vaults
Her steps directed oft,
To the window's nook, where Lucifer
Would wait for her aloft.

She looked afar how high he rose
And shone with his bright rays,
Thus giving the great argosies
On ocean's moving ways.

She day by day, again, again
With longing looked above,
He also, seeing her so oft,
With her soon fell in love.

And as in dream, entranced, she leaned
Upon the window sill,
A yearning deep for him began
Her heart and soul to fill.

And on the castle's craggy walls
How brightly shone his light,
When waiting there he knew that she
Would come again by night.

       • • •

And on her footsteps, step by step,
He slipped into the room,
With cold rays a glowing web
He wove there in the gloom.

And when she lay in bed to sleep,
Her arms across her breast,
He softly hands and eyelids kissed,
And lulled her into rest.

And from the mirror, while she slept,
He shone with trembling gleam
On her closed eyes and smiling face,
To charm her soul in dream.

       • • •

And thus, addressing him, in sleep,
She said with heavy sigh:
"Why does thou tarry, my night's lord?
O, sweet my lord, come nigh!

Kind Lucifer, come on a ray,
Come to my house and mind,
O, come to light my life and thought,
Come down, come down, most kind!"

He listened trembling to her voice,
And brighter still was he,
And like the lightning down he leapt
And plunged into the sea.

The water where he fell with rings
Whirled round and round about,
And from the deep unknown at once
A handsome youth came out.

As on the threshold stepping light
Upon the window sill,
A staff with reed-grass wreathed in hand,
Her wish did he fulfill.

A fair young king, most bright he looked,
With smooth and golden hair,
A long, blue shroud tied with a knot
He bore on shoulders bare.

And his diaphanous, clear face
Like purest wax was white
A lovely dead with living eyes,
That sparkled in the night.

"Out of my sphere, so far away,
I hastened here to thee,
The heaven bright my father is,
My mother is the sea.

To see thee in thy chamber near,
By pangs of yearning torn,
Came I with my serenity,
From waters I was born.

My treasure, O my peerless love,
Come, leave thy world aside,
I am the morning star on high
And thou shalt be my bride.

In coral palaces we'll live
For long, long ages there,
In ocean's kingdom, queen of all
Thou shalt be everywhere."

"So beautiful and bright thou art,
As only angels are,
But to thy kingdom, on that way,
I'll never go so far.

So strange in bearing and in words,
So lifeless are thy rays,
For I am living, thou art dead,
And freezing is thy gaze."

. . .

A day went by, and two, and three,
And now again, at night,
Came Lucifer and shone above
With rays serene and bright.

And now again she every night
Remembered him in sleep,
And for billows' lord her heart
Was seized with longing deep:

"Kind Lucifer, come on a ray,
Come to my house and mind,
O come to light my life and thought,
Come down, come down, most kind!"

And as he heard her, lost with grief,
His light at once died out,
And in the place where he was lost
The sky whirled round about.

And glowing red flames blazed at once
Throughout the whole world's sphere,
And from the vales of chaos deep
A young god did appear.

On his dark locks his brilliant crown
Was blazing like a pyre,
As he came gliding down he looked
Bathed in the sun's great fire.

His arms like marble white did shine
Out of his sable shroud,
His pensive forehead, his pale face,
Did sadness overcloud.

His wonderful great eyes, so deep,
So phantom-like did gleam,
Like unquenched passion full of dark
And full of light did seem.

"Again I hastened to thy call
Out of my sphere so bright,
The beauteous sun my father is,
My mother is the night.

My treasure, O my peerless love,
Come, leave thy world aside,
I am the morning star on high,
And thou shalt be my bride.

Lucifer

A. Bordenache

With wreathes of stars thy head I'll crown,
Entwine them in thy hair,
When in my heaven thou wilt rise,
No one will be so fair."

"Thou'rt beautiful as in a dream
A demon's features are,
But on the way thou showest me
I'll never go so far!

Thy love so terrible doth tear
The strings of my poor heart,
And under thine eyes' burning look
My soul with pain doth smart."

"But how can I forever leave
My world, descend to thee?
That I'm immortal, mortal thou,
Dost thou not feel and see?"

"I cannot find the fittest words,
Nor to begin do know,
Though all thou say'st is clear to me
Its meaning is not so.

If thou dost wish me to believe
And love thee faithfully,
O, leave thy world, come down to earth,
Be mortal too like me."

"To give my immortality
Thou askest for a kiss?
But thou shalt see how much I love,
How much thy love I miss.

I shall be born again from sin,
To new laws I'll agree,
I with eternity am bound,
From it I shall be free."

And for a maiden's sake he went
Away for days and days,
Went on, and from his place above
For long were lost his rays.

. . .

And in this time young Catalin
Sly boy, with beauty vain,
A page who filled the cups with wine
Or held the queen's long train,

A stray young foundling, but with cheeks
Like roses red and soft,
And daring eyes to the young maid
Gazed stealthily too oft.

. . .

How charming is she, gracious God,
A handsome maid, in truth!
Now, Catalin, it is high time
To try thy luck, my youth!

And softly in a little nook,
He caught her by the way.
"What art thou doing, Catalin?
O, leave me, go away!"

"Why always pensive and alone?
I want thee full of bliss,
Come, let's be merry, come and laugh,
And give me but one kiss."

"I do not know what thou dost ask,
O, go, leave me alone,
O, for the morning star on high
I long and I must moan!"

"If thou dost not know what is love,
Full well I'll show it thee,
But softly, be not angry, soon
How good 'tis thou wilt see.

Like hunters spring to catch a bird,
Without fear and alarm,
When I shall stretch my left arm, thou
Must catch me in thy arms;

When I look down to thee, thou shalt
In mine keep fixed thine eyes,
When I embracing lift thee up,
On tip-toe thou shalt rise.

So looking steadfast, eye to eye,
So with an unquenched thirst
Our whole lives we shall live and find
The last day like the first.

So that with highest rapture love
To thee be fully known,
When I kiss thee, thou too must kiss,
And feel thou art mine own."

She listened absently, surprised,
Much pleased withal, and so
With bashful look, so sweet and good,
Allowed him, saying "no."

She lowly said: "Since thou wert child
I fully well knew thee,
So garrulous, for nothing good,
Quite the best match for me;

But now a star rose from eterne
Oblivion's quietude,
And infinite horizon gives
To ocean's solitude;

And secretly I have to weep,
I cannot stop my tears,
When all the ocean's billows go
Towards him when he appears;

With an ineffable great love
He shines to soothe my pain,
But higher, higher still he soars,
I cannot there attain.

His cold rays down he sends to me,
So sad his glances are,
Forever I shall love him, he
Forever will be far.

And therefore all my days are bare,
Like deserts waste they seem,
But of my nights a holy charm
Makes an enchanted dream."

"Thou art a child, and that is all!
Come, far away, somewhere
In this wide world to lose our trace,
How happy we'll be there!

We shall be healthy, wise and gay,
And nothing we'll regret,
Thou wilt forget thy parents' home,
The star-dream wilt forget."

. . .

And Lucifer came down, so fast
His wings grew on the sky,
That flights of centuries did last
The twinkling of an eye.

A sky with myriad stars above,
Below it other skies,
He a continuous lightning seemed
As through them all he hies.

And from the vales of chaos deep
Around him, round about,
He saw as on the first world's day
How myriad lights spring out.

How springing forth, like seas, the lights
On every side abound,
He flies, a thought on longing's wings,
Until all perish round.

Where he arrives no limits are,
No eye its bound can guess,

And time tries vainly to be born
From gulfs of emptiness.

An unquenched thirst there swallows all
In utter nothingness,
A deep abyss, where all things fall,
Like blind forgetfulness.

"From dark eternity's great weight
My Lord, deliver me,
And everywhere throughout the world
Forever praised be.

Give me another fate, my Lord,
Of all eternal spring,
Thou givest life, thou givest death,
Thou givest everything.

O, take my immortality,
My nimbus here above,
My fiery looks, give me for all
One single hour of love...

To chaos, from which I was born
To do my high behest,
I would return, from rest I'm torn,
I thirst again for rest."

"Hyperion, who from deep abyss
With a whole world dost rise,
Ask not for miracles and signs
Unheard of by the wise.

Thou wishest mortal man to be,
Like all the other men?

But if they perish, all of them,
Men would be born again.

. . .

They have their stars, that bring them luck,
They are pursued by fate,
For us there's neither space, nor time,
Nor death that can abate.

Out of eternal past lives now
What will by death be torn,
And if a shining sun dies out,
Another will be born.

They seem to rise, death on their heels,
In their eternal strife,
For all that's born is doomed to die,
And dies but for new life.

But thou, Hyperion, the same
Forever wilt return,
As in the first day thou wilt be
A miracle eterne.

. . .

For whom dost thou now wish to die?
Look down and thou wilt see
What on the wandering earth below
Is waiting now for thee."

. . .

To his predestined place returned
Hyperion, most bright,
And as at first he shone again
And shed on all his light.

The evening now was setting down
And night was coming soon,
For on the waters trembling rose
In quietness the moon.

While with her sparkling light she shone
On pathways in the shade
Of fragrant lime-trees sat alone
A young man and a maid.

"O, my beloved, let me lean
My hand upon thy breast,
Th'ineffable sweet look, serene,
Shall watch upon my rest.

Pervading my tormented thoughts
With that cold charming light,
O, give eternal quietude
To my dark passions' night.

To soothe my sorrow and my pain
On me thy kind looks cast,
Thou art my first, my only love,
Of all my dreams, the last."

Hyperion saw, from far above,
The rapture in their eyes,
And how she held him to her breast,
That heaving was with sighs.

The whole air now embalmed was
With fragrant silver flowers,
And from the trees on golden locks
Rained sweet the silver showers.

She in the ecstasy of love
Her eyes upraised and there
She saw her star, and softly, low
Addressed him her sweet prayer.

"Come, Lucifer, come down to me,
Come to my house and mind,
Alight on fields, on every tree,
And light my luck, most kind!"

He glitters, as he did of old,
On fields, and hills, and woods,
And guides the billows' moving paths,
On ocean's solitudes.

But into seas no longer falls
For new birth, as of old:
"To love but me, or someone else,
What dost thou care, clay mold?

In your narrow circle there
Doth chance your life enfold,
But in my world above I feel
Serene, immortal, cold."

Translated by Petre Grimm

42

I Have Yet One Desire

I have yet one desire:
    In the quiet of the night,
Allow me to expire
    Within the sea's sight;
To have a peaceful sleep
    With the forest near,
    Above, a sky so clear
Over calm waters, deep.
    I want no funeral rite,
I want no coffin rich,
A bed for me just stitch,
    With branches young bind tight.

And let no one bemoan,
    Shed tears on my behalf,
Let autumn stir alone
    The withered leaves, its chaff.
While the brook loudly streams,
    Flows on incessantly,
    May the moon glide gently
Through high tops of evergreens.
    May the bell's echo sow
Through the cold wind of the night,
Let above me, from its height,
    The holy lime shed its bough.

As I will from then be
    A wanderer no more,
Memories, tenderly,
    Will cover me with yore.

Morning stars that ascend
From midst evergreen's hue
Will smile at me anew,
As each remains my friend.
The sea will refrain crude,
Moan with ardor, robust,
But I will then be dust,
In peaceful solitude.

Translated by Kurt W. Treptow and Irina Andone

Of the Masts

f the masts by thousands leaving
    Shores which many an ocean laves,
   O, how many will be shattered
By the winds and by the waves.

Of the birds by thousands wand'ring,
    Many a one a grave soon finds,
While still hopeful it is driven
    By the waves and by the winds.

If to high ideals aspiring,
    Or a soul but fortune craves,
Thou art driven wheresoever
    By the winds and by the waves.

Never understood the thought is
    That the song in wing'd words binds,
Ever floating, far off echoed
    By the waves and by the winds.

Translated by Petre Grimm

Satire III

nce upon a time a Sultan, ruler over nomad bands,
Roaming with their herds and seeking pastures new in many lands,
Lay sleeping on the ground, his head resting upon his right arm,
But his eyes, beneath closed lashes, now awoke in dream's sweet charm.
From the sky down gliding gently, all in silver dress arrayed,
Came the moon towards him descending as a pure and lovely maid,
On her pathway, all, around her, as on mild spring's step did bloom,
Yet her eyes were full of shadows born of secret sorrow's gloom,
All the woods with so much beauty charmed were thrilling with delight.
All the brooks and rivers quivered with their limpid faces bright,
Diamond dust was lightly falling from above like finest rain,
Glitt'ring in the air, on flowers, over all in nature's reign,
In the night resplendent rainbows arching on the sky were seen,
And bewitching, softly whispered, sounded music sweet, serene...
Lovely arms she stretched towards him as he lay, her raven hair
Fell like silken waves down streaming on her snowy shoulders bare:
"Let our lives be bound together, come, belovèd, to my breast,
Soothing balm to my sweet sorrow be thy sorrow, near me rest...
This in Life's book for all ages on the stars did Fate record:
I must be thy sovereign lady, thou must be my life's dear lord."
As to her he looked and listened, darkening she disappeared;
From his heart sprang up a tree that towards the sky its branches reared,
And it grew, it grew in moments as in ages long, this tree
Shot its boughs with massy foliage over all, on land and sea,
Underneath the shadows creeping over all the world disperse,
One great shadow now embracing all the boundless universe.
On the four points of th'horizon the gigantic mountain ranges,
Atlas, Caucasus and Taurus, and the Balkans hoar with ages,
And the Tigris, the Euphrates and the Nile, the Danube old,
All the world th'unmeasured shadow of this tree did now enfold.

Vast expanses, Asia, Europe, Africa with deserts wide,
With their sea-shores and their harbors, and strong cities on each side,
On the seas and on the rivers galleons rocking on the waves,
And the undulating corn-fields, riches, all that man's heart craves,
Linked together, countries, nations, wheresoe'er his eyes would stray
A vast carpet intermingling countless hues before him lay.
Through a greyish mist transparent there before his eager view,
Under one tree's shadow only an all-powerful empire grew.

Towards the sky eagles flying to its branches could not soar;
Loud and victory presaging, a strong wind began to roar,
And the rustling foliage wildly in the stormy blast was rent,
Cries of battle, Allah! Allah! to the highest clouds were sent.
And the tumult grew tremendous like a high tempestuous sea,
Shouts of triumph, shouts of horror, howling now unceasingly;
But with spear-like leaves the branches in the tossing winds contending,
Over the new Rome inclining to the earth were lowly bending.

. . .

Shaken by his dream the Sultan wakened... looking upwards, there
On the sky the moon was gliding o'er the hills of Eski-Shehr,
And behind a latticed window smiling was a face so meek,
'Twas the graceful child, the daughter of Edèbali, the sheik,
Like a hazel twig so slender, haloed by the bright full moon,
Dreaming on the casement leaning stood the fair maid Malcatoon.
Then he knew that the great Prophet had imagined this device,
That in dream he had ascended in Mohammed's paradise.
And that from his love an empire would be born and wide would grow.
But its destined years and limits Heaven could alone foreknow.

So, as Fate decreed, the passing ages proved his vision true,
Like an eagle soaring upwards every year the empire grew,
Sultan after sultan followed, their green banner rose still higher,
Nation after nation conquered was by them with sword and fire,

Country after country open all the ways for them did set...
Full of glory to the Danube came the stormy Bajazet.

At a sign the way was opened, to the tent with nobleness
The whole army crossing over to the martial trumpets' sound.
Janissaries, Allah's children, spahis, with their spears and shields,
Swarmed like bees, the whole earth dark'ning on Rovine's marshy fields,
Numberless their high tents pitching, waiting for the battle grim;
Ominous the oak-woods rustled looming in the distance dim.

A peace messenger came bearing on a rod a kerchief white.
Bajazet then asked him, looking as to one whom he did slight:
  "Say, what wantest thou?"
          "Your Highness, peace is all we come to seek,
If you grant it, fain our lord would with the gracious emperor speak."
At a sign the way opened, to the tent with nobleness
Came on old man plain and simple in his words and his dress.
      "Thou are Mircea?"
          "Yes, High Sultan!"
              "For thine homage here came I,
Lest thy crown to thorns be changèd, with my will thou must comply."
"Howsoe'er thou camest, Sultan, and whate'er thy thought may be,
While we are in peace and quiet, as a friend I welcome thee.
As for vassal's homage, pardon! but our honor this denies:
Would'st thou with thy warring armies this poor country now chastise?
Give us rather, mighty Sultan, a high token of thy grace...
And magnanimously leave us, back again thy way retrace...
Be the one or be the other, what our fate may have in store,
Gladly shall we bear it always, be it peace or be it war."
"When the world to me is open, thinkest thou that I can bear
That my mighty host should stumble on a stump that's lying there?
O, thou knowest not how many in my way with armies pressed!
All the heroes bold and famous, all the glory of the West.
All that 'neath the cross was gathered, kings and emperors great did form
An innumerable army 'gainst the crescent's furious storm.

Satire III

A. Bordenache

In their shining mail, well armored, and in martial proud array
Came the dauntless knights of Malta bold and eager for the fray;
And the Pope, the triple-crownèd, all his gathered thunders sent
'Gainst the thunder that most direful earth and sea with rage had rent,
At a sign, like rivers flooding from the mountain, field and wood,
The whole West sent forth its nations, for the glory of the Rood.
And they came, the whole world shaking from its deepest quietness,
Darkening the far horizon with their shields, spears numberless.
On the land like moving forests they advanced in awful might,
By their daring galleons shaken, trembled e'en the sea with fright...
At Nicopolis thou sawest how they camped, assembling all,
To my power there opposing an unshaken bulwark wall;
When I saw them there as many as the sands are on the shore,
With an unquenched hate I muttered in my beard, an oath I swore,
Over them to tread, to crush them, ruthlessly my way to force,
And in Rome, on Peter's altar, make a manger for my horse.
And my hurricane, that's sweeping all away like dust and chaff,
Thinkest thou that thou canst stay it only with an old man's staff?"
"Yes, 'tis true, an old man, Sultan! but the man thou dost behold
Is a man not of the common, but Wallachia's ruler bold.
I wish not that thou shouldst ever come our direful wrath to know,
That thy mighty hosts should perish in the Danube's angry flow.
Yet in olden times full many, on their way all conquering,
First of all and the most famous, great Darius, Persian king,
Built a bridge on our old Danube, battling o'er with might and main,
Fright'ning all around and thinking the whole world was their domain:
Emperors, whom the vastest empires could within their bounds not hold,
Came here asking earth and water, as in olden tales is told,
And I do not wish to frighten, nor do I now wish to boast,
They were turned to earth and water, nought was left of all their host.
Thou dost boast that thou couldst conquer, all before thee crushing down,
Emperors' proud, great hosts, well armored, bravest knights of high renown,
Thou dost boast the Western powers all their armies 'gainst thee pressed,
But what urged them to the battle, what allured the glorious West?
They would fain have torn the laurels from thy iron brow so bright,

Victory for faith and glory — this was sought by every knight.
I do here defend my country, my poor nation in distress...
Therefore all that here is stirring, friends to me with help will press:
Men, all creatures, woods and rivers, everything will be thy foe,
And the meaning of our hatred to its fullness thou wilt know.
Armies have we not, but know it, love of country is a wall
That by fear is never shaken, nothing ever makes it fall!"

Scarce the old man had departed, when with storm the forest torn
Rustled, roared with shouts and clangor, sounds of arms and sounds
                                                               of horn.
Coming from the dark, deep shadows, on the green skirts of the wood,
Thousands, thousands of bright helmets, long-haired yeomen
                                                      gathered stood.
At a sign together swarming, on their horses, wild and fleet,
On the panting flanks the riders with their wooden stirrups beat,
Like a dust cloud, storm foretelling, lightly, swiftly on they sped,
Shield on shield gave back the sunlight, spear points glittered over head,
As from cooper clouds in autumn hail storms driven by the blast,
Hide in darkness the horizon, so sharp arrows flashing passed,
Whizzing, singing, hurtling, ringing, filled the air with dread alarms,
And to thundering horsehoofs echoed cries of battle, clash of arms.
Vainly like the fiercest lion did the sultan roar and rage,
Death's grim shadow grew still greater on all those who war did wage:
Vainly to arouse their spirits did they lift the Prophet's flag,
For on front, on flanks fast seizing Death did all to ruin drag;
Wavering whole troops were shaken, thinned fell down long battle rows,
The Arabians fell like grass-blades, when a man his meadow mows,
Horsemen from their steeds were tumbled, footmen beaten to their kness.
And the arrows came like billows surging on tempestuous seas,
Like the frost from all sides biting, and it seemed as if the world
To the darkest depths was falling, heaven and hell on earth were hurled.
Mircea led himself in battle this fierce storm so wildly rushing,
Coming on and on, in furry, all beneath it trampling, crushing.
Vanquished were the foe's great armies, scattered, cast away, like rags.

And victoriously advancing came the country's blessed flags.
As in wind the chaff is winnowed, so the pagans were dispersed,
To the Danube they were driven, as within a flood immersed,
That doth carry all resistless to the raging sea's wild coast,
And behind them came in triumph the Romanian glorious host.

As to rest the army settled, gorgeously the sun went down,
As if victory's bright nimbus the land's highest crests would crown,
Like a long and lasting lightning, that with splendor now did rest,
O'er the dark high rising mountains, our land's bulwark toward the West.
From the deep night of the ages, one by one, the stars came, soon
From the mists, o'er dark green forests, shimmering appeared the moon.
The great queen of night and oceans, peace and sleep to all things sent.
A young son of our bold ruler watchful sat beside his tent,
Smiling with a dear remembrance, while the calm moon shone above,
On his knee a letter writing, home to send it to his love:

From Rovine, in a dale
Lady mine, I send this mail.
Many things I have to say,
But thou art so far away.
I must send all in a letter,
Since I cannot now do better.
Lady dear this soul of mine
Yearns for all that's truly thine.
For thine eyes, sweet, smiling, good,
For the springs, the fields, the wood.
Send them, for I too send, dear,
All that is most lovely here,
My proud host with banners glorious,
Over out great foes victorious,
And with them will come together
My bright helm with pea-cock feather
And my brows, my loving eyes:
All to thee, with longing hies,

Satire III

A. Bordenache

Thanking Christ, God save my soul!
I am safe and sound and whole,
With my love I send thee this,
Thy sweet lips, sweet soul, I kiss.

. . .

Such were those old times that happy chroniclers and poets knew,
Our own age is full of jugglers, mountebanks and all their crew.
In the legends and old annals may the heroes still be found.
Shall I greet with dreamy music, with my lyre and flute's sweet sound
All these patriots who later in their heritage did follow?
Oh! before all these, with horror, veil and hide thyself, Apollo!
You were hid in glorious shadows of the past, O heroes bold!
But it is the newest fashion, with your fame from annals old
Our own hollow times to brighten, and to drape with it those fools,
Who your golden age are smirching with their prose, their filthy pools.
Basarabs, Mushats, in holy shadows stay, you noble race,
Settlers of the land and givers of new laws, you who did trace
With the spade and plow new frontiers for a country large and free,
Far extending from the mountains to the Danube and the sea.

Is not great our present? Does not all that one can wish abound?
In our throng is there not any precious jewel to be found?
Is not here the Sybaritic temple of false glories, none
But are offsprings of the taverns, reputations cheaply won!
See we not the fighting heroes, who with rhetor's lances meet,
Thus exciting the loud plaudits of the rabble in the street?
Dancers on the rope, impostors, jugglers, rivals for the prize,
Famous masquerading actors in the comedy of lies.
Does the liberal not always speak of virtue, country-love?
One would think his life is crystal, like the purest sky above.
You would not think that before you is a coffee-house supporter,
Who at his own words is laughing, a mere ape, a word distorter.
See that soulless, heartless, being, with big jaws, and swollen face,

Monster in whom all the vices find the fittest meeting place,
Swarthy, hunchbacked, greedy, wily, he with all the ruffians leagues,
And imparts to his low fellows all his venomous intrigues.
On their lips is always virtue, but their souls are hollow shells,
Worthlessness in these mere nothings, void from top to bottom, dwells.
Mustering his army's numbers, eagerly and well pleased spies
Over all that hideous monster with his swollen, frog-like eyes.
Such are those whom our land choosing representatives must call,
Men who fitly would be gathered all behind some bedlam's wall,
In long shirt and with a fool's cap: these assemble now and thus,
Making laws and fixing taxes, they our public weal discuss.
Patriots and pious founders of establishments like those
Where in words, in deeds, in gestures lewdness, only lewdness shows.
They in parliament assemble, sit admiring there each other's
Thick, stiff necks or long, thin noses, all these Greek, Bulgarian brothers,
Heirs of the great Roman empire are they all, and everyone
On his ancestors is boasting, being Trajan's great grandson!
And this mob, this scum, this vermin, this our country's desolation,
They should now become our leaders, rulers of this once great nation!
All that in the neighb'ring countries was deformed and misbegotten,
All that's stained with foul corruption's mark by nature, all that's rotten,
All these helots, mean and greedy, which the Phanar here has sent,
Self-styled patriots, so-called brothers, on their selfish schemes intent,
Babblers, stutterers, and cretins, wry-mouthed wretches, now grown great
Are your masters — yes, these prattlers are the pillars of the state.

You the heirs of Rome? You, eunuchs, of her fame are boasting when
All the world, with horror shrinking, is ashamed to call you men!
And this pestilence, these creatures with their nasty mouths proclaim
That they are the country's saviors, and they dare, they have no shame,
All the glory of our nation with their filth but to besmear
And thy holy name pronouncing to disgrace it, country dear!

In the lupanars, in Paris, day and night you have been seen
With the most depraved of women and in revelry obscene,

You have lost your youth and fortune, gambling, drinking, wild and lewd,
How could Paris make you better, since in you was nothing good?
Wearing monocles like dandies, with a little walking cane,
You came back, your heads pomaded, in your brains did nought remain
But some waltz learnt in the ballrooms, nothing else was left behind;
And all prematurely withered, with an empty, childish mind,
And a harlot's dancing slippers, all the wealth you did acquire...
I admire you, proudest offspring of the Romans, I admire!
Now you look amazed and frightened to our cold and sceptic eyes,
And you wonder why no longer we can listen to your lies?
When we see that all these loafers, who with great words make such din,
Are but chasing after money, cheaply, without work to win.
If these polished, empty phrases, all this idle talk, by brothers,
Cannot cheat us any longer, is it now the fault of others?
Too much did you this poor country with our foes to pieces tear,
Too much did you shame our nation, too much, too much did you dare
Our most holy things, our customs, language, ancestors defile!
But we have now all your measure, O, you scoundrels mean and vile!
Yes, to gain without an effort is your end, and rich to be,
Virtue is the merest folly, genius is but misery!

Let the ancestors sleep soundly in their annals' dusty book,
From their glorious past they surely down on you with scorn would look.
Where art thou, old prince, Vlad Tzepesh, on them all to lay thy hands
Treating them as rogues and madmen, to divide them into bands,
Throw them into two big houses, as with others thou didst whilom,
Setting fire unto the prison, and the lunatic asylum.

Translated by Petre Grimm

Over Tree Tops

Over tree tops moon is floating,
  The woods gently shiver leaves,
  Through branches of alder trees
Mournfully the horn is sounding.

Ever farther, ever farther,
Ever softer, ever softer,
It my troubled soul brings grace
With a wish for death's embrace.

Why keep silent, when enchanted,
I my heart to you do give?
Will you ever, while I live,
Sound sweet horn for me departed?

Translated by Kurt W. Treptow and Irina Andone

Like Clouds O'er Plains...

ike clouds o'er plains have passed the years so long,
And back again they'll never more be wiled,
They charm no longer as they charmed, beguiled
The youth, those tales and riddles, that sweet song,

Scarce understood, delightful for the child,
With meaning full, for which I much did long —
In vain surrounds me now thy shadows' throng
O hour of mystery, O twilight mild!

Of life's dear past how can I hear the chimes,
And make thee tremble now again, my soul?
In vain I play my lyre, in vain I hearken:

'Tis dumb the lovely voice of those old times,
My youth is far, my joy is lost, the whole,
And Time runs fast behind... My mind doth darken!

Translated by Petre Grimm

Like Clouds O'er Plains...

A. Bordenache

Emperor and Proletarian

On dreary wooden benches, in low-ceiled tavern squalid,
Where day but palely falters, through smoke-bemurked glass,
Beside long cheerless tables, with sullen looks and pallid,
A group of outcast wanderers forlornly there hath tarried;
The poor and sceptic children of proletarian class.

Dost say man shines effulgent, quoth one with cynic sneer,
In this dark world of hardship, of bitterness and pain;
No spark in him appeareth of candid light and clear;
His ray is dull and clouded, like this be-mudded sphere,
Whereon he ruleth sovereign, unchallenged in his reign.

What's justice? See the mighty, behind their fortune's shielding,
Erect their laws and edicts, to serve them as a foil,
Against ye ever plotting, with wealth stolen from your yielding,
Whom they to labor sentence, by boundless powers they're wielding
And hold in subjugation your lives of ceaseless toil.

With sated langor gorge they the sweets their lives o'ercumber,
Bright hours upon them smiling, their day in dalliance flies;
In winter, 'mid green gardens, they quaff the wine's rich amber,
In heat of summer sweltering 'mid Alpine peaks they clamber,
And night to morn transforming, they close day's sleepy eyes.

For them what folk call virtue exists not; yet vicarious,
To ye, they falsely preach it; your doughty brawn and sweat
Their lumbering States are needing, for their expansion glorious;
Their fiery wars need fighting, that they may rise victorious;
That by your bloody slaughter your rulers may be great.

Their navies flaunting proudly, and armies high-belauded,
The crowns, by reigning monarchs, on haughty foreheads borne,
Those millions piled on millions, in lavish heaps, safe-hoarded,
Rich vampires are amassing, depress the poor, defrauded,
And from o'er-burdened toiling of weary mobs are drawn.

Religion — 'tis but phrasing, created for your deceiving,
That by its lure enthralling, your yokèd necks ye'll bow;;
For held the heart no vision of recompense relieving,
After your bitter labors and life of constant grieving,
Would ye the curse still carry, like oxen at the plow?

With shadows vague and formless your sight they have extinguished;
By faith in last requital, mendaciously have led;
Ah, no; when life lies dying, all joy must be relinquished;
To whom this world naught gifted, save sorrow, sore and anguished
Gains no redress post-mortal; for they who died are dead.

Vain lies, empty phrases alone the States sustaining;
Pretence that destined order they cunningly portray;
To make ye strong defenders, their wealth and power maintaining,
In armèd ranks conscribing, by discipline constraining;
To fight your very brothers, they drive ye to the fray.

Unto malignant millions why are ye subjugated;
Ye that a mere subsistence scarce wring from ceaseless toil?
To early death and wastage why are ye dedicated,
Whilst they in easeful comfort have aye luxuriated;
Scarce time amid their feasting to cast the mortal coil?

Bethink thee; power and numbers are yours for liberation!
It needs but that ye will it, to part the soil by might.
Build no more walls and ramparts to serve wealth's preservation;
Or make for ye a prison, when, thrust, by desperation,
Ye fancy to life's bounty, ye also have the right.

Emperor and Proletarian

A. Bordenache

By their own laws encompassed, they take their fill of treasure,
And drain earth's sweetest juices, till sweets, from surfeit, cloy,
Calling in gay carousals and revel-sated leisure,
For your fair daughters virgin, as tools to serve their pleasure;
Their foul lascivious ancients our lovely youth destroy.

Know ye what bitter portion to ye is harshly fated?
Hard toil, wherefrom their riches they draw unto excess,
Black bread your tears have moistened, a life of serfdom hated,
Your maidens smirched and shameful, their happiness frustrated;
The heaven unto the mighty; to ye, the bitterness!

Rich men require no statutes, for virtue grows concurrent
When every want is furnished; for ye the lawyer's creed;
For ye the regulations, and punishments deterrent,
When forth your hands are reaching, for life's good gifts aspirant;
Exists there no forgiveness, e'en for your direst need.

Crush down the social order, accursèd and unfair,
That 'twixt the poor and wealthy our human kind divides
Since after death remaineth no hope to make repair,
On this old earthly planet let each with other share;
Be like a band of brothers that equally abides.

The naked antique Venus shatter to swift destruction!
Oh, fling in ruthless fury, unto the fire's fierce jaws,
Pictures of snow-nude bodies that wake the vain conception,
Sadly the heart disturbing, of ultimate perfection,
Working our maiden's downfall to lust's destroying claws!

Demolish all, unsparing, that pruriency engender;
Raze palaces and temples that crimes from light defend;
Statues of lords and tyrants to molten lava render;
Wash out the servile footprints of those who basely pander,
Fawing behind the mighty unto the wide world's end.

Yes, shiver unto atoms all pomp and ostentation,
And from its granite clothing our human life disrobe;
Cast off its gold an purple, its grief and nauseation;
Make life a dream unfathomed, a vision's emanation
That moveth to eternity exempt from passion's probe.

Build pyramids gigantic from out the desolation
As a *memento mori* from history to arise;
This is the art shall waken your minds in exaltation
To face the great eternal; not whoring degradation,
With mocking sneers grimacing, with vile and furtive eyes.

Oh, bring ye down the deluge; too long indeed ye waited
To see what goodly outcome would patient goodness get;
Came nothing...! The hyena by chatterers was replaced;
Unto the ancient cruelty was clemency translated;
Only the form is altered; remains the evil yet.

Ye'll turn then to the era of gold without alloying,
Whereof the far blue legends oft whisper to our sense;
Where free and equal pleasures all equal are enjoying;
When to life's transient flicker Death comes at last, destroying,
'Twill seem to ye an angel with tresses fair and dense.

Then shall ye die, untroubled by love or sorrow's savor;
As on this planet ye have lived, your offspring shall succeed;
The death bells cease bewailing, with iron-tonguèd clangor,
Folk, to whom e'en old Fortune, hath shown her tender favor;
None shall have cause for mourning the dead who lived indeed.

The pestilent diseases of poverty's dire paining,
And eke of wealth abnormal, shall scourge not as of yore,
And they whose growth is destined shall grow without restraining;

Until men will to break it, the cup they'll still be draining;
For none shall ever perish, till life can give no more.

. . .

Beside the old Seine's waters, with pallid looks and sombrous,
In coach of gala splendor, the mighty Caesar passed;
His brooding not distracted by thund'rous waves upcast,
Nor yet by stony rumbling of equipages ponderous;
In presence of his people, grown silent and abashed.

With ready smile and subtle, and piercing glances scornful
Probing the mind's recesses where secret thoughts abide;
With raisèd hand controlling a world in pomp and pride
He greets upon his passage the ragged crowd and mournful,
Whereto his mighty grandeur mysteriously is tied.

All loveless and unfriended, in lonely elevation,
Like ye, is he persuaded that malice and untruth
To human nature's bridle alone give orientation;
And thus the scroll of history will wind through Time's duration:
The hammer on the anvil — a tale that knows no truth.

And he, the haughty summit of great oppressors blatant,
Saluteth in his passing his mute defender. Know;
If from the world wert absent, thou, the dark cause and latent
Of mighty overthrowing, in grandeur, high and patent,
The Caesar, aye the Caesar, long since had fallen low.

Your shades, with savage outrage, that conquer kind confiding;
Your pitiless, cold smiling, no mercy can convoke;
Your bitter mind all justice, as vain pretence, deriding;
Dread powers, 'tis by your shadows, your shadows dark misguiding,
He drivers the poor and hostile to toil beneath his yoke.

. . .

Paris in flames is seething, wherein the storm is bathing,
And towers, like inky torches, flare crashing to their doom.
Through fiery tongues devouring, that rend in waves the gloom
Great cries and clash of weapons sound from that ocean blazing:
An epoch on its death-bed, with Paris for its tomb.

Dark streets in conflagration flash glares that daze the vision;
A-top the barricading of heaped-up granite mounds,
To bloody conflict moving, the proletarian legion;
Its pikes and muskets gleaming, and capped with bonnets Phrygian.
The belfries' clangor deafens, with hoarse discordant sounds.

Their arms with weapons laden, passing through vapors lurid,
The women of the people, with gorgeous raven hair
Veiling their tender bosoms; impassible and frigid,
Pallid and cold as marble; the fire of rage and hatred
Fierce in their dark eyes burning; their eyes of deep despair.

Oh! launch thee in the struggle, wrapped in thy splendid tresses!
Today reveals heroic the poor abandoned child.
Aloft the scarlet standard, with common justice blesses.
Hallows thy life besmirchèd thy sins and foul excesses;
Ah, no, not thine, the stigma; but theirs who thee defiled!

. . .

Glistens the tranquil ocean; its plates of gleaming crystal
Move each upon each other, in following sheets of grey,
O'er the mysterious forest with trackless graves sepulchral,
Their dark recesses flooding; in azure fields celestial,
Large-faced, the full moon riseth, with proud triumphal eye.

66

In gentle rocking motion, on billows quietly flowing,
With battered wooden bare-bones, go vessels gaunt and old,
In grey and silent passing, like eerie specters showing;
The moon their bellied canvas is piercing with its glowing;
It lingers as a token, a disk of fiery gold.

Beside the shore eroded, and worn with waves' motion,
The Caesar keeps his vigil, where bent unto the ground,
Mournful the willow weepeth. Wide reaches of the ocean,
In fleet as lightning circles, all humbly make submission
To night's sweet silken breezes, and heave with cadent sound.

Amid the skies be-starrèd, to him a vision wended,
Treading the time-worn forests and splendid waters clear;
Hoar locks and brows be-darkened by sorrow's night, descended;
The crown of straw hangs piteous, that idle winds have rended;
                    The ancient man, King Lear.

With mute amaze, he watches the figment of cloud shadows,
Betwixt the filmy tracery, that fair stars quivering pierce.
A host of changing phantoms across his mind swift follows;
Visions of wealth and radiance — scattered by stormy echoes;
The voices of the people; a world of sorrow fierce.

In every man is bosomed a world of dear endeavor,
Old Demiurgus vainly, but ceaseless, striving yet:
In every mind existing, the world demandeth ever
Whence hath it come, and wherefore it goeth hence, and whither;
The flower of strange desiring, in chaos that was set.

The yearning for perfection: the universal essence,
Immutable it lurketh within the hearts of all;
'Tis sown at large by hazard; the tree in full florescence
Seeketh to find fulfilment in every blossom's naissance;
Yet ere its buds are fruited, the greater part will fall.

Thus frozen in its ripening, the human fruit grows rigid:
One to a slave; the other to emperor concealed,
Covering with tinselled follies his feeble life and arid;
Unto the sun revealing his face, forlorn and wretched;
His face, for in each bosom the same deep self's concealed.

The same desires resurgent — new habits yet enclosing,
For aye, the human fabric remaineth changeless still;
The world's malignant mystery in many shapes reposing;
To none the all-deceiver its secret strange disclosing,
With longing for the infinite the atom doth instill.

And when ye know this semblance will cease with your expiring,
And after ye, unchangèd, dure all ye strove to mend,
This hasting here and thither, in anxious hope, aspiring
Fills with fatiguèd langor; one sole thought proves alluring:
"This world of life is merely a dream of Death eternal."

Translated by Sylvia Pankhurst and I.O. Stefanovici

Solitude

ear my simple firwood table
With the curtains drawn I sit,
In the grate the fire is flick'ring,
Musingly I look at it.

And like swallows sweet illusions
Come in flights and wander all;
Dear remembrances seem crickets
Chirping in a ruined wall,

Or caressing come and sadly,
Heavy in the soul they stop,
Like the wax from candles falling
Near Christ's icon, drop by drop.

In my room in every corner
Spiders have their cobwebs spun,
And among the piled books hiding
Furtively the mice now run.

In this peace mine eye distracted
Upward to the ceiling looks,
And I listen as they slowly
Gnaw the covers of my books.

Oft I thought, the lyre forsaking,
To depart and change my mood,
And to leave off writing verses
In this wasting solitude.

Solitude

A. Bordenache

But then mice with tripping noises,
Chirping crickets bring and nurse
My old thoughts, my melancholy,
And this soon becomes a verse.

Sometimes while the lamp is burning
Late, I'm dreaming without sleep,
When I hear the door-latch clicking,
Suddenly my heart will leap.

It is She. The house so empty,
Now at once is full of light,
In my life's black frame appearing
She, an icon shining bright.

And I cannot now but wonder
Why old Time will never rest,
While I'm with my love here whisp'ring
Hand in hand and breast to breast.

Translated by Petre Grimm

What is Love?

what is love? It is a cause
 Of pain so long and sore,
 That though thou shedd'st a million tears
It still will ask for more.

A passing token but from her
 Forever binds thy soul,
And never wilt forget her now,
 Thy life is here, the whole.

But when on threshold there for thee,
 Or in the shady nooks,
Fulfilling all thy heart's desire,
 She waits with longing looks,

Then earth and heaven disappear,
 And throbbing is thy heart,
All hangs on a half-whispered word,
 New life with it doth start.

A pressure of the hand so sweet,
 An eyelash twinkling, nay,
A lazy gait, an aimless word,
 Pursues thee night and day.

And eyes pursue thee, light thy way,
 Like sun and moon so bright,
And wheresoever, night and day
 They are thy only light.

And it was doomed that all thy life
   For her alone shall long,
For like the water bindweed she
   Has caught thy soul so strong.

Translated by Petre Grimm

In Vain in the Dust of the School...

A. Bordenache

In Vain in the Dust of the School...

In vain in the dust of the school,
    Through authors that alone moths rule,
    You're searching for beauty's vestiges
And principles from the ages,
And on oily pages, therein,
You're searching for secrets, hidden
And with their distorted letter
You would like the world to alter.
There is no book from which to learn
How life's preciousness to discern —
But live and do endure it so
And everything undergo
And then you will hear the grass grow.

Translated by Kurt W. Treplow and Irina Andone

With Daydreams and with Images

A. Bordenache

With Daydreams and with Images

With daydreams and with images
I have covered many pages:
Both of my life and of the book,
This since my youth I undertook.

My example do not follow
As it's filled with errors hollow,
Pursuing throughout the darkness
The spectral dream of life so bliss.

Lacking both learning and maxims,
Fantàsy without form, just whims,
In wandered lost, Oh! then it came:
Thoughts are obscure and verses lame.

And ideals, simply inbred,
That palpitate inside my head,
I've embellished them with dressings,
Such opulent, frivolous things.

All mediocre semblances
Of the Egyptian pyramids:
A tomb of stone in mountainside
With icons, antiques of time died,

In corridors the sphinx reflects
Great monoliths and ancient wrecks,
Makes you think that beyond the gates
There a whole land dead awaits.

You go in, up the stairs your drawn,
You know not what awaits beyond.
Alone with dim candlelight nigh
Does one king in a coffin lie.

Translated by Kurt W. Treptow

A Charm Obscure and Sad

A charm obscure and sad
    It binds in all my power,
And by it always led,
    Of life I've gained no hour.

It is a morning star that rose
    Out from oblivion's mist,
An infinite horizon shows
    To lonely sea amidst.

Remains forever withered
    And its descent is nigh,
When, wandering with it,
    The water's cold waves sigh.

With so many hidden yearnings,
    With so many whispers trite,
With so many tears burning,
    Shed all day and all the night.

You've prayed to it: unspeakable desire
    Out from your soul to cast,
But it rises ever higher,
    Out of your reach it's passed.

It will forever be unknown
    And it will shine above,
From past its light is shown
    To the forsaken love.

Upon horizon it is flaring
    Over desert of steppe and sea,
Without my comprehending
    Its weary charm subdued me.

Translated by Kurt W. Treptow and Irina Andone

Prose

Prince Charming
The Tear-Begotten

In the days of yore when people, as they are nowadays, lay dormant in the seeds of the future, when God's holy feet still paced the earth's rocky deserts, in those days of yore there lived an emperor sullen and brooding as dark as midnight, though his empress was youthful and smiling as bright as the light of day.

Two score and ten years had passed and the emperor was still waging war on his neighbor. The latter had since passed away bequeathing his legacy of hatred and ill-blood to his sons and grandsons. Two score years and ten years had gone by and the emperor was living his lonely life, like a weather-worn lion, shrivelled by battles and suffering — he who all his life had never lent his voice to the sound of laughter, who would smile neither at the innocent song of a child, nor at the amorous glances of his young wife, nor at the old, oft-recounted merry yarns of his soldiers grown hoary in battles and troubles. He was feeling weak, he could sense death hovering about, and he had no offspring to inherit the legacy of his hatred. He was gloomy when leaving his royal bed and the embraces of his young empress — a bed of gold, yet barren and unblessed — and gloomy when going to war with an unbridled heart, while his empress, left to solitude, shed a widow's tears. Her hair, yellow as the most precious gold, was left to stream over her milky round breasts and fluid strings of pearls kept welling from her large blue eyes down a face whiter than silvery lilies. Deep dark rings circled her eyes and blue veins furrowed her face, as white as marble.

Out of her bed, she let her knees drop onto the flagstone steps of a vault wherein the silver-bound icon of the Mother of All Suffering was keeping vigil above a quivering votive light. Moved by the prayers of the kneeling empress, the cold icon's eyelids grew wet and a teardrop trickled down from the dark eye of the Mother of God. The empress raised her shapely frame, let her dried-up lips touch the cold tear and sucked it into the innermost nook of her soul. At that moment she grew heavy with child.

A month passed, then two, and nine, and the empress gave birth to a son, as white as the cream of milk, his hair fair like the light of moonbeams. The emperor's face creased into a smile, the sun himself smiled in his fiery kingdom and arrested his flight so that for three whole days there was no night, but only sunshine and joy, with wine flowing freely from opened casks and cheers of merriment flying up to the gates of heaven.

And his mother christened him: Prince Charming, the Tear-Begotten.

And he grew as tall and straight as a fir-tree in the forest, for in one single month he grew as big as others in a year.

When he was old enough, he had an iron mace forged which he hurled up so high as to bang on the gates of heaven; yet when he caught it on his little finger, the mace splintered in two. So he had a heavier one made, which he hurled up to the moon's palace of clouds. When falling down from the clouds it did not splinter on his finger.

By and by Prince Charming took leave of his parents and set on his way to do single-handed battle against the armies of the emperor who had such a deadly feud with his father. He arrayed his princely frame in a shepherd's outfit with a floss silk shirt woven from his mother's tears and a splendid flowered hat with a band of ribbons and pearls from the necklaces of emperors' daughters, slipped two pipes under his green belt, one for doinas, the other for horas, and, when the sun had hardly begun his journey across the sky, he set out to scour the wide world, as his calling spurred him.

On his way he took turns at doinas and horas and he would hurl his mace so high into the clouds that it fell down as far as a whole day's walking distance. The dales and hills woke at harking of his strains, the waters raised their waves higher, the better to listen, the springs stirred their beds to let their ripples flow upon their banks, so that each of them could hear him and repeat his verses when murmuring to dales and flowers.

The streams gurgling below the range of melancholy rocks set to learning the love songs from the princely shepherd and the eagles perched in stately silence on the barren hoary crags took over from him the wailing dirge.

All stood in awe as the princely shepherd was passing by, piping his doinas and horas: the wenches' dark eyes were tear-stained with pining for love, while in the breasts of the youthful shepherds, lying with one elbow resting on some boulder and one hand holding the staff, a deeper, more mysterious and ardent yearning was sprouting — the yearning for adventure.

All stood still while only Prince Charming kept going, with his song following the yearning of his heart, and his gaze on the mace sparkling among the clouds and through the air like an iron eagle, like a magic star.

Toward the evening of the third day, the falling mace struck a brass gate with a resounding rumble. The gate was shattered into pieces, and the young man walked in. The moon had risen from behind the hills and was mirroring her face in a vast lake, limpid like a clear sky. Golden sand was glittering on its untroubled bed and in its centre, on an islet of emerald girdled by a grove of leafy green trees, stood a stately palace of milky marble, shiny and white — so shiny that its walls reflected like a silver mirror the grove and the everglade, the lake and the waterside alike. By the gate, a gilded boat was rocking in wait on the clear ripples of the lake, and the sound of wondrous merry songs was wafting from the palace out into the serene air of the vesper. Prince Charming set foot into the boat and rowed up to the marble steps of the palace. In there he beheld chandeliers with hundreds of candlesticks hanging from the arches of the staircases, a fiery star glowing in each candlestick. He entered the hall. It was a lofty hall, supported by columns and arches of gold and a resplendent table spread with white cloth was in its middle, every platter on it carved into one large pearl; and the boyars seated around the table on the red velvet chairs, arrayed in gold-embroidered clothes, were as handsome as in the days of their youth and as merry as their songs of joy. But especially one of the party, with his brow girt by a band of gold inlaid with diamonds and dressed in sparkling, rich attire, looked as wondrously fair as the moon of a summer night. But our prince was even more handsome.

"A hearty welcome, Prince Charming," said the emperor. "Your fame has reached our ears, though we have never set eyes upon you until now."

"Good day, Your Highness, though I fear we shall not part company as friendly, for I am here to fight you to the death, that I might avenge your evil doings against my father."

"I have never wrought evil deeds against your father, for I have always fought him in lawful combat. I shall not fight you though, but would rather have the fiddlers play and sing, and the cup-bearers fill the cups with wine, and entreat you to be my sworn brother for as long as we shall live."

Forthwith the two princely sons embraced and, amidst the cheers of the noblemen, drank to each other's health and talked.

The emperor enquired of Prince Charming: "Whom do you fear most in this world?"

"No one in this world, save God. How about you?"

"I fear no one myself, save God and the Witch of the Woods, a hideous old hag who has taken to haunting my realm with the thunderstorm in tow. Wherever she shows her ugly face, she turns the earth barren, the villages into wastelands, and the boroughs into rubble. I did battle against her, but to no avail. So that she should not wreak havoc over my entire realm, I was left no choice but to comply to her terms and yield to her in tribute every tenth of the offspring of my subjects and this is the day she is coming to collect her dues."

When midnight struck, the revellers' visages clouded over with gloom for, flying astride the darkness of the night, with wings of gale, her face shrivelled like a bloated stream-furrowed rock, with a forest where her hair should have been, the raging Witch of the Woods came howling through the sullen air. Her eyes were two stormy nights, her mouth — a gaping chasm, her teeth — two rows of grindstones.

As she came howling down Prince Charming clasped her waist in his iron grip and hurled her with all his might deep inside a large stone cask, as deep as he could. Then he rolled a boulder over the mouth and knotted it to the cask with seven iron chains at seven sides. Inside, the hag was hissing through her teeth and wriggling like a confined gale, but to no avail.

No sooner had he returned to the feast than, through the arched windows, they beheld two large waves of water rising in the moonlight. What had come to pass? The Witch of the Woods, unable to wriggle free from her prison, was whirling across the water in her cask, splitting it into two huge waves. So she whirled on like a bedevilled rock, rending her way through the woods, delving deep furrows into the earth, until she vanished into the dark distance.

Prince Charming finished wining and dining and then, placing his mace on his shoulder, he followed the track left by the cask, which led him to a delightful white house gleaming in the moonlight in the middle of a garden. The flowers grew on green beds and gave blue, russet, and white glimmers. Swarms of delicate butterflies twinkling like as many golden stars hovered among them. Both the garden and the house were bathed in their fragrance and in the unending soft, sweet hum of the fluttering butterflies and honeybees. By the porch steps stood two large barrels of water and a lovely young maiden was spinning on the porch.

Her long white gown looked like a cloud of rays and shadows, her golden hair was plaited and hung down her back, and she wore a string of pearls on her smooth brow. The moonlight cast about her an air of molten gold. Her fingers, white as wax, were holding a gold distaff and out of a silvery tow of wool she was spinning a white, flimsy, shiny thread looking like a vibrant moonbeam piercing the air rather than a homely yarn.

Hearing Prince Charming's light footsteps, the maid raised her eyes, blue as two ripples on a lake.

"Welcome, Prince Charming," she said, her clear eyes half-closed, "it has been so long since I first dreamed of you. While my fingers were spinning a yarn, my thoughts were weaving a dream, such a beautiful dream, in which we were in love. It was a silver tow I was spinning, Prince Charming, and I meant to weave a garment spun with charms and laced with happiness for you to wear... that you might love me for ever. I would weave you a cloak out of my yarn and a life of endearment out of my living days."

As she was gazing at him so humbly, she dropped the spindle from her hand and the distaff fell at her side. She rose and, blushing at her daring words, she let her hands hang down as if she were a guilty child, with her large eyes staring at the ground. He reached one hand for her waist, caressed her brow and hair with the other and whispered:

"How beautiful you are, and how I care for you! Whose daughter are you, my sweet maid?"

"I am the daughter of the Witch of the Woods" she answered with a sob. "Will you love me now that you have come to learn the truth?" She threw her naked arms round his neck, her eyes gazing into his.

"Why should I care whose daughter you are?" he said. "It is enough that I love you."

"Take me away if you love me," she said, nestling closer to his breast. "If mother should find you, she is sure to slay you, and should you die, I would go mad or die with you."

"Never fear," he reassured her, smiling and disengaging himself from her embrace. "Were is your mother?"

"She has been struggling in the cask wherein you locked her ever since she returned, gnawing at her chains with her fangs."

"I'm not worried," he said and hurried to look for her.

"Prince Charming," the maid said, two large tears glimmering in her eyes, "wait here awhile! I will teach you how to get the better of my mother. You see these two barrels? One holds water, the other vigor. Let us change their places. While fighting her enemies, if she gets tired, mother will cry out: 'Stay your hand awhile for a drink of water!' Then she drinks vigor while her enemy's share is sloppy water. So, let us shift them that she will not know and drink only water when fighting you."

No sooner said than done.

Then he went around to the back of the house.

"How are you feeling, old hag?" he jeered.

The hag, full of rage, broke loose of the cask tearing off the chains, and curled her long thin frame up to the clouds.

"My, what a sight for sore eyes, Prince Charming!" she croaked, shrinking back to her natural height, "and now let's fight it out to see who will carry the day!"

"I can hardly wait," replied Prince Charming.

The hag caught him by the waist and curled up again soaring to the clouds, then hurled him down to earth so forcefully that he went ankle-deep into the ground.

Prince Charming flung her into the ground down to her knees.

"Stay your hand for a drink of water," the Witch said, when her strength gave way.

They paused to recover their breaths. The hag drank water whereas Prince Charming drank vigor and he felt a blazing fire run along his weakened sinews and veins, with a thrilling sensation of freshness.

With doubled strength and iron arms he clasped the hag by the waist and flung her into the ground down to her throat. Then he banged his mace against her head so forcefully that her brains were scattered over the ground. Presently the sky grew hoary with clouds and the wind gave a bloodcurdling growl, shaking the house at all its joints. Red snakes were rending the black ridges of the clouds with a mighty roar, the waters seemed to howl, and the thunder sang a low-keyed dirge, like a prophet of doom.

In that dense, impenetrable dark, Prince Charming spied the shimmer of a silvery shadow, her golden hair streaming down her shoulders, groping about, pale and with outstretched arms. He went to her and took her in his arms. She dropped to his breast in overwhelming dread and her cold hands fumbled for shelter against his bosom. He kissed her eyes to make her come to her senses. The clouds were scattering their torn sheets about the sky, letting the fiery moon cast an occasional glimpse through their slits, while Prince Charming was watching two blue stars, limpid, though amazed, blooming on his breast — the eyes of his bride. He cuddled her into the crook of his arms and set off carrying her at a run through the storm. She had let her head rest on his bosom and looked asleep. Outside the emperor's garden he laid her gently into the boat as in a cradle and took her across the lake, culled some grass, fragrant hay, and flowers and contrived a snug bed on which he nestled her.

The sun rising in the east cast beams of endearment over them. Her rain-soaked garment moulded about her sweet round limbs, her visage of the moist pallor of white wax, her dainty hands joined on her bosom, her unplaited hair spread over the hay, her large eyes closed and sunk beneath her brow — so beautiful she was, though looking like dead. Prince Charming strew some blue flowers on her flawless milky brow, then sat at her side and started playing doinas tenderly. The vast clear sky — a sea, the sun — a fiery visage, the fresh grasses, the dewy fragrance of the enlivened flowers lulled her into a long, sweet slumber wherein she was joined on her dreamy path by the plaintive strain of the pipe. When the sun was at high noon all nature was quiet and Prince Charming could hear her contented breathing, warm and dewy. Ever so gently he bent over her upturned cheek and kissed it. Whereupon she opened her still dream-laden eyes and stretching drowsily, said with a smile:

"Is it you here by my side?"

"Only a shadow of me; can you not see that I am away?" he replied, choking back a tear of happiness.

As he was lying by her she reached out an arm slipping it about his waist.

"Get up," he said caressing her, "it is high noon already."

She rose to her feet, brushed aside the hair over her brow and threw it back, where it belonged. He took her waist in his arm, she put her arm around his neck and they walked entwined among the flower beds and entered the emperor's marble palace.

He led her to the emperor and presented her as his bride. The emperor beamed at them, then took Prince Charming by the hand, as though he would unbosom a painful secret, and walked him over to a large window overlooking the vast lake. He let no word pass his lips, but stood gazing in wonder at the sheen over the water with tear-stained eyes. A swan had hoisted her wings like two silver sails and was rippling the untroubled sheet of the lake, with its head sunk under the water.

"Why are you sobbing, Your Highness?" asked Prince Charming.

"Prince Charming," the emperor said, "I could not possibly repay the good you have done me; yet, in spite of that I turn to you for more."

"What might that be?"

"Can you see that swan caressed by the waves? Still in the prime of my youth, I ought to take delight in living still, but I cannot recount how many times I contemplated bringing an end to my life. I am in love with a beautiful maiden with brooding eyes, as sweet as the dreams of the sea might be — the daughter of January, a haughty wild giant who passes the days of his life hunting in old forests. Alas, how harsh in appearance he is, yet how beautiful his daughter! All my attempts at stealing her have proved in vain. Now, your turn has come to try your hand!"

Prince Charming would have stayed where he was, but his pledge of brotherhood was dearer than dear life, dearer than his dear bride, as befits a sterling knight.

"Mighty Emperor, of all the trumps fortune might have dealt you, this is the luckiest: that Prince Charming has pledged himself to be your sworn brother. Come what may, I will go steal the giant's daughter for you."

Forthwith he chose swift racers, steeds with whirlwinds for souls, and made ready to depart. Whereupon his bride — Elaine was her name — whispered in his ear, while kissing him sweetly:

"Remember, Prince Charming, that as long as you are away from me I shall pass my days weeping."

He looked at her tenderly, caressed her, then detaching himself from her embrace, bounced onto the saddle and set out into the wide world.

He rode through untrodden forests, over snow-capped mountains and when the moon showed her face above the hoary rocks, pale as a lifeless maiden, he had occasional glimpses of some huge rags hanging from the sky and surrounding the peaks with their shreds, the night torn into tatters, some glorious past turned into ruin, some castle weather-worn into broken walls and rubble.

At the break of day Prince Charming beheld the mountain range rolling down into a green expanse of sea, throbbing alive in myriads of serene shimmering waves thrashing the sea floor softly and melodiously toward the far distance, where sight loses itself in the blue of the sky and the green of the sea. At the far end of the range, towering above the sea, a stately granite cliff cast its image into the depths. A wondrous fortress was perched upon it, white as if bound in silver. Tall, brightly-lit windows were encased in the arches, and the head of a maid appeared among the flower-pots at an open window, dark and dreamy as a summer night. She was the giant's daughter.

"Welcome, Prince Charming," she said, and hurried down from the open window to open the gates of the stately castle wherein she dwelt by herself like a genius in a desert. "Last night I thought I was conversing with a star who foretold me of your coming on behalf of the emperor, my beloved."

In the great hall of the castle, cuddled in the cinders of the hearth, a seven-headed tomcat was keeping watch; when howling from one head he could be heard at a day's distance and when howling from all seven he was heard at a distance of seven days.

The giant, gone about his savage hunting, was at a day's distance.

Prince Charming lifted the maid in his arms and, having mounted her astride his racer, they set off darting across the desert by the sea like two bodiless specks of wind.

Yet the giant, tall and full of mettle though he was, had a magic steed with two hearts. When the cat in the castle meowed from one head, the giant's steed neighed in his brass voice.

"What is ailing you?" the giant asked of his magic steed. "Are you perchance fed up with your easy life?"

"There's nothing wrong with my life; it's yours I'm worried about. Prince Charming has stolen your daughter."

"Shall we make haste to catch up with them?"

"No hurry, for we can do that easily."

The giant mounted his steed and they darted through the air like a raging plague, in chase of the runaways. Forthwith they caught up with them. Prince Charming was no match for the giant, for the latter had been christened, so his might originated from God, rather than from the spirits of darkness.

"Prince," growled the giant, "since you are so handsome, I will take pity on you. I will not harm you this once, but you'd better think twice in the future!"

Whereupon he mounted his daughter on his own steed and vanished into the wind as though he had never been there.

But Prince Charming was brave of heart and, besides, he knew the way back. He retraced his course and found the maiden alone again. Though pale and tear-stained she looked more beautiful than ever. The giant was away hunting again, this time at two days' distance. Prince Charming picked two other racers from the giant's own stable.

This time they set out under cover of night. They ran as the moonbeams run over the deep waves of the sea, like two cherished dreams in the cold solitary night; yet they could hear the long redoubled meows of the cat in the castle's hearth. Forthwith it seemed they could make no further progress, as befalls people struggling hard though idly to flee in a dream. A cloud of dust covered them, for the giant was racing his steed, its hoofs scarcely touching the ground.

Revenge was writ all over his face and his eyes were flashing forth thirsting for blood. Without a word he gripped Prince Charming in his clasp and hurled him up to the black stormy clouds in the sky. Then he went on his way, taking his daughter with him.

Prince Charming was consumed by lightning and he was a scant handful of ashes when he fell back onto the hot barren sand of the desert. Yet his ashes turned into a crystal-clear stream running on a sand of diamonds bordered with tall, green, leafy trees which spread a cool, fragrant shade. Had any soul lent a watchful ear to the stream's murmur, he would have been aware that its plaintive doina was bewailing Elaine, Prince Charming's fair-haired princess. But who should be there to understand the stream's murmur in a yet untrodden desert?

Yet in those days the Lord God was still wont to pace the earth. One day two men were wayfaring across the desert. The garb and visage of one of them were shiny as the white light of the sun; the other, more humble, looked like a shadow of the former. They were the Lord and Saint Peter. They let their feet, scorched by the desert sand, dip into the cool clear stream gushing from the spring. With their feet ankle-deep they paced the wavelets up to the shady spring. Thither the Lord quenched His thirst and washed His glorious holy face and His miracle-working hands. Then both took shelter in the shade, the Lord musing on His Heavenly Father, while Saint Peter listened pensively to the doina of the wailing spring. When they rose to their feet to continue on their way, Saint Peter pleaded:

"Lord, pray turn this spring into what it used to be."

"So be it!" said the Lord raising His saintly hand in blessing, whereupon they headed for the sea, never looking back.

By the power of magic the spring and trees vanished and Prince Charming looked around him as if awakening from a long slumber. He spied the hallowed visage of the Lord Who was pacing the sea, its waves bowing to Him, as though He were walking on land, and Saint Peter following Him who, prodded by his human nature, was casting glances of encouragement over his shoulder and nodding at Prince Charming. Prince Charming kept them in sight until Saint Peter disappeared in the offing. Only the Lord's hallowed visage could still be gleaned by the streak of light radiating over the sheet of water, so bright that, had the sun not been at high noon, one would have thought it was twilight! The miracle of his resurrection dawned on him and he knelt down facing the setting of that godly sun.

But forthwith he recalled his promise to steal the giant's daughter and a knight is in honor bound to be as good as his word.

He proceeded on his way and toward evening he was at the gates of the giant's castle, towering in the dusk like a huge shadow. He entered and found the giant's daughter in tears; on seeing him, her visage brightened as a wave brightens under a moonbeam. After listening to the miracle of his resurrection, she said:

"There is no way of stealing me; not until you secure a steed to match my father's, for his has two hearts; but I shall ask him from where he has his steed so that you can secure one like it for yourself. Until then I shall turn you into a flower so you can stay here unbeknownst to my father."

He sat on a chair, she uttered a sweet charm and no sooner had she kissed his brow than he turned into a russet flower, the color of a ripe cherry. She set him among the flowers on the window-sill and started singing for joy, making the walls of her father's castle ring out.

Forthwith the giant returned.

"Being merry, my lass? Why so merry?" he enquired of her.

"For Prince Charming is no more of this earth to steal me away from you," she retorted between rings of laughter.

They sat to supper.

"Father", asked the maid, "wherefrom have you your steed, the one you hunt on?"

"What is that to you?," he retorted knitting his eyebrows.

"You know only too well," the maid replied, "that my sole reason for knowing it is that I wish to know and that's all there is to it, now that there is no Prince Charming to steal me away."

"How well you know that I will indulge your every whim," the giant said.

"Far from here, somewhere by the sea, lives a harridan with seven mares. Every year she hires a hand to mind them (though her year be only three days long) and if he should succeed in minding them well, she rewards him with a colt of his own choosing. If he should fail, she slays him and impales his skull high on a pole. Yet, even if a lad should do his duty well, she still tricks him, for she culls the hearts from the breasts of all the horses and places them into one horse and so, he is bound to pick a horse with no heart, worse than an ordinary one... Are you satisfied, my lass?"

"I am," she answered with a smile.

With his last words, the giant waved a flimsy and scented red kerchief over her face. The maid stared in bewilderment into her father's eyes, as if awakened from a dream she could not recall. She had forgotten every single word he had uttered. Yet the flower at the window was awake in the shelter of its leaves like a red star in the folds of a cloud.

On the morrow at break of day the giant went about his hunting again.

The maid kissed the russet flower, whispered a few words over it, and lo, there stood Prince Charming, as if reembodied from thin air.

"Remember anything?' he asked her.

"Nothing at all," she said ruefully, brushing the back of her hand against her brow, "for I have forgotten every word."

"But I heard every single word," he replied. "Farewell for now. I will return before long."

He mounted a steed and vanished into the desert.

In the sweltering heat of day he spied a gnat writhing in the hot sand at the skirt of a forest.

In the sweltering heat of day he spied a gnat writhing in the hot sand at the edge of a forest.

"Prince Charming," pleaded the gnat, "take me into the forest for I might also do you a good turn some time, I am the emperor of the gnats."

Prince Charming felt pity and took him to the forest through which he was to pass.

Clear of the forest again, he rode across the desert by the seashore and who should he spy this time but a crawfish, so scorched by the sun that he had no strength left in his limbs to crawl back to the sea...

"Prince Charming," he pleaded, "cast me back into the sea, for I might also do you a good turn some time. I am the emperor of the crawfish."

Prince Charming felt pity and cast him back into the sea and proceeded on his journey.

Toward evening he arrived at an unsightly hovel with horse manure spread over for roofing. There was no regular fencing around it, but a handful of wooden stakes, six of which were holding human skulls, while the skull-less seventh was shaking in the wind, screaming at the top of its voice: "skull! skull! skull! skull!"

On the porch there was a wrinkled harridan lying on a threadbare sheepskin coat, her ashen head resting in the lap of a young comely servant girl who was hunting for lice.

"Good day to you," hailed Prince Charming.

"Welcome, my lad," said the harridan, struggling to her feet. "What wind blows you hither? You are willing to take my mares to pasture, I presume?"

"Right you are."

"My mares will only graze at night... You can take them to pasture right away. You, wench, go fetch the lad the food I cooked and see that he sets about his task!"

Beside the hovel there was a cellar dug in the ground. He betook himself to it and clapped eyes on seven glossy mares, jet-black like as many nights, which had not yet seen the light of day. They were neighing and stamping their hoofs.

Having gone without a crumb of bread all day, he stilled his hunger on the food the harridan gave him, then mounted a mare, and drove the others out into the dark, cool air of the night. By and by he felt a numbing drowsiness creep along his veins, his eyesight blurred, and he fell off his horse onto the grass in a sleep of death. He woke up at the break of dawn. The mares had vanished into thin air. He was already envisaging his skull high on a stake when — lo and behold! — the seven mares came trotting out of a distant forest driven mercilessly by a swarm of gnats. He heard a shrill voice buzzing in his ear:

"You did me a good turn once; now I have returned the favor in your hour of need."

When he returned with the horses the harridan flew into a rage, turned the house upside down and poured out a stream of abuse and blows on the innocent girl.

"Something amiss, auntie?" enquired Prince Charming.

"Not a thing," she mumbled, "it's only the tantrums visiting me, now and then. No grudge against you... I'm pleased as pleased can be."

With that she betook herself to the stable and set to whipping the horses and yelling at them:

"Look for a better hiding-place next time, for hell and damnation, so he won't find you again, the devil take him for all he's worth!"

On the morrow while out with the horses, he fell off again and slept like a log till break of day. In utter despair he would have taken to his heels when he spied the seven horses coming out of the sea with a host of crawfish thick and fast on their tails.

"You did me a good turn once, now I have returned the favor in your hour of need."

It was the emperor of the crawfish.

He drove the horses home and the same scene ensued.

That day the harridan's servant girl came to him, took him by the hand, and told him under her breath:

"I know you are Prince Charming. Forbear from eating the victuals the harridan cooks for you, for she mixes the herb-of-sleep in them. I shall cook other victuals for you."

Stealthily the girl cooked other victuals and toward evening, when time was due to drive the horses to pasture, he felt his head uncommonly clear. Nigh to midnight he returned home, stabled the horses, locked them in, and entered the room. A few coals were still glowing in the hearth under the cinders. The harridan was lying on a low chest, her limbs still as in the sleep of death. He took her for dead and set to shaking her, yet she stayed stiff as a log and showed no sign of life. He woke the girl who was sleeping on the hearth.

"Alas," he said "your harridan has given up the ghost."

"Puff! She, dead? Not likely!", she replied with a sob. "True enough, she might look dead for the moment. It is midnight... and a numbing sleep seizes her body... yet there is no knowing at what crossroads her soul might be keeping watch, or what deadly witchcraft she might be fostering. Till the rooster crows at dawn she is wont to suck the blood of the dying or gaunt the soul of the wretched. Brother, when your year is up tomorrow, please take me with you, for I may serve you in good stead. I may see you through the many dangers the harridan has in store for you."

She produced a whetstone, a brush, and a headkerchief from the bottom of an old wreck of a chest.

On the morning of the morrow Prince Charming's year was up. The harridan was to give him a horse and let him resume his journey. Having given them their lunch, the harridan left for the stable and culled the hearts from the chests of all seven horses only to stow them into a three year-old weakling, all skin and ribs. Prince Charming finished his lunch and, goaded by the harridan, followed her to pick a horse for his pay. The heartless horses were glossy and jet-black, whereas the seven-hearted colt was lying in a corner, on a heap of dung.

"I will have this one," said Prince Charming, pointing to the weakling.

"For shame, I won't have you leave here empty-handed," said the shrewd harridan. "Take your rightful due, my lad. Choose one of these beauties — it is not more than you deserve."

"My mind is settled and my choice is made," said Prince Charming resolutely.

The harridan gnashed her teeth in rage yet she held back the flow of her words lest the venom seething in her evil heart should find vent out of her battered mill of a mouth.

"As you will," she mumbled at last.

He mounted his horse with his mace on his shoulder. The expanse of the sand seemed to draw aside as he was darting through the air, quick as lightning, his steed's hoofs raising eddies of sand.

The runaway girl was waiting for him in the forest. He took her up on his steed and kept it a swift gallop.

Night had flooded its chill black air over the earth.

"My back is burning," the girl cried out.

Prince Charming glanced over his shoulder. He spied two immobile red-hot eyes in a whirling green cloud, whose fiery beams were piercing their way into the girl's insides.

"Throw the brush back," said the girl.

He did as he was told. Forthwith they beheld a forest sprouting forth behind them, dark, entangled, and vast, resounding with a fluttering rustle of leaves and the howl of a ravenous pack of wolves.

"Straight ahead!" Prince Charming spurred his steed who darted forth like a curse-chased demon through the darkness of the night. The pale moon was careening through the hoary clouds like a smiling visage in a blurred idle dream.

Prince Charming kept darting forth with never a moment of respite.

"My back is burning!" cried out the girl, with a long suppressed moan after a vain struggle to hold her pain in check.

Prince Charming glanced over his shoulder and spied a big hoary owl, her red eyes flashing forth like two bolts of lightning chained to a cloud.

"Throw the whetstone back," said the girl.

Prince Charming did as he was told.

Forthwith a huge mass of rock, grey, straight, and unscalable, soared from the ground — a terrifying giant with his head towering over the clouds.

Prince Charming was whizzing through the air as if shooting down from the vault of heaven into a bottomless abyss. His was no ordinary flight.

"My back is burning!" the girl again cried out.

The harridan had pierced the rock and was squeezing through the hole in a whirl of smoke, its forepart blazing like a live coal.

"Throw the kerchief back," said the girl.

Prince Charming did as he was told.

Forthwith they beheld a vast, clear, and deep sheet of water stretching along their track, in whose golden translucent deep the silvery moon and the fiery stars were swimming.

Prince Charming heard a charm pervading the air and turned his gaze up toward the sky. Two hours away — somewhere in the vault of heaven — old Midnight was gliding along the blue on her wings of brass.

The harridan swimming for her life had hardly reached the middle of the white lake when Prince Charming hurled his mace up to the clouds and hit Midnight right on the wing. She shot down to the dirt, heavy as lead, and gave out twelve groaning croaks.

The moon had hidden her visage behind a cloud and the harridan, overcome with heavy sleep, sank into the bewitched unfathomable deep. A tall black tuft of weeds sprouted in the middle of the lake out her hell-bound soul.

"We are rid of her," said the maid.

"We are well rid of her," repeated the seven-hearted steed. "Master," the steed added, "you have hit Midnight forcing her to fall to earth two hours ahead of time, and I can feel the sand stirring under my hoofs. The skeletons buried by the eddies of the desert's scorching sand are making ready to rise and head for the moon for their feasts. It is a dangerous time to travel, for the poisonous and chilling breath of their souls could slay you. So you had better snatch some sleep while I return to mother to let her suckle me at the white flame of the milk of her teats, that I may become beauteous and glossy again."

Prince Charming followed his advice. He dismounted his horse and spread his cloak out on the still hot sand.

Uncanny to behold... The girl's eyes had sunk deep into their sockets, the bones of her body and cheeks had jutted out, her skin had turned bluish and her hand was as heavy as lead and ice-cold to boot.

"What is ailing you?" Prince Charming asked her.

"Nothing, not a thing," she said in a faltering voice. She lay down on the sand, seized by a fit of trembling.

Prince Charming unharnessed his steed and lay down on his cloak. He fell asleep, but as though he was awake. The lids of his eyes turned flaming red and it seemed to him he could spy the moon looming larger and wafting down toward the earth like a silvery and saintly city hanging from the sky and quivering in a halo of light... with lofty white palaces... with thousands of rosy windows — while from the moon a majestic bridge was unfolding itself to the earth, covered with silvery gravel, and studded with stardust.

Tall skeletons were writhing out of the sand of the vast desert... their skulls hollow... wrapped in long white cloaks woven of sparse silver yarn, letting their bones bleached from dryness be seen through. They were crowned with rays and long gilt thorns... Mounted on skeleton-horses, they were advancing in a slow-moving pageant... in long files... moving streaks of silvery shadows... climbing the path to the moon and disappearing into the marble palaces in the city thither, through whose windows a mystical music was wafting out... the music of dreams.

Then he seemed to spy the girl beside him rising so slowly... her body dissolving into the air, leaving the bare bones fleshless... and, wrapped in a silvery cloak, pacing the shiny path to the moon. She was heading for the misty kingdom of the shadows, whence she had come to earth, summoned by the harridan's witchcraft.

The lids of his eyes turned green... then black... and darkness took over.

When he opened his eyes afresh, the sun was high in the sky. There was no trace of the girl, only the steed was neighing in the barren desert, beautiful and shiny, as he was thirstily drinking in the golden light of the sun of which he was now having his first glimpse.

Prince Charming bounced astride and hardly had he spun a few happy thoughts when he reached the giant's crenellated castle.

This time the giant was hunting at a distance of seven days.

He set the maid on his racer. She threw her arms about his neck and let her head rest on his breast while the hem of her white gown was brushing the desert sand in their flight. So speedily were they racing that the desert and the waves seemed to be running, while they were standing still. And ever so faintly they could hear the cat exerting all his seven heads in long meows.

Rambling in the woods the giant heard his steed neigh.

"What's amiss?" he asked.

"Prince Charming is stealing your daughter," the magic steed replied.

"Can we overtake him this time?" the giant enquired in surprise for, as far as he knew, he had settled his accounts with Prince Charming once and for all.

"Not this time, I fear," replied the steed, "for he is riding a brother of mine with seven hearts and my two hearts are no match for him."

The giant stabbed his spurs into the ribs of his steed who, though seeing stars before his eyes, darted forth like a whirlwind. When spying Prince Charming in the desert, he said to his steed:

"Ask your brother to hurl his master up to the clouds and come over to me, for I will feed him on walnut kernels and water him on fresh milk."

The giant's steed neighed his master's words across to his brother and the latter passed them on to Prince Charming.

"Ask your brother," Prince Charming said to his steed, "to hurl his master up to the clouds, for I will feed him on glowing coals and water him on blazing flames."

Prince Charming's steed neighed his words across to his brother and the latter hurled the giant up to the clouds, which turned into a stately palace of grey marble. Two sky-blue eyes darted forth forked bolts of lightning through two rifts in the clouds. They were the eyes of the giant banished to the kingdom of the air.

Prince Charming slowed down his steed and set the maid astride the one that had been her father's. They rode for another day at the end of which they arrived at the stately palace of the emperor.

Word had spread abroad of Prince Charming's death so, when the good tidings of his return was received, the day sprinkled festive light about the air and the people gathered to wait for him, their voices hardly above a whisper, as a field of wheat will rustle under a breath of wind.

But how had Princess Elaine spent her lonesome days and nights in the meanwhile?

No sooner had Prince Charming departed than she secluded herself in a garden surrounded by a lofty iron fence and, lying down on cold stones with her head on a flint boulder, she gave vent to her sorrow over a golden cauldron placed at her side, shedding limpid tears like as many diamonds.

In the formerly blooming garden, now unwatered and untended, out of the barren gravel, the sweltering heat of day, the dryness of night, there sprouted forth a scattering of yellow-leafed flowers, the pale hue of the murky eyes of the dead — the flowers of sorrow.

Princess Elaine's eyes, turned blind with weeping, had lost the gift of sight, yet she imagined she could behold the visage of her beloved bridegroom in the sheen of the brimful cauldron, as if in a dream. Her eyes, two dried-up wells, had no more tears to shed. Her long yellow hair, unplaited, and streaming over her cold bosom like the creases of a golden mantle, her face with pent-up grief chiselled into its every trait, made her look like a marble water sprite knelt over a tomb in the gravel.

Yet, no sooner had she got wind of his return than her face brightened. She took a handful of tears out the cauldron and sprinkled them over the garden. As if by magic the yellow leaves of the trees bordering the walk turned emerald-green. The melancholy murky flowers in the valley grew white like as many shiny pearls and being thus baptized they donned the proud name of "lilies-of-the-valley."

The blind, snow-white empress felt her way among the beds, picked a rich bunch of flowers, laid them beside the golden cauldron fashioning a bed of flowers.

Forthwith Prince Charming entered the garden.

She threw her arms around his neck, speechless with joy, she could only fix her withered blank gaze on him, though she would have feasted her eyes on such a sight. She threaded her fingers through his hand and walked him over to the cauldron.

The full moon was in bloom like a golden visage on the deep blue sky. In the air of the night, Prince Charming washed his face in the cauldron, then, wrapping himself in the cloak she had woven of moonbeams, he went to sleep on the bed of flowers. The princess lay by his side and dreamed a

"They had a great and rich wedding, the likes of which
has never been seen on this earth, before or after..."

A. Bordenache

dream in which the Mother of God had unloosed two bluish morning stars from the vault of heaven to place them beneath her brow.

On the morrow on waking up she regained her sight...

On the third day the emperor married the giant's daughter.

Prince Charming's wedding was to follow on the fourth day.

A flight of heaven-sent beams taught the fiddlers the songs the angels sing when saints are beatified and a swarm of waves undulating from the very soul of the earth taught them the carol of the Three Graces when wishing happiness to men. The fiddlers fashioned lofty paeans and fervent carols of good wishes.

The fiery rose, the silvery lilies, the pearl-grey lilies-of-the-valley, the fragrant violet, and all the other flowers clustered together and held a long council in the language of their own particular perfumes as to what gems should be arrayed on the bride's gown and in what pattern, then entrusted their secret to a well-bred gold-freckled, blue butterfly. He fluttered many rings over the face of the sleeping empress making her envisage in a crystal-clear dream the attire she was to wear. She smiled in her dream, marvelling at how beautiful she was to look.

The bridegroom donned a shirt woven of moonbeams, a pearl-studded belt, and a snow-white cloak.

They had a great and rich wedding, the likes of which has never been seen on this earth, before or after.

And they lived a life of peace and goodwill for many happy years and, if what people say is true — that time stands still for fairy princes — they might be living still.

Translated by Joan Giurgea
Revised by Kurt W. Treptow

FINIS

Poor, Forsaken Dionis

nd likewise, if I were to close one eye, my hand would look smaller than when keeping both open. Were I to have three eyes, I should see it larger still and, the more eyes I were to have, the larger everything about me would look. Yet, born with a myriad eyes, offspring of some colossal creatures, their size in direct ratio to mine, they would look to me neither larger nor smaller than they would now. Imagine a world shrunk down to the size of a rifle-ball and everything in it shrunken accordingly; the inhabitants of such a world, if endowed with our kind of senses, would perceive all things to the sameness and proportions as we do ourselves. Imagine that world, *caeteris paribus*, a thousandfold larger — still no change. Within unchanged proportions, a thousandfold larger world and a thousandfold smaller one would look to us of the same size. Thus, the things I contemplate seem smaller when looked at with one eye and larger with both; whatever is their real dimension? We might even be inhabitants of some microscopic world and due to our eyesight it is that we perceive it of this particular size. How are we to know that not every single one of us perceives things differently and hears sounds differently — and it is only language, the identity in naming an object perceived like this or like that by different persons, that levels our understanding?

Language it is? Definitely not. Each vocal is likely to shape a different sound in the ears of different people, yet, the individual, staying the same, hears it to the same tune.

And, in an imaginary limitless space, is not any stretch, however large or small, a mere drop in the ocean of boundlessness? Likewise, in the boundless eternity, does any stretch of time, however long or brief, mean anything more than a suspended second? This is why. Supposing the world ' shrunken to a dewdrop and time relations to a tick of time, the centuries in the history of that microscopic world would become fleeting moments, seconds wherein people would work and think just as extensively as we do in our aeons — for their aeons would be to them as long as ours are to us. The millions of germs of their researchers would drift in a microscopic indefiniteness, their moments of joy stretched to an infinitude of time, whereas everything, every single one of these, would mean to them what our daily life means to us.

...Actually the world is but the dream of our soul. There is neither time nor space — they exist only in the soul. Past and present are but in my soul, as a wood in an acorn and so is the infinite, as the reflection of the starry sky in a dewdrop. Could we unveil the mystery to let us commune with these two orders of things secreted in our innermost selves, the mystery which the Egyptian and Assyrian magi might have mastered, then, probing into the recesses of our soul, we could actually live in the past and inhabit the worlds of the sun and stars. The sciences of necromancy and astrology have been shamefully lost to us — for there is no knowing how many such mysteries they would have unveiled! If the world be a dream, there is no reason why we could not coordinate the play of its phenomena according to our will. There is really no past — consecutiveness emanates from our thinking — so the causes of phenomena, though consecutive to us, staying always the same, are always there and simultaneously at work. Would it be a dire impossibility for me to live in the ages of Mircea the Old or Alexander the Good? A mathematical point loses itself into the boundlessness of its placement, a moment of time into its infinitesimal divisibility, which goes on without end. What infinitude within these atoms of space and time! If only I could lose myself into the infinitude of my soul down to that stage of its emergence which we call the age of Alexander the Good, for instance... though...

• • •

The reader may have rightly shaken his head wondering what brand of mortal could foster such unheard-of ideas. The ideal existence of these reflections had as their source of emanation a head covered with long, savagely irregular locks, hardly seen from under a lamb fur cap. It was a night with a fine drizzle pattering on the narrow and muddy uncobbled streets winding among the cluster of low ramshackle houses which make up most of the capital of Romania, with mud-pools splashing the unwary venturer, heedless of his deluge-proof knee-high boots with rims taking in the trousers of the man who put them on as soon as the weather turned unpredictable. The shadow of our hero grew dim in the pelting rain, which made his head look like a soaked ram, and it was to be wondered which it was that resisted the rain: his soaked clothes or his metaphysics. A dingy light was filtering out through the unwashed multi-paned windows of pubs and shops, turned even weaker by the raindrops splashing the glass. Here and there some romantic was passing by, whistling a tune under his breath; a lout or two, three sheets to the wind, breathing the fumes of wine, made conversation to the walls and the wind; an occasional woman, her face deep into her hood betook her walking shadow along the misty space like some dark goddess descended from a Norse saga... From an open pub floated out the jarring notes of an ill-used violin. Our metaphysician drew nearer for a closer look, allowing the beams of light coming out of the door to focus on his visage.

Dionis's was no unsightly head. His face was of the bluish-white soft-ness of shady marble, rather wan, yet not dry, and his almond-shaped eyes had the embracing voluptuousness of black velvet. They set to swimming in their sockets when a gentle though candid smile lit up his visage at the spec-tacle he was contemplating. What was going on? A Gypsy urchin, his small head in a hat whose stretched-out brim made it a fit symbol of boundless-ness, with boots that could take in his whole body, with a greatcoat falling down to his heels and, obviously, not made for him, was ill-using a sparsely-haired bow, while his dried-up fingers were pinching the off-key strings, resulting in an uncanny squeal, and a spindly Hungarian, his bare feet in large, straw-stuffed slippers, was trotting on the dirt floor. However unsightly this spectacle to the aesthetic sense of my wayfarer, it had a wel-come influence on our hero, who, shaken off of the high horse of his meta-physical reflections, noticed at last that the rain had soaked him through. He entered a nearby coffee-house to dry his clothes. On taking off his fur hat he revealed the smooth, white, perfect arch of his brow, which went well with the pleasant face of my hero. His hair, a little too long, fell back in tresses, yet its unkempt dark dryness made a pleasant contrast to the lad's fine, sweet, and childish face. He hung his wet greatcoat on a hook and, while relishing the flavor of a Turkish coffee, his soft, bright eyes wandered back into the purposeful dreaminess that is at times so becoming to boys, for gravity will always make a winsome contrast to a boyish countenance.

Within these smoky walls whereon the odor of tobacco, the rattling of the domino players, and the regular clang of a wooden grandfather clock had left their imprint, a few slumbering lamps were burning, scattering forth yellow streaks of light through the stuffy air. Dionis set to pencilling a mathematical calculus on the old table of polished wood, often smiling to himself. He had a quite candid smile, sweet one might call it, though toned down by some deep-rooted melancholy. At his age melancholy is the token of orphans; and an orphan he was, an existence — as there are so many in this country — without hope and of an inborn inclination toward non-positivism to boot.

In the introduction to these lines we have unveiled some of the musing to which he was wont to devote his time — and no one goes far with such brains — especially when poor — and Dionis was as poor as a church mouse. The predispositions of his nature made him still poorer. He was young — he had not turned eighteen yet — so much the worse, for what life expectations could he nurse? Barely earning his life as a scrivener, he set to schooling himself by fits and starts... and this freedom of choice in items of culture predisposed him to read only that which accommodated the propensities of his own soul. Mystical things and subtle metaphysical arguments attracted his mind like a magnet — no wonder that dreaming meant life to him, whereas life was but a dream. No wonder that he was growing superstitious. He had often envisaged the sad, long, and monotonous years that lay ahead — with himself like a leaf adrift on a stream. Unloved — for he had no kin in the whole wide world, a lover of solitude, spiritually misfit to strive for a better fate, he was bitterly aware that he would exhort neither a caring smile nor a tear in this "order of reality," as he was wont to call it, that neither loved nor hated, he would pass out like a spark no one cares about — not a soul. His hermitage, a dark, cobwebbed cubby-hole in the archives of a bookkeeping office and the idle, live-and-let-live atmosphere of the coffee-house were the innards of his life. Not a soul to enquire whether he possessed a heart, whether he would care for smart attire, as so many children are asked, or whether he would wish for love. Love — the mere thought made his heart throb. How he would love! How he would worship a maiden reciprocating with her own heart! He would imagine that silvery shadow with white visage and golden hair — for all ideals are fair-haired — and almost feel her warm, narrow-shaped hand in the grip of his own, her eyes melting to tenderness under his kisses, his soul, being, life, pining away while feasting his eyes on her... forever feasting his eyes on her.

At a scattering of tables there were foursomes of gamblers with dishevelled hair, holding their cards in one shaking hand, snapping their fingers with the other before laying the stakes, speechless lips moving, and gulping noisy mouthfuls of the coffee and beer in front of them — some show of triumph! Over there a man was chalking the green cloth of the billiard table; another one, top hat tilted back and hands clasped at his back, a long cigarette hanging from his mouth barely sticking to his lips, was gaping at a portrait of Dibici-Zabalkansky hung on the smoke-covered wall with real interest or just for the hell of it. The grandfather clock, faithful interpreter of the old time, clang its metal tongue twelve times, to let uncaring people know that the twelfth hour of the night had petered out.

Dionis made himself start for home. Outside, the rain had abated and a wan cold moon was drifting among the meshes and waves of bluish-black clouds. In the center of an untended garden, where the pig-weed and other weeds had overgrown into greenish-black thickets, a derelict house was looking out through its cracked windowpanes, its moss-grown rotten eaves shiny as rime in the cool moonlight. A flight of wooden steps led to its upper floor. The large door ajar on the balcony upstairs was swinging to and fro on its only hinge, the steps were rotten and blackened — some were missing altogether and so one had to skip every other step, and the wooden balcony groaned and rocked under the weight of one's footsteps. He negotiated the wilderness of the garden and the rundown fences and climbed the stairs with sprightly steps. All the doors were open. He entered a large, high-ceilinged, sparsely-furnished room. The walls had turned black with the raindrops trickling in from the attic and the whitewashing had caught a film of green mold; the window sills had given in under the weight of the old walls, the grills had been broken, only their rusty roots showing out of the rotten wood. In the corners of the ceiling supported by long, dark beams, the spiders were going about their silent and peaceful work; in a corner of the room, on the bare floor, several hundreds of old books were slumbering in random stacks, many of which were in Greek, ripe with Byzantine wisdom. There was a bed in another corner, a contraption of a few boards set on two horses, spread over with a straw pallet and a red quilt. In front of the bed there was a dingy table the top of which, turned ruddy with time, stencilled in Latin and Gothic lettering, was covered with sheets of paper, verses, tattered newspapers, and short-lived pamphlets that were handed out gratis; a truly ungodly disorder. The moon was pouring down her fantastic light through the large windows, bleaching the floor chalk-white; the moonlight reflected by the windows painted two silvery squares on the bleak walls; the cobwebs were shining gaily in the moonlight.

Above the books slumbering in their corner rose the angel-like shadow of a man. A hook supported the full-sized bust of an eighteen-year-old boy, his hair dark and long, his lips thin and rosy, his face flawless and marble-white, his eyes large and a blue beneath thick eyebrows and long dark lashes. The blue eyes of the boy were so bright, so deep and clear that they made the spectator warm up to their innocent, tender, rather feminine look. Though the portrait of a manly-clad person, his delicate, small, white hands, the finely-drawn, dewy, shiny, and soft pallor of his visage, his unfathomably deep eyes, his smooth, girlishly-narrow brow, his longish wavy hair might have led one into taking it for the image of a woman in disguise. The starry-eyed Dionis stopped before the portrait breathing life-like in the light of the full moon and his eyes dazed with superstitious foolishness; he uttered quietly in a tear-choked voice:

"Good evening, Papa!" The shadow seemed to smile in its wooden frame, so he drew closer and kissed the portrait's hands, face, lips, and bluish, glowing eyes.

Overwhelmed by the love for a long-bygone being, he would have had this cool moonlit night stretch into eternity with this sweet, incomprehensible, yet so blissful madness lasting forever. So, it was on this figure, a mere portrait, that he focused his love, that much shape had his wretched, wasted life! Truly, it was his father at his age. His mother, a pale, tall, fair-haired woman with dark eyes, had often told him about his father, lost while still a child among the lower classes by some whim of fate. Unfathomable, keeping to himself the secret of his name, he found lodgings with an old priest who had a daughter, Maria. They fell in love. Day after day he kept giving her his word that the secret of his soul would come to be unveiled, that he would make her his spouse and that a bright future was to be her reward. Up to the day when he received a letter sealed in black, opened it, read it, and tore it to pieces; with it, he fell to pieces as well. As far as she could make out, the torn pieces put together again read like a copy of a will. He passed away in an insane asylum... pale and mute to his expiring breath, seemingly set on taking with him some dreadful secret.

Dionis came into the world as the fruit of their love.

His widowed mother brought him up as best she could by the work of her two hands — fine ladylike ones at that — her pale visage, her soft dark eyes showing tenderness and understanding only to her two wards — himself and the portrait. Since early boyhood he admired the beautiful eyes of the portrait glittering lifelike in their sockets.

"How handsome my Papa was!" he would say with a smile, and his mother, on hearing his words, would dry a furtive tear.

"It is his eyes, isn't it, Dionis? His eyes!"

"Yes, mamma."

"Those eyes!... Had you only seen those eyes once in your life, they would have appeared to you afresh in each bluish morning star, in each blue wave, through each rift in the clouds. How beautiful the boy was and how young when he passed away! Beauteous have his eyes stayed in the dark mist of my thoughts, like two bluish stars, only two, twinkling on the dark dome of heaven between the rifts in the clouds..." Then she would hug, fondle, and kiss him. Save the black eyes, inherited from her, he was *his* spitting image, the boy's in the portrait. She pampered him — what else was she to do? — she loved him so! With him as her only joy in a life without hope, expectations, or satisfaction, she experienced neither pain nor joy but those of her child. Her very soul was but a sad, shady reflection of his childish soul. Every conceit the child devised in his naive mind, words and dreams alike, were nourishment for whole days of her life — and for whole days she could ponder on some chance remark uttered by his playful lips. One day, however, want-bedridden, she passed away. In her delirium she nestled her child's hand against her breast, nigh to her heart, to warm it — a symbol of her whole life!

Thence his appearance and his smile had acquired that gentle shade of sadness which made him so attractive — and irresistible — to unexperienced boarding-school girls. Yet it did not even cross his mind that there might be someone to love him — no one had, except his mother — for, how could they love *him*, so alone, so poor, so futureless! "Has not every one," he thought, "a family, friends, kinsmen, his own people to love — but who cares about me? I shall die the way I have lived with no soul to mourn me, as no soul has ever shown me love."

The moon hid her face behind a black could splintered apart by two long red flashes of lighting, the house fell into darkness and both shadows — that of the portrait on the wall and Dionis's tall one — vanished. He lit a candle.

Let us now have a look at the dire poverty half-disclosed by the beams of a tallow candle shoved into the neck of a bottle for want of a candlestick. What a lair — and this was the room wherein he saw both summer and winter in and out. In the bitterest cold of winter the beams in his room would splint, the firewood and the stones would crack with a groan, the wind would growl through the snow-laden fences and branches; he wished he could go to sleep and dream away, but the freezing cold would clog his eyelashes and eyeballs with cobwebs of frost. To cap it all his coat was warp rather than weft, frilled at the hems and frayed at the elbows, so the wind itself seemed to laugh at his expense. People would gape at him with a leer... Yet would you imagine that at such moments, during the endless frosty winter nights, he would be sad? He felt at home. A long train of humorous imaginings would flood his brain, as eerie and impossible as can be. He would become aware of his thoughts shaping themselves into rhythmic sequences with rhyming tags and could not help jotting them down on paper... the empty bottle, of all things, leading him to melancholy reflections...

For a candlestick is serving my dear old big-bellied bottle!
And the tallow of the candle sizzling burns and sizzling dies...
In this penury, oh, minstrel, raise the songs unto the skies!
Money I've not seen for ages, I've not washed for weeks my throttle

For a cigarette a kingdom! The snow-bringing clouds I'll pamper
With chimeras! Whence?... The window in the tempest knows no rest,
Cats are wailing in the garret, turkeys with benumbéd crest
Strut about the courtyard brooding in a melancholy temper.

Breath, like steam, allays the coldness, and my fur cap is pulled tighter
O'er my ears — as to my elbows, little, indeed, for them I care!
Like the fingers of a Gypsy fumbling through the meshes rare
Of a net, they scan the weather: will it get any brighter?

Were I but a mouse, o, Heavens! he is furred, upon my life!
I would feed upon my volumes and the frost I would outwit;
I would think a piece of Homer the most toothsome dainty bit,
The wall-hole a stately palace, and an icon my dear wife!

On the walls long over-dusty, on the cobweb-ridden ceiling,
Bed bugs swarm — it is delightful just to watch them walk and ply;
They don't fancy the straw-mattress, and my skin is now so dry,
They won't suck it any longer. — Cluster in a frenzy rolling,

They enjoy short excursion. — And the sight will drive me frantic.
Oh, how coyly that old matron strolls and spreads about her stench!
And the bachelor how nimble! Does he actually speak French?
Over there besieged by legions, you may see a girl romantic.

With the biting chill I shiver... On my hand a flea's sight-seeing;
In my mouth I'll wet my finger. I shall catch him on the spot.
If he sojourned with a woman, of then he would get it hot!
But I care so very little — why destroy the helpless being?

And the blasé cat is purring by the fireside. Tommy, hello!
Let us have a chat together, my sole time-piece and sole brother!
In a pussy-peopled village I'd make you a judge, none other,
So that you may lord it, learning what is to be rich, my fellow!

Is the slyboots thinking of it, as he purrs, rolled over there?
What ideas flutter gently in his cat's imagination?
Has some white-furred lady led him into love's most sweet temptation?
Will there be an assignation in a loft or shed or lair?

I would still remain a poet if but cats the world should people;
I would, tragically mewing, set up eulogies — like Garrick —
Watch, while basking in the sunlight, the mouse tails beside a hay-rick,
And by moonlight walk the garret, ramble on the roof and steeple!

If I were a sage, my feelings would experience mad division;
In a hall of public lectures for ideals I'd boldly fight,
And I'd show the gen'rous youngsters, the young ladies gay and bright
That this world is merely dreamland and a tom-cat's senseless vision.

As a priest, in yonder temple, dedicated to the power
Which, repeating its own image, has created the catkind,
I would shout, "O tribe of tommies! woe to you and yours! for, mind,
You have disregarded fasting! Kneel in awe, o cats and cower!

Are there such as hold the tables in a reverence uncivil,
Disbelieving the Almighty and the greatest mind of all
Who the destiny of kittens can upon demand unroll!
Don't they fear the Godless creatures, Hell and bats, its spirits evil?

Anathema sit! — Spit on him honest cats, and — with no nonsense!
Don't you see what lavish wisdom lies concealed in you? Your claws,
Soulless brutes, he gave for scratching, whiskers — to purr with, and paws
To feel gently — is it with them that you mean to touch his essence?

Ah! the wick in my poor bottle is diminishing to naught.
Go to sleep, my dear old Tommy. It is night, and we'll be dreaming,
Each on his own wretched bedstead, dreams of gold and fortune beaming.
If I could but sleep, yet can I? — Sleep, thou balm of my sick thought,

Wrap my being in thy still harmony — come, restitution,
Sleep, or death — whiche'er is willing? It's same to me — all's rot.
Whether cats and fleas and moonshine will be still my mates or not,
I don't care button, do I! — Poetry is destitution.

    Yet this night of all nights Dionis was unreasonably cheerful. Seated
by the candle in the bottle neck frittering away its stub into quivering beams
of red light, he opened an ancient moth-eaten, leather-bound book — the
manuscript of a zodiac. He was a superstitious atheist — like so many oth-

ers. The initials on this hand-written book were strangely illuminated in blood-red ink, in Slavic script, shapely pious, hunch-backed, and fantastical all in one. An astrology of rather Byzantine extraction based on the geocentric system which offers the Earth as the center of all cosmic architecture with man as the sole reason and beneficiary of God's creation. The title was also written in Latin: "Architecturae cosmicae sive astronomiae geocentricae compendium" beneath which — "an enquiry into the world's godly order showing how the Lord God of Mercy hath created all things on Earth — turned from Greek into Romanian and enclosing an appendix on the influence of the constellations on human lives." A dedication followed: "To him Whose own Self is boundless, Wondrous Lord over the creatures of His own making, to everlasting worship and glory." The pages were scrawled over with charts of an imaginary cosmic system, their corners taken up with the portraits of Plato and Pythagoras encircled with sentences in Greek. Two interlocked triangles were surrounded with the phrase "Director coeli vigilat noctesque diesque, qui sistit fixas horas terrigenae." Constellations painted in red, geometric charts drawn according to some fantastical mystical system, followed by interpretations of dreams in alphabetical entries — in short, a book doing its utmost to cater to superstitious brains addicted to such food. At the end of the book there was a picture of St. George doing battle with the Dragon — an appropriate symbol of truth getting the better of ignorance. The gold on the back of the leather binding had peeled off in some places and gave off a spattering of tinsel-like glitter in others. Dionis propped his head in his hands and immersed himself in making heads and tails of the arcane text until the candle stub started sizzling into smoke. It burned out. He drew his chair to the window, opened it, and in the pale moonlight went on leafing through the pages and contemplating the strange constellations. Turning a page he came across a host of overlapping circles, as many as to resemble a ball of red yarn or a cobweb spattered with red blood. Then he raised his eyes and gazed dreamily at the smooth face of the moon — she was journeying, beautiful and limpid, in a translucent, deep and clear sky, across silvery-fluid clouds and large stars of molten gold. Another thousands skies seemed to stretch farther beyond, their supposed entities shimmering through the blue depth of the one beneath... "Whoever could tell," Dionis was musing "whether the sign be in this book, which might enable one to probe into the recesses of one's soul, into the worlds that come into being the way you wish them, into spaces spread over with a splendid, dewy floating blue?"

A beautiful white house stood opposite that of Dionis. By the open window on the upper floor there floated to him, in the night air, the sweet notes of a harpsichord along with the tremulous youthful voice of a maiden, breathing forth a gentle prayer with a fantastic, scented sound. He closed his eyes to give his dreams free rein. He envisaged himself in a desert, barren, wide, and sand-bound like the drought itself with a fantastic pale moon glimmering above like the visage of a dying maid. Midnight. The desert is silent, no breeze stirs the air, the only things alive are his breath and his eyesight, so he can spy high up in the sky a white angel kneeling on a silvery cloud, her hands joined, chanting a divine, deep, tremulous prayer: a maiden's prayer. He half-opened his eyes and beheld beyond the open bow window in a brightly-lit drawing room a youthful maid, a white gown floating about her, enthralling the keyboard of a responsive piano with her thin, long, delicate fingers and accompanying the gentle sounds of some divine score with her sweet tender voice; as if the genius of Shakespeare, the divine Briton, had breathed out into the world another lunatic angel, another Ophelia. He closed his eyes afresh and kept them closed until, back in the wide desert, the white palace merged into the silvery cloud and the youthful maiden into the kneeling angel. Then, forcing his eyes to close tighter, he drowned his dream into a sea of darkness, shutting out the images, yet he could still hear receding farther and farther away, like a dim memory, the prayer of a maiden. The music had long ceased and he, a willful prey to his imagination, still kept his eyes closed.

When awakening from his reverie, the upper window of the palace was still open, but the drawing-room was in darkness, its panes glittering in the white moonlight. A scent of summer suffused the translucent air and the moonbeams, coming into Dionis's chamber, flooded his pale face and repleted his mournful soul with an undefinable melancholy. "Verily," he murmured his favorite quote, "the world, that endless wasteland, is all there, beneath our own brow — but wherefore the space only without the time, the past?" He gazed again at the red-striped spiderweb — and the stripes quivered into movement. He placed a finger on their center and a sensation of spiritual voluptuousness flooded his soul — at first he seemed to hear the murmur of those old sages who, while a boy cuddled on their knees, would pass the winter nights recounting fantastic tales with fairies

"He placed a finger on their center and a sensation
of spiritual voluptuousness flooded his soul..."

A. Bordenache

clad in gold and beams of light living their untroubled lives in crystal pal-
aces — and he had a yesteryear feeling of entangling his fingers in the tufts
of their white beards and listening to their soft all-wise voices — the good
bygone past, the sages' tidings... Doubtless... an invisible hand was beckon-
ing him to the past. He envisaged a train of princes in gold and sable attire,
on their thrones in ageless castles, he beheld the wise old men's council and
elated Christian throng undulating like waves on the sea within the walls
of the princely court — but the images were still mixed and blurred.

The lines of the astrological sign kept writhing like as many serpents
of fire. The spider was looming larger and larger.

"Where shall we stop?" he heard a voice out of the glowing center of
the book.

"Alexander the Good!," he whispered in a low, yet compelling voice,
joy and wonder filling in his soul, while... ever so slowly the red spiderweb
grew larger, more immaterial, turning into a reddish sunset. He was lying
sprawled in a freshly-mown field, the stacked hay fragrant, the blue twilight
sky clear and deep above him, clouds of fire and gold scattered all over the
sky, the hills dented with loads of purple, the birds on the wing, the mirrors
of the rivers turned reddish, the tremulous chime of a bell pealing out in the
dusk calling worshippers to evensong, while he, himself — what a strange
garb! A sackcloth surplice, a black hat, the book of astrology in his hand.
Everything looked so familiar! He was no longer his old self. It seemed only
natural that he should find himself in this particular world. He knew for cer-
tain that he had strolled out into the fields to read and he had fallen asleep
over his book. That dismal room, the bygone life of a man by the name of
Dionis was but a strange dream! "Alas," he thought, "my book has played
this trick on me, making me dream such extraordinary things. What a
strange world — what strange people, what a language — sounding like
ours, though different and alien..."

Odd! Brother Dan had dreamed he was a layman by the name of Dio-
nis... in apparently other times and among other people! Odd!

"Alas, Master Ruben," he said with a smile, "truly wondrous is your
book!... if only it would not befuddle the brain; at long last have I, a humble
monk, grasped that the soul journeys from century to century, staying for-
ever the same, but for death that makes it oblivious of its former lives. Right
you are, Master Ruben, that the Egyptians did justice to metempsychosis.
Right you are that boundless time and space are within our own soul and its

magic wand we need to move to any particular point we might wish. Here I am, living during Prince Alexander's reign, and I was dragged by an unknown hand into times coiled within the future of my soul. How many selves are there in one man? As many as the stars in a dewdrop beneath the sky of a clear night. And should one enlarge that drop so that one could gaze into its depth, one would re-encounter all the myriad stars in the sky, each one a self-sufficient world with its own countries and nations, as well as its own history — a universe within an ephemeral drop. How profound this Jew can be!" he mused on his teacher Ruben.

He got up from the grass, the ancient book in his hand. In the far distance were the mountains with their forest-crowned brows, their sides sloping into white-brooked vales. Large round clouds boding of storms were sailing across the deep blue sky. The mountains showed through them a prodigality of precipices and slopes; black rocks and tree-trunks occasionally broke through the mist and a thunderstruck fir-tree was perched in solitude on a peak in front of the setting sun. The sun hid behind the clouds painting them red and bluish with golden fringes. They ensconced the light of the heavenly Lord into clusters of lofty vaults and deep caves with purple pools overflowing through an occasional crevice in their dark ruins. Then, ever so slowly, they scattered into bluish-grey folds. The setting sun seemed to linger on the top of the solitary fir-tree like a hallowed brow perched on dark shoulders; then, climbing down, it looked like a ruby-nest among the boughs, then from behind the broad trunk he let rosy shafts fly at the rocks, rekindling the silvery embers of their brows, and it gradually sank behind the tall black mountain, painting its hemmed edges red against the blue air. Night was slowly closing in, large stars were budding forth in the blue plains of the sky, quivering voluptuously in the vesperal soft clear air and this pastoral harmony suffused the evening with its myriad voices, each different, yet each doing its bit for the moon's sweet and voluptuous drowsiness.

Our monk was passing through a world turned russet in the beauteous twilight, heedless of the spellbinding mood of nature, his soul still immersed in his strange adventure. From far away he could spy the glittering church steeples of Iasi, the beautifully painted houses, their eaves violet in the light of the rising moon. He walked into the borough at a hasty pace and found himself in a narrow lane lined with old tumble-down houses, their upper stories jutting out over the lower, so that the former rested half on wooden stilts with the other half upon the ground floor. Tall verandas protruded from beneath long, stodgy ramshackle houses overgrown with black-green moss; old men sitting on the verandas, talking of this and that; young lasses, their faces as fresh as ripe apples, leaning their heads over the sills of opened latticed windows lined with potted gold-yellow flowers. Hither and thither the moon shed a long and narrow streak in the darkness of the alley, hither and tither some passer-by was whistling under his breath — gradually the lanes fell into slumber, the shutters were pulled down, the candles were put out, the night guards strutted by, their heads ducked down into their white greatcoats, while our monk moved on like a half-embodied shadow along the long benighted lanes.

He stopped before a house standing by itself in the middle of a waste-land. Light was coming out through the slits in the shutters. The house had a tapered roofing and walls of small stones like those used to metal wells, from which any trace of former whitewashing had peeled off, so that it had taken on the look of a ruined citadel. The shutters were far wider than the narrow windows and, from the side of the verandah supported by four-sided stone pillars, a long flight of steps led to half the height of the house. There were neither trees nor outhouses around the homestead; the large yard with its dry grass stretched yellow in the moonlight with only a well sweep groaning in the wind. He mounted the stairs at a run and knocked loudly at the door. There was a thud of footsteps in the hall.

"Who's there?" asked a deep, but quiet voice.

"Me, Dan." The door was opened and a tall man stood before Dan, grey-bearded and wide-browed, wearing a small fez like a Jewish skull-cap on the crown of his head. He shook hands with the monk and showed him into the room. In old plank cases there were ancient leather-bound books, human skulls and stuffed birds on the shelves lining the walls, a bed and a desk, both cluttered with parchments and papers. A torch was casting its dim red-yellow drowsy light in an atmosphere heavy with the stench of bottled substances.

Master Ruben was an old man of ancient-type good looks. His high bald brow wrinkled with meditation, his grey eyes arched and deep-set in the head of a sage, his long beard, flowing down from beneath the cheek-bones onto his bent chest, made him look like a sage of yore. His visage was composed, though not meek. Round his well drawn mouth lurked a doubt-embittered tenderness. He was a scholarly Jew who had wandered from

Spain to Poland, whence, having been banned from public teaching for stay-
ing faithful to his creed, the prince of Moldavia had invited him to be master
of Mathematics and Philosophy at the Socola Academy. Brother Dan was
one of the Academy's students, of Ruben's particularly, who shared with
him both his doubts and his secret discoveries. The wise Jew took in Dan's
dreamy countenance with a spark of curiosity.

"Well?"

"It is fully as you have taught me, Master," Dan said "and now I
stand convinced that boundless time is a creation of our immortal soul. I
have lived in the future. Verily, there are two entirely different selves within
me — one of them, Brother Dan, now addressing you, and living in Prince
Alexander's reign, the other by another name, living five hundred years in
the future."

Ruben replied: "You could live successively the lives of those that
have caused you into the world and of all those whose lives you might be the
cause of. Therefore men cherish an awe-inspired feeling toward the preser-
vation and enlargement of their lineage. It is they that are reborn in their
descendants... And therein lies the difference between God and man. Man
is a mere link in the chain of bygone men and men to come. God holds in
His bosom all nations, past and future; man occupies a place in time; God is
time itself and everything that comes to pass in it, time coiled back onto
itself like a brook whose water flows back into its own spring or a wheel
which holds all its ever-revolving spokes within its hub. Our own soul is
itself eternal — but in piecemeal fashion only. Imagine a moving wheel and
a grain of dust glued to it. This grain will pass through all the spots the
revolving wheel does, but successively, whereas the wheel is present at the
same moment in all the spots it touches."

"I stand persuaded, Master, as to time, but how about boundlessness,
how about space?"

"The same as with time, for you could be, in piecemeal fashion, in any
desired place, which you cannot leave vacant. You know that in virtue of a
law: there is no empty space. Yet there is a means of negotiating that snag...
a snag enforced by the perishable human body. As you have seen, there is an
endless chain of people in one man. Out of this chain, leave one of them in
your place for as long as you will be gone. Unquestionably he cannot be all-
sufficient since, becoming so, he would refute your own existence. In actual-
ity, however, the eternal self, from whom the whole chain of transient people

springs, is beside everyone at every moment — you can see him though you cannot lay hold of him — he is your shadow. You could swap natures for a while — with you giving over your transient nature to your shadow, whereas he will lend you his eternal nature, so much so that, as a shadow endowed with immortality, you will even partake of God's omnipotence. Your every wish will be no sooner thought than materialized... observing the right formulae, of course, since they are as eternal as the words God uttered when he created the world, and they are all writ in the book which I lent you."

"Master Ruben, however could I bring myself to penetrate the depths of your wisdom?"

"My wisdom is all there within your own self, only yet unveiled. Do you imagine you could make sense of my words without partaking of my own nature? Do you imagine I should have singled you out as my disciple if I had not considered you worthy and thoroughgoing? You are like a violin with all the strains lying expectant for an accomplished hand to resurrect them, and I am the hand that will resurrect your innermost self."

"Suppose this night I should attempt to project myself to a place of my own devising?"

"That lies within your power... for it is already there in your immortal soul, unfathomably deep. On the seventh leaf of the book you will find all the formulae you might need for your venture. And also on the seventh leaf you will learn what you must do further on. Doubtless, we shall have to part forever for, in self-devised spaces, our days are century-long so, on your return, you will find no trace of Ruben, but some other man, similar to me, whom you will find easily — only that he might not recognize you, having lost the secrets of his wisdom and become a run-of-the-mill individual.

Further advice from me would be useless, for when your shadow, still a shadow to you, starts speaking, he will be all-wise and will instruct you how to proceed. As soon as you take over his nature, you will become all-wise yourself and will not need me any longer. Yet, you will have noticed one thing: my book, when perused line by line, stays incomprehensible... whereas, whatever the starting-place, if you skip to every seventh leaf, you will be astounded by a godlike clarity. That is a mystery I do not grasp myself, and it is writ that no Christian can ever even conceive of the reasoning hidden within this odd numeration. No use enquiring of your shadow... the secret is beyond his understanding. It is writ that the Devil, before his fall, had devised this obtuse idea which might have precipitated his destitution. Should you set your mind on unveiling it, everything around you would vanish into thin air, time and space would forsake your soul, and you would wither away like a dry branch, likewise forsaken by time. Myself, ignorant of that secret, for, as I have said, I am unable even to conceive of it, I can give you no further advice."

Ruben smoothed his beard thoughtfully, deep grief on his withered, wise face. Dan kissed his hand: were not they to part forever? When Ruben tore with his fingers the fallen candle-end, tears glimmered in his eyes. Both stood up. Dan threw his arms round Ruben's neck, sobbing like a son never to see his father again.

Yet, no sooner had Dan left the room and climbed down the stairs, holding the book under an armpit and raising the long tail of his surplice clear of the steps with the other hand than... the house turned into a black-walled cave, the wax candle into a floating live coal, the books into large glass bubbles tied with parchment at the mouths, wherein, swimming in a fluid glittering violet-blue, little devils were dithering, hanging by their horns and spinning their legs about. Ruben's face was creased by countless wrinkles, his shaggy beard forked into two goatees, his eyes grew glittery like two live embers, his nose twisted and withered like a tree stump. Scratching his shaggy horned head, he burst out into hideous roars of laughter then, splitting his sides with bleating, he crowed:

"Haw, haw, one more soul gone to the devil!" The devils made faces, jeered, and made somersaults in their bubbles, while Satan stretched his stallion legs, gasping for air.

"Long have I had to wait to ensnare this pious monk yet, at long last... haw, haw... yet... my old enemy will destroy him yet. I have had him think the idea secreted in the pages of the book will not flash through his mind... yet it must... it must... How on earth did it dawn on me? It was meant to!"

Meanwhile Dan was passing with a sprightly step through the boyars' district. The silver-white courtyards with verandas and outer stair-cases, their scrubbed and wax-polished planks shining in the moonlight, hardly showed through the clumps of fruit-trees in the orchards, the lower branches of which overhung the fences... rows of palm-leafed walnut trees, quince trees, and cherry trees... Hither and thither an occasional yellow streak from an opening in the shutters would stray through the dark verdure of the gardens... He was walking at a hasty pace... Now and then a gallant passed by him, long-stapled hat on his head, wrapped in a cloak whose tail was raised by the sword on which he was resting his hand... in other places he would spy gallants jumping over fences into gardens, under windows opening in the moonlight, some white shadow leaning its youthful head over the ledge toward the shadow below. At another place a shadow was heaving itself onto the grating and studying the flowers, its lips meeting the lips of another shadow whose head was leaning out through the bars. Every now and then he would hear dogs howling at the moon, the night guards bellowing, or see bands of gallants staggering back from some belated spree. They would tear twigs off the overhanging branches and throw them after the beardless pale monk... Stars were keeping vigil on the dome of heaven, the moon was gliding like a silver shield through the darkness of the clouds, there was gold in the air and a deep violet-bluish shade in the fragrant gardens, dappled by white shafts of light dripping through the leafy meshes as if through light strainers.

He made it home. He dwelt in a tiny cell in the house of a rich boyar. Minding his footsteps, he walked across the long veranda with overhanging eaves supported by white pillars... Noiseless as a shadow he passed and, on entering his cell, he heaved a deep sigh. Was he not to undertake an unheard-of venture? The darkness of his cell, stuffy with the smell of incense, was scattered only by the red speck of an icon lamp flickering away on a shelf stacked with dried basil and flowers, under the silver-bound icon of the Saviour. In the hearth, a cricket was chirping in its hoarse voice. He lit a black lamp burning on cooking oil; its light gave out flickering fumes. In the sluggishly enlivening light he sat at his table and opened the old book in Cyrillic script with faded letters and occult meanings. In the ear-ringing silence he seemed to hear the very thoughts, scent, and sprouting of a pretty red carnation set in a pot between the curtains at his window. He sat staring at his own shadow, looming huge and fantastic on the smoky wall. The light was fluttering as if to reach the ceiling, while his shadow... sprawled like a beak-nosed net, the fur hat over his eyes, looked as if having engaged Dan in a friendly conversation. It seemed to him he was posing his shadow pointed questions... the latter replying in long-winded sentences... a dialogue of sorts yet, when attempting to account for its reality, it came down to a dialogue between his own reflections, between two sides of his own self. Odd! This split of his personality resulted in a strange idea. He cast a long stern gaze at his shadow who... irked by that gaze took sharper and sharper outlines on the wall, growing clearer, like an old oil-painting. He blinked — and the shadow turned back into what it used to be.

"This is a momentous hour, I ought to give it some pause," he mused. "Have I ever nursed a wish for my own benefit? Mine alone? Definitely not. Have I ever left her out of my prayers? Has there ever been a moment when she was not in my thoughts? Maria? Oh, no! Whenever I beseeched some extraordinary power, it was on her behalf that I did so. Alas! — that I could take her to a desert with no living soul about — no one but the two of us; bring down the stars in the sky onto the white expanse of sand, turn them into hosts of gold and silver flowers; lay out laurel groves with shady paths and crystal-clear blue lakes for her to hie along the paths ensconced beneath the foliage, feigning to shun my love, with me chasing her... Nay, heaven itself would be a wasteland without her!"

And what a gem Maria was!

She was the daughter of Tudor Mesteacǎn, the sword-bearer, an angel blond as a golden teardrop, lissome as a wax lily, with pious blue eyes, as pious and blue as the deep of the sky for all its divine eternity. Oft would she raise her eyes from the prayer book to cast one more look at the monk's pale, haggard face; oft had he spied her sprouting — like a flower at the window — and, on moonlit nights he would throw aside his surplice to don a gallant's cloak and keep vigil beneath her lighted windows... until they opened revealing her visage wan with sleeplessness and love, the rays of her eyes gliding deeply into his dark eyes. A few words, a touch of the hands, and she would vanish back into her balmy alcove having enriched his nights with sweet, unforgettable dreams... Now his thoughts flew out to her again.

The lamp was flickering more oddly, the ancient letters in the book were taking on meanings, creeping into his dreams and thoughts, whirling in his weak-willed head, his shadow started again to take on the outlines of an oil icon, his wide brow, pale and smooth, his lips bluish, grey streaks in his hair, his deep-set eyes focused on the book lying open in front of Dan. His shadow was whispering in thoughts the very answers he was long grappling with.

"You are aware," his shadow was thinking, and he could hear the train of his thoughts, "well aware that since the dawn of the world up to this very moment your soul has been making a wearisome journey in thousands of bodies now long turned to dust. It knows it not, since every time it took the shape of a new body, it had drunk of Lethe's tasteless water of oblivion; and no one but me has accompanied it on its forgotten journey — me, the shadow of the bodies it has dwelt in; me, your shadow. I was present at every burial and at every birth; I was present by your cradle and so shall I be by your grave. Your soul, though today it remembers not, once dwelt in Zoroaster's breast. He who could command the stars to change their places with his almighty word and the combined operation of his numbers. Zoroaster's book, with all the mysteries of his science, is lying there before your eyes. For centuries, many have endeavored to unravel its secrets, but none have succeeded completely; it is only I who can unravel it, for I used to converse with Zoroaster from high on my wall as I am doing now with you."

Dan realized clearly that his nature was made up of two sides: one side eternal, the other transient. Zoroaster's book was his rightful possession. He turned seven leaves and the shadow took on the outlines of a bas-relief, then another seven and by slow degrees he detached himself as if from within a frame, leaped down from the wall, stood by him translucent and smiling and uttered in a clear, respectful voice:

"Good evening!"

The red flame of the lamp stood between Dan and the newly-embodied shadow.

"Let us proceed," said the shadow resuming the train of his ideas, which Dan could hear as if they were his own. "Your appropriating my essence by force of magic in exchange for yours compels me to turn into an ordinary man, my past washed out of my memory, whereas you are to become eternal and all-wise like me and, by the agency of the book, all-powerful as well. You will leave me in your former milieu with the embodied shadow of your sweetheart and your friends; you have doomed me to forget my visionary essence, whereas you will be setting out on journey, your sweetheart at your side, to any place in the universe that you might wish: to the moon, for instance. Living there, a century will seem no longer than a day. You could even take the whole Earth with you and no harm would be done. Turn it into a pearl pendant and hang it on your sweetheart's necklace; and, verily, though thousands of times smaller, humans will consider themselves as big as they are now, provided that you observe their proportions. Their time? An hour of your life will be a century in theirs. Your moments will be decades for them and, during those moments they will find time to wage war, crown kings, nations will be extinguished and born, in short, all of today's follies will be reenacted, on a diminished scale, of course, but exactly the same follies."

"Very well," said Dan, taking hold of the shadow's cool diaphanous hand, "Yet I entreat you to write down the memoirs of your life, for me to find and read when I return to Earth. Yours is a cool judgement, so you are well fit to record the visionary and delusive nature of all earthly things from the flower lying with naivety from beneath its dazzling attire that it is happy, within its tender organs, up to the man who coats with idle prattle and all-pervading hypocrisy, as old as the history of mankind, the dark evil kernel which is the nethermost root of his life and deeds — his egotism. You will see how we are fed lies in school, in Church, in government: namely, that we are to enter a world of justice, love, and saintliness, the more bitterly to realize on our death bed that it has been one of injustice and hatred. Alas! Whoever would wish for life if, while still a toddler, instead of fairy-tales, he were apprised of the real plight of things before turning him loose into the thick of life?"

"A philosopher's calling?" said the shadow with a bitter smile. "So be it! Your words have settled my fate. I shall light my lamp and go out into the street in search of men. You will find the memories of my life in the drawer of the desk over there when you come back. As for me, I shall be long dead and buried when you return, since the hours of your life will be long years on the Earth. Turn another seven leaves and hold me by the hand! What are you feeling?"

"My arms melting away into thin air, yet gaining gigantic powers; the dull cells of my brain splitting asunder, leaving my mind as clear as the light of day."

"I feel," said the shadow in a low voice, "the awareness of my immortality darkening and melting away... my thoughts heavy as lead... Turn another seven leaves, and the mutual metamorphosis will be completed."

Dan turned the leaves, whispered something, and the shadow became man. The man, his spitting image, stood staring at Dan, as at an apparition, diffident and oblivious, his lips trembling and his legs unsure. Dan was a gleaming shadow. He raised his long, strong arm. "Go to sleep!" he commanded. The grandfather clock announced the hour hoarsely... the embodied shadow slumped onto the bed in a sound sleep. Dan threw his long cloak over his shoulders, put out the lamp, tiptoed across the veranda, got out, closed the door, and started at a slow pace along the moonlit wide street of the town, with shuttered windows and barred gates, with its white walls turned yellow in the moonlight, drawn curtains, an occasional night guard, his mustache tucked up in the collar and the hood of his cloak and a truncheon under his armpit; finally, the slumberous, quiet, warm summer air, with the moon shining bright, golden stars blinking, their eyes shut and open again, a blue cloudless sky, tall houses, their tile eaves gazing up at the moon — that was the picture! His shadow's footsteps roused no sound in the street. He was wrapped in his cloak, the brim of his hat slouched down over his eyes, walking along the brightly-lit streets, and the moonlight cast no shadow on the walls. Having left his own at home, he looked like a clumsy shadow running along the walls of the lined houses. The house in the far corner of the lane was yellow, with windows gilt by the moonlight, with white curtains. He tapped gently on the pane.

"Is it you?" answered a soft beloved voice.

"Me... open the window... there is no one in the streets, no soul can see you, and even if someone could..."

The window was opened slowly, the curtain drawn aside and between its folds appeared, lovely and pale, the blond head of an angel. The moonlight flooded her visage, making her blue eyes shine bluer still, and blink as if smarting under a sunbeam. Under the white nightgown, beneath the neckline, her budding breasts were throbbing. She held out her bare hands and arms and he covered them with kisses. A moment later he jumped over the window sill, folded her bare neck into his arms, then cuddled her face in the cup of his hands and kissed her so ardently, hugged her so passionately, as if he would have drained out her life through their pressed lips.

"Dearest," he said caressing her golden hair — "dearest, follow me into the wide world!"

"Where?"

"Where? Anywhere. We shall live such happy lives, troubled by no one, wherever we might go, you for me and I for you. We shall build castles of our dreams, spread out seas with myriads of wavy mirrors of our thoughts, weave centuries of bliss of our days together. Come!"

"What will mother say?" she blurted out with tears in her eyes.

Her shadow loomed on the wall. Dan stared at it; forthwith it came off, floated on a moonbeam, and slumped onto the bed.

"Who is there?" asked Maria, shivering against his chest.

"Only your shadow" he answered with a smile — "it will stay behind... behold how it sleeps."

"Oh! how free and weightless I feel," she exclaimed, a golden tingle in her voice. "No pang nor passion in my breast. Oh, thank you... How handsome you look to me now... as if a novel one... from another world!"

"Come with me," he whispered into her ear, "come through swarms of stars and throngs of rays until, far from this wretched, dismal earth, we will forget all and have only our own selves in mind."

"Let us go then" she whispered, encircling his neck with her white arms and pressing her mouth against his lips.

Her kiss inspired him with genius and new power. Holding her in his embrace he wrapped his glossy black cloak about her white shoulders, reached his arms about her waist, nestled her at his chest and, fluttering the tail of his cloak with the other hand, they rose ever so slowly up through the shimmering moonlight-bathed air, through the black clouds in the sky, through clusters of stars, until they reached the moon. Their journey had felt like one long kiss.

He let go of his sweet load on the redolent bank of a blue lake that mirrored all the encircling wreath of groves, delighting the eye with the world of its depths. He resumed his journey to the Earth. Nigh to the Earth, he sat on the edge of a black cloud and gave the Earth a long, brooding last look. He produced Zoroaster's book, leafed through some pages and started to read the judgement on the Earth, every letter in the book a whole year, every line a century of truth. It was terrifying how many crimes had been perpetrated on this puny atom, so small in the boundless ocean of the universe, on this black inconsequential clod of dirt called Earth. The grains of this clod are called empires, the barely discernible germs emperors, with the remaining myriads of germs playing the subjects in this nightmarish dream... His hand reached out toward the Earth. Together with the sphere around it, ever more and faster, it shrank into a blue pearl, gold-speckled outside and black-cored inside. Size being only relative, it stands to reason that the atoms at the pearl's core, whose bounds were the sky, whose speckles were the sun, the moon, and the stars, though infinitesimal dwarfs, still crowned kings kept waging wars, while their poets racked their brains for the most appropriate metaphors and similes in the universe in order to extol their heroes. Dan took the telescope and gazed through the pearl's husk wondering what it was that prevented it from bursting into smithereens from all the hatred it had amassed. He took it in the palm of his hand and, back on the Moon, he hung the blue pearl on his sweetheart's necklace.

And how beautiful he had made the moonscape!

Endowed with a gigantic imagination, he hung two suns and three moons in the blue deep of the sky and built his residential palace out of the rocks of a mountain range. The colonnades — hoary rocks, the eaves — an ancient forest soaring up to the clouds. Lofty staircases climbed down the caved-in mountain sides, patches of forest slanted down into gorges and into a vast valley watered by a stately river, its floating islands like as many tree-covered ships. The glittering mirrors of its waves reverberated the starry icons into the deep so much so that gazing into it was like gazing at the sky itself.

The islands were covered with hallowed incense-trees and amber gravel. The shady groves along the banks cast their image into the river bed, so it seemed that the same root was the starting-point of a heaven soaring up into the light of dawn and of another one submerged in the waters. Rows of cherry trees shed the rosy load of snow of their wealth of blossoms, for the wind to amass into snowdrifts; flowers made the air resound, their leaves alive with gold-speckled beetles, their murmur a world of voluptuous thrill. Husky grasshoppers were chirping like as many grandfather clocks scattered about the grass, and emerald spiders had woven across an island a bridge of adamantine gauze, glittering so violet-blue and transparent that the moonbeams crossing it spread a green glimmer over the myriads of waves on the river. Tall and lithe, and silver-white in the sheen of the night, Maria would pace across the bridge, braiding her hair, golden strands twining around her waxlike fingers, her weightless limbs showing through her silvery gown, her snow-white feet barely touching the bridge... At other times, seated in a cedar boat, they would sail down the submissive waves of the river. He would rest his brow girt with a wreath of blue flowers on her knee, and a magic bird would warble on her shoulder.

The wide river ran deeper into dark forests, where its water gave only sparse glitters under an occasional sunbeam; the tree-trunks reached their branches over the river, in high vaults of virgin verdure. An occasional flashing streak would quiver across the water. The merry waves drove on their dark blue pageant until, all of a sudden, dammed by rocks and mountains, the river gathered its waters amid the forests into the wide mirror of a sea, settling clear under the suns and displaying all the silver jewelry on its floor.

To pass the time they devised a game of cards. The kings, queens, and knaves on the cards were characters from the fairy tales they were wont to tell each other at night. The game itself was a long-winded and complicated tale like the Arabian Nights, wherein the queens were wooed, the kings married, and the poor knaves roamed about love-smitten; yet the yarn never got unwound for they would give up, visited by slumber.

And what a wondrous slumber it was!

Before going to sleep she would join her hands and, under the white stars playing the orison of the universe on airy strings, her lips would breathe out a smiling murmur, then her head, pale in the night's sweet-scented breeze, would sink into the pillows. Oh, that one who could have beheld her at such moments! But no one could, save he who would cover her arm hanging down over the bedside with kisses. He would fall asleep on his knees. They would dream the same dream. Mirror skies, angels gliding on white heavenly wings, lofty portals, marble corridors, layers upon layers of the blue stars on silvery ceilings — everything suffused with a bracing, balmy air. Only one closed gate they were not allowed to open. A fiery eye within a triangle was over it and a tag written in the twisting script of dark Arabic above the eye. It led to the dome of God. The tag, an enigma to the angles themselves.

How come man is never to drain dry the cup of happiness? The Arabic sign on the dome of God was always on Dan's mind and vain was his search in Zoroaster's book — it remained deaf to his questioning. Yet, the same dream haunted him every night; every single night he would take Maria for a stroll about the sunny world of heaven. And in every dream he had Zoroaster's book with him and searched for the answer to his question between its covers. To no avail would the angels fetching the mortal's prayers in their laps cast him telling glances; to no avail was an angel's placating whisper in his ear: "Why seek for that which is beyond your understanding?" And another's: "Why belabor brass and expect it to sound like gold? It is beyond you." Yet it seemed odd that whenever he wanted the angels to carry out his wishes, they should willingly obey his unuttered thoughts. He could not grasp that preordained harmony between his dawning ideas and the life of the flight of angels.

"Can you not see, Maria, that I have the angels at my beck and call?"

She gently shut his mouth with the palm of her hand. Then she whispered in his ear:

"When rainfall comes, all the grain rejoices; when God wills it, your thoughts partake of the angels' thoughts."

All to no avail. His mind was set and the gaze of his large eyes stayed riveted on the eternally closed gate.

"I wish to behold the face of God," he confided in an angel passing by.

"If you have Him not within your own soul, he will eschew you for ever and searching for Him will be like chasing the wind," the angel replied sternly.

Once he felt his head alive with songs. The airs were humming limpid, sweet and clear in his infatuated mind as if in a beehive, the stars themselves twinkling to their time and the angels gleefully passing by giving voice to the songs in his head. Beauteous angels were passing by, clad in silver, white-browed, their dark-blue eyes glittering in the sunlight, their flawless breasts smooth as marble, the curls of their hair streaming about their shoulders. An angel, the most beauteous he had ever beheld in his sunny dreams, was playing such a well-known tune on his harp that he could anticipate every note of it... and the air itself turned reddish with its voluptuousness. Only the Arabic sign was still glowing red, like live embers in the night.

"That is the question," Dan muttered, "the enigma holding sway over my soul. Will they not play whatever I might be thinking?... Will not the world move according to my wishes?" He hugged Maria to his breast in foreboding pain. The pearl of the Earth was flashing forth fiery beams from her necklace... Could it be that I myself, without knowing it, am G..." Bang! the peal of a gigantic bell — the sea's death, the sky's collapse — the vaults were caving in, their blue enamel splitting apart, and Dan felt thunderstruck and marooned into boundlessness. Flashes of lightning chased him with hordes of old thunder — all the uproar of boundlessness roused into motion. "Alas, you wretched thought!" he blubbered. He kept hold of Zoroaster's book in spasmodic grips and instinctively broke loose the Earth's bead from Maria's necklace. She was torn off from his arms... like a willow reaching its boughs out to him in the mist while crying in its fall: "Dan! What have you done to me?"

A voice boomed out in his wake: "What have you dared think, you wretch? Lucky you for not having uttered the whole word!"... Sucked into boundlessness as if by a magnet he was falling quick as lightning, thousands of years in one second. Presently the darkness around him grew still, pitch black devoid of sound or a spark of light. He opened his book, threw the bead away and started reading. The bright bead was falling through the darkness becoming larger and larger. Larger and larger — and glaring-bright — until it was like a moon in the offing — while, book in hand, he was wafting earthwards beneath the thick ceiling of clouds, heading for the Earth — he could already spy the glittering steeples of a city, stray lights, a summer night with golden air, fragrant gardens, and... he opened his eyes.

He somehow struggled out of sleep. The sun was high in the deep-blue sky like a burning sphere of gold. The garden outside the window by which Dionis had been sleeping was dewy-green and cooled after the rainy night, the enlivened flowers lifting their dallying childish heads, their eyes brimming with cool, idle tears. In the house opposite, the white curtains were still drawn, the cherry trees were in blossom and the sweet-scented locust-trees on the alleys of its garden cast a melancholy bluish shade over the criss-crossing walks.

Had his so life-like dream been only a mere dream, or had it been the dream-like reality of the stamp of all human realities? — The curtain opposite was slightly drawn and a maid's blonde head appeared between its folds. She was laughing.

"Maria!" he whispered, his very heartstrings aching.

Her braided blond hair fell over her shoulders; a purple rose bloomed by her temple, her mouth was small as a ripe cherry and her face white and red as a ripe apple. Having had her laugh — he had no inkling at what — she dropped the curtain back.

Yet his heart pounded violently in his breast, for the object as well as the idleness of his dreams had dawned upon him. Now he knew he was in love. "Wherefore this to top it all!" he brooded, his soul brimful with tears. "Suffice the misery I have been living in — a misery with no yearnings, at least. And my very first wish — my last perhaps — unattainable!" The bittersweet line about his mouth sank deeper. His soul winced at the thought that he could not bring himself to shake off the burden of this love. Hope? None. Was a feeling he had never experienced before to be born together with love?

She reappeared and smiled. This time she drew the curtains aside and, holding a carnation in her white hand, she fixed her thoughtful gaze on its purple calyx.

"The precious gem!" he whispered staring at her. "Alas! she ought to be kind, yet... why was she smiling? At that window, of all places? Could she not see him? What if she did see him, if her smiles were meant for him... the little wily flirt... yet, yet..." She disappeared.

"I shall write to beg... to beg her to cease smiling, lest she should instill an idle, painful illusion into my soul. She cannot deny me that much. She is so kind; I will entreat her to be wicked."

In a painful, excruciating voluptuousness he wrote to her:

My star,

Bereft of fortune, beauty, and wit, my heart is ailing like sunlight strayed in the night, for I love you. Your eyes, two molten morning stars, pierce so deeply, so blessedly deep into the darkness of my soul, that they make me daydream of you and, if asleep, I awaken at the recollection of their light.

If you could only divine the feeling I have unbosomed into these lines, my angel!

...Nay! Not a shadow of the pain that tears at my heart to break it apart could have crossed your serene life. It breaks it! Imagine a man endowed with sense, a man of flesh and blood reduced to the undying embodiment of despair. You would not know of such creatures. They do not belong in the company you keep. They are rabble. When a soul in misery, in torment, unworthy of loftier feelings, for such feelings will abide in mightier breasts, when such a soul would raise its aspirations to you, unwillingly, struggling to smother them, yet powerless to keep them in check, which feeling would get the better of such a soul? Grief? That is not what grief is made of. Despair? Not despair, either. It is the soul's agony, an idle, cruel, and foredoomed struggle. Despair will slay, this feeling tortures. Love, martyrdom is thy name. In every broken heartstring lies a boundless world of pain and my heart is being broken string by string instead of bursting once and for all. Death is but a moment, despair is lifelong — such a feeling is what hell is made of.

Maria! Could you imagine such torture without shedding tears — of pity? Nay — of horror. However callous a heart, there must be some feeling to move it; however embittered a soul, there

must be some pain to soften it and there is no pain greater than
mine. Why did I happen on this earth at a time when it was pre-
ordained that you should live? Why did I set eyes on you? Why
did I see you? Had I been blind, I should have been spared all this
suffering! Had I not been born at all, I should have been spared a
tortured, barren, purposeless life. My flower! How you smile
amid the garden of your life, little knowing that a soul is writhing
in the agony of death nearby. And your ignorance renders you
even more beauteous, so much the more the cause of my cruel
pain. Alas! the more beauteous you are, the more unhappy you
make me — and the more unhappy, poor me, the more beauteous
you are! I was not given to cherishing any hopes and little did I
care; I cherished no wishes, not one in my whole wretched life
and little did I care. One durst I have, one only, to fill my whole
life, and even that unattainable — you! However great your pity,
it cannot come down so low. Do not smile at me! Your smile
would fill me with idle hopes. Since you cannot bring yourself to
love me, lend me your contempt instead! Pray! Your contempt
might fortunately kill me and death will be a godsend after my
present pain. I worship the ground under your feet, the walls your
shadow may once have glided along, yet I beg for your contempt!
I cannot forbear loving you. You would not know why and it is
beyond me to explain, yet the shade you have cast over the web
of my thoughts is the only happiness I have ever known in this
world.

Maria!... that is your name for sure!... the only name worthy
of you... you!... I cannot call you by any other name... Farewell!
Farewell!

Albeit he had finished the letter, a bittersweet hope, as idle as single-
minded, intoxicated his soul. He was imagining she could be his. Maria! A
whole universe in one single word. Dreaming of her golden head in the cup
of his hands, of her eyes melting away under his kisses, of her dainty waist
resting in the crook of his arm, of how he would hold her white delicate hand
gazing at her diaphanous fingers for hours and hours, he felt he was losing
his mind. What is life after all? He felt an hour next to her would mean more
than a whole lifetime. What intense, excruciating, unspeakable bliss in an
hour of love! And how he would talk to her! What words he would summon

to life, outdoing each other in tenderness beyond meaning and unheard of — for a smile of her lips, a fleeting smile, the shadow of a happy thought. What gratitude for a look; what thankfulness for a moment with her sweet fingers in the palms of his hand — and he actually felt them nestled close to his pounding heart. Like a child, he would weep and laugh for joy and he would go mad at last to dream forever of that incomparable hour.

Whence this unbridled feeling, whence this unrefrained madness? He could not feel his head or his heart, everything was swimming around him in a rosy light; he could only see the white curtains and from behind them her head appeared smiling with diffident and childish wiliness. In love with her? Far beyond that. Not with her, but with her every thought, step, smile — a thousandfold love. Had he been God, he would have forsaken His universe to look for another in her blue eyes, and who knows that He would have found it... for the search would have gone on forever. How he loved her! Had she scorned him, he would have loved her scorn; an inkling of her hatred would have kindled his love for a lifetime.

"Alas!" he smiled in painful intoxication, "that I could kiss her once at least! I would wish for nothing more... or to caress her hands, or to unbraid her hair, or to kiss her shoulders. Angel of mine!"

He had sent the letter. He was standing at the window restless as if he had been expecting a death sentence, not knowing what to think. Nay, not thinking at all, a rambling medley of hazy, intoxicating images fleeting through his mind. Alas! He had asked for scorn and was hoping for love.

She appeared at the window. He hid behind the curtain to spy on her. His eyes were dry with fever and blazing with morbid desire. There she was, his beauty, her large, deep eyes stained with tears, gazing at her lowered joined hands holding the letter, a wavering expression on her face, about to cry like a guilty child. He showed up at his window and her tear-stained eyes took him in... deep, compassionate, swimming... She crumpled the letter, raised it to her heart... and... a sharp, violent ache darted through his heart. His life seemed to fail him, his heart to split apart, a white haze filmed his eyes... then nothing... nothing. He had fallen headlong on the floor of his chamber.

The maiden ran away from the window in fright.

. . .

"What letter is that in your hand, Maria? And what has happened to your looks? What's amiss?" said a friendly, elderly man who had just come to the window, raising the maiden's oval chin in his finely-shaped hand. She made an attempt to smile, but painfully and uneasily...

"Let's have it!"...half-smilingly he unfolded the crumpled letter in her hand... read it, and his countenance grew more and more thoughtful. He arrived at the signature.

"From whom have you received this letter, and where does he live?"

Tears flooded her eyes and she took shelter against her father's chest, sobbing.

"You see," she said haltingly, "he dwells over there, in that deserted house across the road... I saw him collapse like a corpse... no telling whether he be not dead already. Make haste, father... it might not be too late."

"What did he look like?" the elderly man asked, apparently under the burden of an obscure thought.

"Oh! he is so handsome!" she let slip... and she bit her smiling lips.

A bespectacled bald man appeared, whom the elderly man addressed in a flustered low voice, proffering the letter. The bald man shook his head.

They sped down the stairs and reached the house opposite in no time. Though both elderly men, their haste betrayed their lively concern in Dionis. They opened the door. Dionis lay sprawled headlong on the floor, his hair dishevelled, his eyes closed tight. The bald-headed man lifted him from the floor and bared his chest.

"Within an ace of having a vein burst in his heart," he muttered in a hushed voice. "Seems very high strung. Too great a joy could be the end of him. Dangerous even to wake... I shall chloroform him to make this swoon turn into a deep sleep."

While the doctor (for you many have guessed that was the calling of our bald-headed man) was muttering to himself and nodding his head, lifting his eyebrows and moving his spectacles up unto his brow, Maria's father kept staring at the portrait on the wall. A brief word of explanation: the person now under the care of our Aesculapius had rights to a certain inheritance. Evidence was adduced by his likeness to the portrait, as well as by several other circumstances beyond our scope, yet all of them connected with Dionis's so far obscure extraction. Suffice it to say that his financial standing knew an instant change for the better.

He was lying on his bed. His head propped up on the pillows reclining against his chest and the peaceful marble-like pallor of his face were at variance with his dishevelled hair. One hand was pressing hard on his chest, convulsively alleviating the pain inside, the other was hanging over the bedside. He was covered with a black cloak, the creases of which revealed his gentle, finely-built frame. Maria's father bent over him, a pleased purposeful look about his face.

"Aha!," the doctor mused slyly.

. . .

A thick mist, grey and shimmery... then a sky of eternal blue darkness, stars turned mellow under the night's breath, wrinkled clouds, warm air... and again, the old city with narrow streets, cramped houses, moldy eaves in the moonlight, while Dan was pacing briskly along the streets... with the moon darting forth occasional streaks through their darkness... and back into the house, his brain fully conscious of his prolonged dreams.

"So, the wretched idea did flash through my mind," he exclaimed "that Ruben had thought beyond human understanding."

His shadow was sleeping on the bed.

He started leafing Zoroaster's book... the shadow got up slowly... with eyes shut... grew thinner... became one with the wall and took an ironic, fantastic position looming alongside him.

Dan was feeling ill, dejected, cowered under the burden of his thoughts. Besides, a flash of lightning had pierced his heart in his fall. He could still feel the lightening knifing through his heart. He lay on his bed and spread the surplice over him. Uncanny creatures, the like of which he had never set eyes on, were fleeting to and fro before his eyes. "Alas!" he thought, "my hour of death has come and these must be shadows from the netherworld." His own shadow alone was looming erect, apparently smiling and — how odd! — its eyes were blue. "What the hell," he thought, "I have become the laughing-stock of my own shadow."

The door opened letting Master Ruben in.

"What the deuce. Master, why have you been growing whiskers and wearing that Jewish gown?"

"For a long a time, sir, so help me God! — for as long as I can remember," said Ruben smoothing his beard. "Have you ever seen me in another guise by the Old Court?"

"By the Old Court... dwells someone called Riven... the book-seller... not you, Master Ruben."

Ruben gave him a thoughtful look.

"You are not quite yourself, sir," he said gravely.

"I am dying, Master Ruben... Have a look in my desk, there are the memoirs of my shadow, the one you see on the wall, while I was on the moon."

The Jew gave the ailing boy another thoughtful look and shook his head.

"That shadow of yours is only a portrait which resembles you a great deal" he said.

"Master Ruben, either your judgement hasn't changed for the better since I last saw you," said the youth with a smile, "or I have turned into a being superior to my master... which might be true."

The Jew went to the desk the ailing boy had pointed to, opened its drawer, and, true enough, found some bundles of yellowed, antiquated papers tied together with blue strings. He took them out, leafed through them, then put them down on the desk. Thereupon two men entered Dan's cell, who he had never seen before. One of them, bald-headed and withered, came to him to feel his pulse, while the other was talking to Ruben.

Ruben pointed to the papers... the man gave them a cursory examination... "Not a shadow of a doubt," he said to himself. "How long have you known him?" he added, turning to the Jew.

"A long time. He buys books from me. Usually the oldest and the most unsalable. I used to buy them wholesale from destitute libraries of old people whose heirs sold them for a song, books hardly worth the value of their paper. And he would steep himself in such books with a kind of passion, buying the most obscure and incomprehensible. I have brought some such old curiosities with me to show him and make a quick sale... Yet now that I have found him in this plight... besides, he does not call me 'sirrah Riven' any longer, but 'Master Ruben!' God only knows why the strings in the poor boy's brain have gone haywire!"

The ailing boy overheard all this and did not know what to make of it. "These men must be mad," he was thinking, "and Master Ruben is completely out his mind... he does not talk sense. Aha!" he thought at last, "I must be dead, so Ruben has brought the doctors with him to sell my corpse. He has every right to it... my body must have become phenomenal owing to the changes I have been passing through. But are these two real doctors?... Both look like Satan to me... Or are they one man split into two apparitions, so the crafty Ruben can poke fun at me... one half with hair, the other bald. The bald-headed half is feeling my pulse, while the hairy one is scanning my shadow hung on that nail on the wall. Lo! He is taking it down from the wall and handing it to Ruben. "Well done! Master Ruben," he cried, "your devils are skillful in taking shadows off the wall, and now the bald one is going to grab me... for I can see through him, though he is playing the doctor... Well done! Well done!"

He started clapping his hands in a fit of laughter.

Ruben took his shadow and the papers on the desk and left the house slamming the door behind him...

"You have left me, old Jew... after selling me to the Tormentor of Souls," he murmured in painful resignation and let his head drop onto the pillows.

"He is feverish... in delirium," the bald-headed man said gravely.

• • •

Night. A fragrant cool is coming in by the open window while Dionis, lying in his bed, is shivering with fever, his lips dry, beads of sweat on his brow, his mind in a haze. He seems to have awakened from a succession of never-ending, obscure, meaningless dreams and he is scanning the reality around him with misgiving. His father's portrait is missing from the wall and so are the ancient books... yet the house is the same, with fashionable new furniture, the floor spread over with carpets, the old bed alone the same. "Odd," he mused, "wonder succeeding wonder... I no longer know what is happening to me." The moon was flooding his room with golden light and the furniture and the carpets gave a smooth, slumbery shimmer under this translucent enamel; a high-pitched grandfather clock was ticking sluggishly on the wall and a train of fleeting, hazy, and blurred images of recent occurrences was flickering through his mind. And they all had the inconsistency of dreams, for he felt his present mood refreshed, cool and clear as compared to the previous plight. The shady world of his youth had vanished from around him and he was envisaging his future as if gazing at the bottom of a quiet, crystal-clear lake. He could not account for that clearness of mind. He closed his eyes. All of a sudden he felt someone at his bedside, seated on his legs. Then he felt the touch of a sweet, small hand on his brow. He half-opened his eyes. He beheld a boy with an oval, pale, rather haggard face, his golden hair straying out of a wide-brimmed, black velvet hat, clad in a velvet singlet and the daintiest waist imaginable, girt with a shiny belt. Dionis's half-closed eyes did not betray his attention. He took him in from his gold-flooded head to his tiny boots, shining radiantly on the flowered carpet.

"Ah!" he thought, his heart pounding, "it is Maria!"

Yes, it was she, his dearest. She was talking to herself, as girls are wont to do... He felt the air smell sweeter under her whispers.

"I have left home surreptitiously in this guise... they kept putting me off day after day... that sawbones of a doctor mumbling it would be danger-ous for him to... dangerous, my foot! Me, dangerous?" she uttered sharply. "If he should wake up, then, oh then really... Sleep! Sleep!" She whispered, touching his brow with her lips... He felt a cool dew running through his hair... but by then his arms had taken her neck hostage... She tried to draw away in fear, but his arm still held her tight to his breast... he sat up, "Let go of me," she said, blushing.

But he had enchained her and was now caressing her white brow, caus-ing her hat to fall and the waves of blond hair to stream down her shoul-ders... then he took both her tiny hands into his... she offered no more resistance... he sat gazing at them, kissing her fingers... she offered no resis-tance at all...

"Maria, do you love me?"

"What if my name is not Maria?" she said, under the urge of some unaccountable malice.

"What might it be, then?"

"But it is! Really!" she answered with silvery tinkles in her voice, "yet will you kindly be silent now, for you are not allowed to talk... not yet... and do not get out of bed, for you are not allowed that either..." She pushed him back onto the pillows... He would have liked to talk, but his mouth was being covered with kisses... He closed his eyes and felt that his heart stopped free from the confines of his breast... then he opened them again to let them feast on that sweet load childishly making fun of his smile as well as of her own surprise and fear... of everything under the sun...

Many a time, on long winter nights, when she had become the jewel of his wedlock, when they were willingly living in the seclusion of some remote village to keep their love away from the hubbub of the world, Maria would put in an unexpected appearance in the warm drawing-room, its only light the red beams of the live embers on the hearth, in a boy's attire, as on the night they had first seen each other at close range — her slender limbs in the black velvet singlet, the same wide-brimmed hat on her blonde hair and the tiniest feet ever in men's footwear. She drew nigh to him, her milky, diaphanous, wax-like hands even whiter against the soft black sleeves, and they would pace arm in arm in the warm semi-darkness of the room; time and again their lips would meet, time and again they would stop in front of a mirror, their heads resting against each other, and they would burst out laughing. It was a prepossessing contrast: his drawn fine countenance still bearing the imprints of the bitterness of a tormented youth with just a touch of inexpressible naiveté round the mouth, against her milk-white oval physiognomy... the visage of a young demon nigh to the visage of an angel never visited by doubt.

· · ·

A few concluding words. Is Dan the real hero of these incidents or is it Dionis? Many of our readers may have been hunting for the clue to his events in his surroundings. They may have found the ingredients of his spiritual life in reality: Ruben is Riven; the shadow on the wall, playing such an important role, is the blue-eyed portrait — with it out of the way, what you might be goaded to consider a fixed idea disappears in its turn; finally, in possession of the thread of causality, many will have thought to have conjectured the meaning of his incidents reducing them to as many dreams of a diseased imagination.

Were they dreams or were they not? — that is the question. Might not there be a stage manager behind the scene of life whose existence we cannot ascertain? Might we not be cut in the likeness of those dummies who, ordered to represent a great army, will strut across the stage, skirt the backstage, and come back onto the stage again? Might not all mankind throughout history be likened to such an army of itinerant players disappearing hither only to put in a new appearance thither, an army numerous to the onlooking spectator, though of the same limited number to the manager? Are not the actors the same, though the plays be changed? Fair enough, we are not in a position to pry behind the stage. Likewise, might not there be some living person experiencing such moments of retrospective clearness of mind that they might seem to us reminiscences of a long bygone man?

We will not refrain from quoting a few lines from one of Théophile Gautier's epistles, which render this idea more colorful: "We do not unfailing belong in the country that gave us birth, and that is why we keep searching for our rightful homeland. People cast of that mould will feel themselves exiles in their own city, strangers in their own home, and belabored by a reversed homesickness... It would be easy to assign not only the country, but also the particular century wherein their real lives should have been lived. It seems to me I must have lived in the East at some time or other so, when during the carnival I disguise myself in a Muslim caftan, I feel as if I was wearing my customary attire. I have always been surprised at not understanding every word of Arabic. I must have forgotten it."

Translated by Ioan Giurgea
Revised by Kurt W. Treptow

FINIS

Wasted Genius

Tasso in Scotland

Dumas holds that the novel is as old as mankind. He may be right. It is the metaphor of life. Have a look at the gilt tail-side of a fake coin, listen to the idle song of a day with no claim to raise more ado in the world than any other ordinary day, unveil the poetry lying dormant in them, and the novel is all there.

In a stack of dusty old books (for I have a bias for such old curiosities), I came across a more recent volume: *Novellas with Six Engravings*. I opened it and came across the history of a Scottish king on the verge of falling prey to death on account of an embalmed human skull. And could you imagine whom the lithographer had to play the king of Scotland in his engravings? Tasso! The explanation is easy to provide: economy. I produced Tasso's portrait for the purpose of comparing them. It was he, trait for trait. What bizarre coincidences can occur on this earth, I said to myself, a smile lighting up my dreaminess. Could a similar history such as that which I was reading ever befall a Tasso?

Yet I had overlooked that all objective impossibilities are none the less possible in our mind and that, in the long run, everything we behold, hear, think, and consider comes down to all too arbitrary creations of our own subjectivity rather than to real things. Life is but a dream.

It was a gloomy night. A fine drizzle was pattering on the uncobbled streets of Bucharest, winding, narrow, and muddy, among the cluster of low ramshackle houses which make up most of the self-styled capital of Romania. You would find yourself trampling in the mudpools splashing you with their clammy water as soon as you ventured to put your foot down a step forward. A dingy light was filtering out through the large unwashed windows of pubs and shops, turned even weaker by the raindrops splashing against the glass. Now and then you would pass by some red-curtained window wherein some woman showed her charms in the semidarkness. Here and there I would spy some romantic passing by, whistling a tune under his breath. Some drunkard would give a raucous call under the windows of perdition and the painted woman behind the pane would readily light a match to display her salve-greased face and her withered naked breast — perhaps the last means of smothering filthy passions in misshapen souls ravaged by corruption and drink. The drunkard would enter, the semidarkness would turn pitch dark, and the twilight of contemplation would decline into a lead-heavy midnight when I was thinking that such creatures were apt to style themselves as men or women. Yet you have to make allowances, for such are three quarters of this race and — as to the remaining fourth — God only knows the scarcity of characters worthy of the name "humans."

From the door of an open pub I heard the shrieks of some off-key strings, ill-used by a poor Gypsy urchin, his dried-up fingers clenched about a shaggy bow while a foolish slattern and a ragged spindly Gypsy, his feet in large, straw-stuffed shoes, were bounding and bouncing about him. Grotesque, unsightly mirth was painted on the faces of both.

There was a coffee-house next door. The rain and cold that had pierced to my bones left me no choice but enter it. The stench of tobacco and the unrelenting clatter of the domino players took their toll on my senses, already dazed by the rain and the cold. The grandfather clock, faithful interpreter of the old time, clang its metal tongue a dozen times to let the uncaring people know that the twelfth hour of the night had petered out. At a scattering of tables there were foursomes of card players with dishevelled hair, holding the cards in one shaking hand, snapping the fingers of the other before laying the stakes, with staring looks, taciturn, biting their lips without a word and, occasionally, gulping noisy mouthfuls of the coffee or beer in front of them — some show of triumph!

A youth bent over a billiard table kept chalking on the green cloth the word *Ilma*. He made me think he was one of Arpad's race and that he was either bringing to light some dear sweetheart's name from the recesses of his memory or else some Hungarian ideal from the novels of Mauriciu Jokay. I gave no other thought to the person of this youth, disappointed in love, perhaps, but turned to thumbing through some foreign newspapers, literary and art magazines, etc. (Ours have nothing to say on these matters, nor do they show the slightest concern).

The youth came up to me.

"I'll wait for my turn," he said with a bow.

A perfect Romanian accent — he is no Hungarian.

"Here you are," I said, proffering the paper, surprised at the sudden interest he roused in me as soon as I had uplifted my eyes.

A man I knew without ever having met him, one of those faces that you feel you must have seen at some time in your past without ever having seen it, a phenomenon which may be accounted for only by assuming some spiritual affinity. I set to observing him at length. He was handsome — demonically handsome. A brow serene and impassive like the meditation of a philosopher rose above his pale, muscular, and expressive face and, from above his brow, his glossy black hair, a savage mark of genius, streamed down onto his well-made sinewy shoulders. His large hazel eyes were glowing like a dark flame beneath his thick, bushy, knit eyebrows, and his tightly closed bluish lips showed uncommon sternness. One would have easily taken him for an atheist poet of the race of the fallen angels, a Satan, yet not wizened, hideous, loathsome, as painters would have him, but a handsome Satan, unspeakably handsome, a Satan taking pride in his fall, on whose brow God had writ genius, and Hell had writ obstinacy, a godly Satan who, endowed with life in heaven, had partaken of the most saintly light, had feasted his eyes on the most sublime ideals, had bathed his soul in the most precious dreams, to be left with bleak disappointment, engraved about his lips, after his fall to the earth, and sorrow at having forfeited his place in heaven. His fast-fluttering nostrils and quick-sparkling eyes were tokens of an unbridled heart and fiery character. His fine sparing frame and his white hand with long, aristocratic fingers revealed, however, an iron strength. All his appearance exuded a generous yet infernal power.

He picked up a Romanian newspaper. At the advertising page he read out in a low, sarcastic voice: "The Italian Opera... *The Huguenots.*"

"Would you rather it were Romanian?" I uttered unconcernedly.

"No mistake about it. Could we not have an opera... sweeter and more beautiful than the Italian?"

"You haven't been here long."

"Right."

"I see," I said.

"What?"

"Our countrymen," I went on, "are dry, bitter, skeptical cosmopolitans — and what is worse, they boast the nice trait of loving anything foreign and hating everything Romanian. We have severed all ties with the past, whether it be language, ideas, or ways of thinking and reasoning, for otherwise we might not pass for a civilized nation in the eyes of Europe."

"Yet... are you actually what you wish to be taken for?"

"Hmm... you do not belong here... that much I can see."

"Right."

"So... There's more to it... Well, take it from me that no one here takes pains to be what he claims. You will encounter historians ignorant of history, men of letters and journalists unable to write, actors unable to act, ministers unable to govern, financiers unable to calculate, all this resulting in so much paper soiled uselessly, so much beastly yelling resounding in the theatre houses, so many cabinet reshuffles, and so many bankruptcies. You can sooner find men polling pro and con the existence of God than souls in love with the tongue and customs of their forbearers, than hearts in love with the expressive trait of our people — or minds concerned with the daily problems of this people on whom we brand all the phantasmagorias of our fake civilization. Divorce and adultery strut their sickly, thickly-smeared faces along our streets, like live puppets: their smile renders our women fruitless, their smile withers our men, yet we throw parties in their honor, sacrifice our winter nights, squander away our youth which ought to be consecrated to striving for the ideals wished for by all mankind and to establishing a family... The women of our nation do not work... they have means of earning their living; men do not work either, for there is no work for them — all the factories in the world compete with their miserable trades. As to our intelligentsia — a generation of hirelings... of smatterers... men lying in wait to seize power... a misguided intelligentsia more conversant with the history of France than with the history of Romania, scions of men blown here by all the winds of the world, for the Romanian children themselves are not yet deemed worthy of book learning... in short, men whose visage and character come down from their Greek or Bulgarian ancestors, their name only appropriated from their mother — the disgraced Romania. If only they had done any small deed to deserve the name of Romanians! Far from it. They hate their country more bitterly than any aliens. They consider her a place of exile, a sorry plight in their existence... being, according to themselves, Romanian by birth, French by allegiance — and, if France cared to bestow on our smatterers the privileges they enjoy in their unhappy homeland, they would have surely moved there long ago — every single one of them!"

"By my honor," I continued drying my brow "single me out a man to write the novel of the miseries of this generation and he is likely to fall like a bomb amid our dried-up intelligentsia, a demigod to myself and a possible saviour of his country."

"Swerve the public opinion, swerve its bias, rouse up the national genius, its genuine and unmistakable spirit from the recesses wherein it lies in slumber — stir an all-pervading moral reaction, a revolution of ideas, whereby the notion of Romanian should mean more than human, great, beautiful, in short, be Romanian in flesh and spirit," he said in a throaty voice.

"Whoever will you have accomplish that? Everyone is cut of the same mould. All nations are responsive — whether French, Italians, Spaniards or whatever — barring us, Romanians."

"Nay, strength does not lie in number... The public spirit is the making of a handful of men. It is within the power of one God-anointed brow to gather the whole ocean of human reflections into one gigantic whirlpool which could sore from that abyss up to the clouds of wisdom surrounding the morning star, and that is what genius means. Let them face the ghost of the future and they will become frightened... Let them envisage where the path they are following now is leading, and they will turn back... Yet, in the teeth of that," he added with a sceptic smile, "why should we carry the burden of our generation upon our shoulders? All earthly means lead to their proper ends. If it be written that they should come to nought, then so they shall, no matter what our pains."

"Cosmopolitans?" he added under his breath, "Hmm! I am a cosmopolitan myself; oh, that the world were a prism, one only, sparkling and suffused with light, though beaming forth ever so many colors. A prism with a myriad of colors, a rainbow with a myriad of shades. Nations are mere shades of the prism of Humankind, and the differences among them are as natural and explainable as the differences among this individual and that, all due to circumstances. Render these colors equally bright, equally polished, equally bathed in the Light which shapes them out of the void of nothingness — for in the darkness of injustice and barbarism all nations are equal in brutishness, beastliness, fanaticism, and vulgarity — yet let one streak of light shine on them and they will display prismatic colors. A wave is the soul of one man, but the soul of a nation is an ocean. As long as the wind of misty wings and the night of darkish air and grey clouds reign above the sea and her waves, she will still slumber, untroubled and dark, coiled on her floor, amid indiscernible whispers; whereas, when the Light blooms forth in the serene and blue kingdom of heaven like a fiery flower, each wave will don a sun on its brow, the sea herself partaking of the color of the sky and the limpidity of his greatness, wafting them back her deep, untroubled sleep. When the nation is kept in the dark, she will slumber voicelessly in the depth of her unfathomable power and greatness, but when liberty and civilization flutter their wings over her, superior men will emerge and let the sun bathe their brows whence they will make it reverberate into far-reaching beams on to the commonest people — so that the bosom of the sea may be as clear as the day mirroring the crystal clear sky on her floor. The poets and philosophers of any nation turn their eyes to the heaven above in search of rhyme or reason and they pass their findings on to their nations. Yet there are such clouds which, once darkening the sky, are apt to spread darkness over the earth beneath. Alas! The clouds, lords over the earth, will drive their unbridled thunderbolts over the hosts of waves forever, albeit those clouds be no more than the icy, gloomy exhalation of the wretched waves themselves. The clouds will pour down thunder and lightning, shielding the gilded Sun beneath an iron curtain and, so long as they hold sway over the brows of the waves, so long as the darkness they let fall from their towering shadow will turn the depth of the soul of the sea into a cold and voiceless night, so long the Lord's Creation is to stay wretched.

The most numerous and venomous clouds are the monarchs.

Next to them, though as full of venom, are the diplomats.

Their thunderbolts, which they wield to ruin, kill, and turn to dust whole nations, are the wars.

Crush all monarchs! Oust their most servile hirelings, the diplomats. Abolish war, call the complaints of the nations before the Tribunal of Nations and you will have the most felicitous cosmopolitanism warm the Earth with its peaceful and righteous rays."

The reasoning of the youth — bizarre as it was — roused my full attention and I sat drinking in, as it were, the words flowing forth from his thin, pale lips. His face was growing ever more thoughtful and expressive, taking on a fantastic look. I let myself drift along the smooth stream of his reflections into an otherworld of dreams.

"Do not think," he said, "that cosmopolitanism as I see it, is without its fervent followers." With these words he produced from the inside pocket of his jacket a small sheet lithographed somewhere in the north of Germany. Originated in an underground printing house from the pens of a group of young apostles of true liberty and of the most feasible and equalitarian cosmopolitanism, the sheet advocated a host of praiseworthy, beautiful, and youthful ideas. It called on all nations to set up a Holy Alliance against the despicable tyrants of this world, with a view to banishing from the affairs of the world the wicked despots, the diplomats trampling on the catchwords of the day, and war which bleeds dry the sacred hearts of nations.

Oh, thou wondrous dream, spread thy wings wider over the face of the earth and, once become rooted conviction, overthrow peacefully, without bloodshed, all despotic crowned heads along with the nations tyrannizing over their sister nations!

An hour chimed. On the stroke of it, he got up, shoved the lithographed sheet into his pocket, proffered his right hand, and put on his hat with his left.

"My name is Toma Nour... What is yours?"

I told him my name. He walked out leaving me prey to the uncanny idea of making him the hero of a novella.

Back home, I had hardly struck a match to light the lamp when in the dimness of the room I caught sight of the story book with its six engravings. The match went out leaving me in darkness.

"I say," I remarked, "is it inconceivable that I might discover a Tasso in this fellow? Shall I examine him more closely?" The darkness about me felt like the metaphor of his name: Toma Nour (cloud).

II

Having set for myself the task of immortalizing his noble image in the marble of a novella, I was now eager to develop a closer acquaintance with my hero.

I met him several times and, as an instinctive attraction drove me toward him, I invited him to visit me. I had a friend in him now, a friend who would only call on me to chide me, who would wear nothing but black clothes, who would laugh his foolish laugh in the company of people, only the more bitterly to lament at home, who professed hating people and was peevish like an old hag so that he would make a nuisance of himself in a society that nauseated him.

He had not yet asked me to visit him. Finally, one day he bestowed upon me that unexpected favour. I went to his place. He lived in a high-ceilinged, large, but sparsely-furnished room. In the corners of the ceiling the spiders were going about their silent and peaceful work; in a corner of the room, on the bare floor, several hundreds of books were slumbering in random stacks, dreaming of their content; there was a wooden bed in another corner spread with a straw pallet and a red quilt, and a dingy table in front of the bed, its top carved with Latin and Gothic lettering by the penknife of some wayward child. On the table — sheets of paper, verses, newspapers, whole or torn to shreds, short-lived pamphlets handed out gratis, in short, an incomprehensible and purposeless confusion.

Yet, above the books slumbering in their corner, hanging on a nail, there was an oil painting of the full-sized bust of an eighteen-year-old boy, his hair dark and long, his lips thin and rosy, his face marble-white, his eyes large and blue beneath thick eyebrows and long dark lashes. The blue eyes of the boy were so shiny, so clear in hue, that they made the spectator warm up to their innocent, tender, rather feminine look. It was a genuine work of art. Though the portrait of a manly-clad person, his delicate, small, white hands, the finely-drawn, dewy, shiny, soft pallor of his face, his unfathomably deep eyes, his arched, *too* narrow brow, as well as his longish wavy hair might have led one into taking him for a woman in disguise.

"Who is the lady?" I inquired of Toma, who was lying sprawled over his red quilt.

"Lady, eh?! "... he laughed, "always dreaming of ladies. I swear on my manhood it was a man like you or me..."

"Nonetheless, those eyes..."

"Those eyes?...Had you only seen those eyes once in your life, you would have imagined seeing them afresh in each bluish morning star, in each blue wave of the sea, and through each azure rift in the clouds. How beautiful the boy was and how young when he passed away! He was a friend, perhaps the only friend I have ever had, and he loved me unselfishly and gave his life to save mine; and if my hand dabbling in painting could daub these eyes which seem beauteous to you, you can but imagine how beauteous they must have been in real life. Beauteous have they stayed in my dark, cold, and mad soul, like two bluish stars, two only, twinkling on the dome of heaven between the rifts in the clouds. My friend, you might end up as a columnist with some newspaper... When I die, I will bequeath a booklet with the story of my life for you to turn its long weary years, sad, monotonous, and sorrowful though they were, into an hour of leisure for some coffee house patron, for some romantic youth, or some mincing girl with nothing to lose and no urge to love, though still eager to learn from novels how to write her love-letters."

"Oh!... such as you who pose as fainting heroes of the French novelists, who would love like the German sentimentalists," I rejoined, "and fill your bellies like the practical English, such as you are apt to live to be as old as the hills and, take it from me, my friend, that you, in spite of your affliction, in spite of your looks, so heroically pale, will outlive me and see me turn to dust. Will you lay the stakes?"

"As I have already told you," Toma replied, "let the stakes be our biographies in the form of novellas. If I should die before you, I will leave you mine, if your turn comes first, I'll inherit yours. That's all."

One night I had come to Toma's. The moon was shining brightly and there was no candle lit inside. Toma was lying on his bed dreaming and drawing lung fulls of smoke from a long chibouk, the embers in his pipe burning in the darkness of the room like an eye of red flame glowing in the night. I was standing by the open window dreamily contemplating the pale face of the moon. Opposite Toma's house there stood the stately palace of... one of our so-called aristocrats... By the open window of the upper floor there floated in the night air the sweet notes of a piano along with the youthful voice of a maiden, breathing forth a gently-perfumed fantastic prayer. I closed my eyes, to let my dreams run loose. I envisaged myself in a desert, barren, wide, and sandy, like the drought itself, with a fantastic pale moon glimmering above like the visage of a dying maiden. Midnight... The desert is silent... no breeze stirs the air, the only things alive are my breath and my eye so it can spy high up in the sky a white angel kneeling on a silvery cloud, her supplicating hands joined, chanting a divine, deep, tremulous prayer: a maiden's prayer. I half-opened my eyes and beheld beyond the open bow window in a brightly-lit drawing-room a youthful maiden, a white gown floating about her, enthralling the keyboard of a responsive piano with her thin, long, and white fingers, and accompanying the soft moans of some divine score with her sweet, tender, and low voice. As if the genius of Shakespeare, the divine Briton, had breathed out into the world another lunatic angel — another Ophelia... I closed my eyes afresh until, back in the endless desert, the white palace merged into the silvery cloud and the youthful white maiden into the kneeling angel. Then, forcing my eyes to close tighter, I drowned my dream into a sea of darkness, I shut out the images, yet I could still hear, receding farther and farther away like a dim memory: the prayer of a maiden.

The music had long ceased yet I, a wilful prey to my imagination, still kept my eyes closed. When awakening from my reverie, the upper window of the palace was closed, there was darkness in the drawing-room, its panes glittering like silver in the white moonlight. A scent of summer suffused the translucent air and the moonbeams coming into Toma's chamber flooded his upturned face. It was paler than I knew it and two moonbeams seemed to pour gold speckles on a couple of tears trickling down his closed eyes.

"Weeping?" I managed to ask, softly and tenderly, for my own soul was brimful with tears.

"Imagine being loved by such an angel, with no love to reciprocate;" he whispered in a husky, bitter voice.

"What's ailing you?" I said.

"Ailing, you call it?" he rejoined. "Alas! had you the dimmest glimpse into my soul, you would shrink back in fright — for you cannot imagine what a wasteland, what a desert it is — an epitome of the idiot and barren thinking of a man whose ears are deaf as clay, whose mouth is dumb as the ground, whose eyes are blind as stone! No feelings are apt to surge within me, yet when a chance tear trickles down my eyes, I call that bliss! You have beheld an angel paying homage to her God — nay, that angel's earthly love is set on an unfeeling, shallow, hard-hearted demon — me. As for myself.... I have no love to return. So many stars in the sky, so many loves on this earth, yet no one star to twinkle in my night and no love to warm my soul. Ever so seldom can I still hear a throb welling up my ravaged soul, ever so seldom the breath stops short in my breast, like the wind vainly buffeting against the ruins turned to rubble by the burden of ages — those are the moments when feelings surge up within me!... Oh, those are the moments I choose to elbow the people in the streets with my eyes shut, living in either the past or the future. Dreaming the dream of the infant who will talk and smile in his sleep to the Mother of God. I betake myself to heaven, spread out wide wings from my shoulders and forsake the earth to abandon my soul to those divine shadows — dreams that will fly me from world to world and from thought to thought. Dead on this earth, but how alive in heaven!

Oh! That I could love!

Can you realize the pain of it — of not being able to love? To pace the earth in so many appointed steps, with your sight turned inward, to toss about within the cold and narrow confines of your soul, struggling to fathom it only to find it dried up with its stream wasted under the sand of social draught or evaporated from the blistering heat of a society of men thriving on their hatred against their peers.

Not to love is of no consequence — not being able to love is terrible."

Toma Nour, having put an end to his apologue of hatred and indifference, got out of bed and began pacing his large room. The moonlight flooded the marble-white face of the icon on the wall, whose eyes seemed to glow with life in the dark.

"Oh, Ioan!," Toma burst out and kissed the icon's eyes of bluish fire, "Ioan forgive me for having fallen into a hell of hatred, you who used to preach for a heaven of love from deep down in your angelic heart!"

The moon had hid beyond a black raincloud split by two red lightning bolts. The house fell into darkness and neither shadow could be perceived any longer — the one on the wall, Ioan, or the other of walking marble, Toma.

"Toma," I whispered, "I'll be on my way... good night. Beware of madness."

I let myself out and went home.

Toma was apparently his old self, but it was clear to me he was going to pieces.

Nonetheless one day I reached a praiseworthy decision and put on a grave mien, though given by nature to sport rather than to mourning, so as to deliver a harangue on morale and sanity to that fellow whom I tended to take for a wasted genius. This is how I am. In my dreams I look on myself as a beastly tyrant, thirsty for bloodshed, slaughter, and gold, whereas I am no better than a smoke without a fire in broad daylight. My grudge against a fellow is as short-lived as his against me. Yet I could be harder on Toma.

"Toma," I said, "you are going to the dogs. For God's sake, come out of your den and socialize a little, before they label you as crazy."

I kept repeating such words, or others of the same importance, for days on end, yet he would not answer, and his face stayed inscrutable and unconcerned at my friendly, though childish reproaches. Until one day when he burst out in a loud, fiery voice — with filmy eyes and jerky breath.

"Keep your counsel, you child! What is it you want?... Do you think — you, or the other pigmy souls about me — that you have the least inkling of who I am? What they see is the carcass of a man — and each one, according to his lights, tailors a soul for this black-clad biped — and there is their man. 'He's mad, the poor devil,' this one says. 'He's a dreamer,' says another.... 'So! He would have us take him for an original,' the third butts in — and all these personalities, ready-made for me, have nothing to do with my real self. I am what I am and suffice it to say that their guesses are preposterous. Their praise does not flatter me for they praise an entity entirely dissimilar from mine... Their jeers do not hurt me for they jeer at an entity I know nothing of... I despise people.... I've had enough of them."

With that, it goes without saying, he stifled any argument that might have flashed into my mind. I chided him no longer — no use reasoning with the door post.

One day he left Bucharest with no word of farewell to me or any of his acquaintances.

A year passed without hearing from him. One day I get a letter from Copenhagen. It read: *"Friend, send me Alecsandri's poems post-haste — under the initials Y.Y."* And that was the long and the short of it.

I obliged. Then I left for the country, to my parents's small estate whereon I spent a beautiful summer, with tales and songs of yore. Yet, on leaving, I put an old charwoman in charge of accepting my letters and stowing them away in the drawer of my desk.

When autumn set in, I took wing from those cold vast plains covered with hoar-frost and took shelter in Bucharest, in my small, yet cosy chamber on the third floor.

I am an incorrigible dreamer. Once I sat nodding over the tabletop spinning gorgeous dreams, musing on those mysteries in the life of nations and in the flow of generations which, alike to the high and the low tide of the sea, are apt to bring about their rise and fall in their awesome pageant. The weather was bleak and wailing like the musings of the dying, the driving rain swished on the windowpanes, the fire in the hearth had turned to cinders, the candle was flickering about to give up its ghost — and I seemed to hear the murmur of those old sages who, while a boy cuddled in their trembling arms, would pass the winter nights recounting fantastic tales with fairies clad in gold and beams of light singing away their untroubled lives in their crystal palaces.

Long years had passed and I still had a yesteryear feeling of entangling my fingers in the tufts of their white beards and listening to their soft-all-wise voices, to the wisdom of the bygone past, to the sages' tidings. How I wished I could have lived my life in the past! To have lived in ages when princes clad in gold and sable sat on their thrones in time-old castles and lent their ear to the eldermen's council — the elated Christian throng undulating like waves on the sea within the walls of the princely court — while I, amid those heads crowned with the white hair of wisdom, amid the elated people, should be their heart fired with genius, their mind ripe with inspiration, their priest for better and for worse, their own bard. To lend more succor to those dreams, I opened some old chronicles and, while thumbing through their pages, I came across a yet unsealed envelope which, doubtless, my housekeeper had received and stowed away in a book. I ripped it open. It went like this:

Turin, date of no consequence.

"Friend,

You have actually sent me Alecsandri's poems. Grateful. I often read Emmi, the only thing in the world able to squeeze a tear from my eyes. Really, you and your fellows in idling your lives away nurse a queer idea of death... you are no wiser than imagining the skeleton of some corpse and calling it death. As for me, it is a beloved thorn-crowned, wan-faced, black-winged angel. An angel it is... the angel of my dreams, such a well-known visage, the sole visage that could call forth the bliss of the world with one smile and the melancholy of the earth with one teardrop. That visage is here no more. Those smiling lips have been closed by the smile of death, or I would rather have it like this: Death, covetous of my soul, took on the guise of a maid, tread the earth and bereft me of my heart first so as, once she was here no more, my soul itself should follow suit. Write to me. My sight is impaired and my ears are ringing with the chant of the shadows I am soon to meet in the netherworld. My angel covers the face of the sun and her black wings gradually turn to darkness my remaining hours, so soon to be ended. I am to die. Write me soon, that I might be still here to get your letter. When I am dead a strange legacy shall fall into your hands. Remember this: my body belongs to the earth and my soul to you.

Yours for the time being,
Toma Nour"

A trembling tear welled out of my eyelashes and I threw the letter into the hearth. My eyes, bleary with tears and sleeplessness, recalled in a wild vision the bluish visage of my unhappy friend, his brains incandescent with meditation, his jaws closed tight in bitterness and misanthropy, his eyes sunken and murky like the eyes of a madman. Doubtless, he was dead by now. I opened the drawer of my desk and took out what few portraits I had scattered among my papers. His portrait was next to Tasso's.

The missive had long lain in the chronicle. It was old.

Another month passed by and I received a parcel from a small town in Germany — the capital of a miniature-king, a parody-king, a satire-king. The parcel contained a manuscript of Toma Nour's biography.

Among its pages, a scrap of paper with these words:

"Friend. I am not dead yet, but I am sentenced to death. My execution will be carried through soon. My dwelling is a stately palace — magnificent guards stand at the gate — though it be rather dark and damp — they call it prison. Do what you will with the manuscript. Farewell. See you again in the next world!

Toma"

This is the manuscript:

III

I saw the dark of the world under a snowdrift, which is to say in one of those cottages whose only claim to existence in winter is the green smoke curling up from their chimneys. My father was as poor as a church mouse, one of the poorest in our hamlet... All I can recollect of my mother is a pale shape, an angel who charmed my infancy with her pained, sad voice. I was still an infant the day I noticed that mother would not answer me, having fallen asleep, white-faced, distaff in hand, her lips half-parted in a smile. She looked like wrapt in some deep thought; I would pull at her sleeve, but she seemed unresponsive! Eventually my father came, some people laid her in state on a table... all villagers came... some of them weeping; I stood there looking up at them, little knowing what had come to pass. As often as not I had seen people lying stiff on a bed they called bier carried away amid chanting and wailing, and had noticed that tears were welling down mother's cheeks when they were passing by our house, the reason escaping me... Night closed in... The men in the house were playing cards, yet mother was lying there still white-faced and unmoving. On the third day they took her to a wooden house topped with a cross — to the church; a white-bearded old man in clothes trailing down to his heels and of the most diverse colors chanted something through his nose — then they laid her into a grave, shovelled earth over her until they covered her.... I returned home. For three days I had let no words pass my lips and this wonder befuddled my inexperienced brain. I cannot recall my every feeling but a terrible fear had overcome me that I was not to see mother any more... I set to looking for her about the house... and in all places... it seemed to me I could hear her low sweet voice with never a glimpse of herself. As soon as darkness set in, I went to church... I saw a mound where they had left mother. A candle of yellow wax was burning in the night like a golden star through the darkness of the clouds. I lay on the grave and put an ear to the ground. "Mother! mother!", I cried out, "get out of there and come on home... The house is empty", I wailed. "Father has not turned up all day, your white doves have gone berserk and flown away... Come here, mother, or take me there with you"... I strained my ear. Yet the mound stayed cold, silent, and wet — a gust of wind blew out the candle letting the pitch-black night rush into my very soul. Mother would not come... tears started welling down my cheeks, wooden claws were clutching at my heart and, overwhelmed with sobbing, I was lulled to sleep by the hooting of a sad owl.

And this is what I dreamed. From very far above, from those floating rocks people call clouds, I beheld a ray descending straight toward me, and a woman was flying downward along the ray, attired in a long white gown... it was mother... She breathed out a charm over me and I spied a white turtle-dove flying out of my bosom into mother's arms... I was lying cold and pale on the grave, as mother had been, yet I felt that I was not my old self any longer, for I was the dove... In mother's arms I turned from dove into a milk-white pretty child with a pair of silver down wings on my shoulders. The golden ray rose up with us... we passed through a night of clouds and a day of stars and finally we alighted in a world of fragrance and sing, a wondrous garden beyond the stars. The trees there had gems for leaves and lights for blossoms and thousands of fiery stars glittered among their boughs in place of apples. All the paths, strewn with silver sand, led to its middle whereat stood a resplendent white table on which wax candles were glittering like gold and the saints seated round it were attired in white, as mother was, and haloes of rays shone round their heads. They were telling tales and singing songs of the ages when there was no world nor people and I listened in wonder... Suddenly a cold darkness lashed my cheeks and the eyes I had opened. I found myself on the same mound of dirt, the hailstones were hitting my face and the black clouds in the sky were torn into thousands of shreds by fiery-red forks of lightning. The hoarse bell gave sickly moans in the steeple and the wooden plate kept striking against the belfry pillars.

I ran clear of the mound, wet and full [of mud] and coiled down in the belfry, soaked through and with teeth chattering, my long hair fallen over my eyes and my cold weak hands drawn back into my wet sleeves. I stayed like that all night. About cockcrow I summoned my bare feet to plod the way back home in the mud. I entered the hut... there was no firewood left on the hearth... inside it the cinders were hardly glowing and father was sitting on a low stool with bitter tears trickling down his unshaven sunburnt face.

"Where have you been?" he asked, taking my freezing hands into his tender grip.

"Looking for mother... where's mother?"

His breast swelled as if to burst, he took me in his arms, hugged me lovingly, and covered my cold face with hot kisses.

"The hoarse bell gave sickly moans in the steeple and the wooden plate
kept striking against the belfry pillars."

A. Bordenache

"Your mother, poor child," he whispered, "your mother? You are mother-less now..."

I was now the only consolation my aggrieved father was to know. I was the apple of his eye, the food for his thoughts, the hope of his old age. While still an infant I would go to our old curate who, seating me on his knees, gave me my first lessons in reading. An overwhelming yearning, an unquenchable thirst for knowledge had stirred up within me, which also was to be my doom. Had I stayed in my mountains and let my heart take delight in doinas and my mind in the delusions of fairy tales, I might have been a happy man.

Father sent me to school. What I learnt there I do not know, but this I know: that my days felt like a barren winter, like a meaningless dream.

Of those poor children who sit at their school desks and drink in thirstily the voice of knowledge, of those for whom study is not a drudgery but their very calling and destiny, of those with a spark of the heavenly fire burning in their heads and hearts, two categories stand out — though both have a point in common: poverty, which is self-assumed for some and dire straitened circumstances for others. The former will squander their money as if to gild the cobblestones of main street until, turned out of doors into that street themselves, they are forced to drain the cup of poverty to the dregs; the later are left no choice in the matter.

Amid the four yellowish walls of a low-ceilinged and narrow garret, forever doomed to stay clear of the touch of a broom, five fellows lived in the most complete and peaceful disorder. A two-legged table stood by the only window with the other edge propped against the wall. Two or three crippled beds, a three-legged one, another with a couple of legs at one end, with the other end on the bare floor, so that one would lie on it aslant, a straw chair with a gigantic hole in its seat, a few earthen candlesticks donning proud tallow candles, an ancient lamp with a genuine pedigree down to the lamps of Greek philosophers whose writings stank of burning oil, stacks of books piled at random on the table, on the window ledge, and along the smoky rafters of the ceiling of the dingy color of burnt wood [made up the furniture of the room]. There were pallets and woolen rugs on the beds and a mat on the floor on which my fellows would sprawl when playing cards and puffing away at the stinking tobacco in their pipes, making unbreathable the already stuffy air in the garret. We were at the age when one bellows opera airs, scans lines from classical authors, writes love poems, wants to be taken for a romp and womanizer, gives so much credit to one's budding moustache, is so cocksure of one's winsome smile and darting eye — in any case, at that priggish trying age one is at a loss what name to tag to. While my fellows killed their time playing cards, making merry, and telling frivolous and funny jokes about the village jest, Gypsies and priests, I sat wasting my time with my head cupped in my hands, my elbows propped against the edge of the table, unheedful to them and reading away bloody and fantastic romances that inflamed my brains. Among my numerous colleagues one stood out with his feminine good looks. Though pale and delicately built he was foremost in our academic excesses. He would drink twice as much as any of us yet, when his companions lost the use of their legs and let their tongues run loose, yelling and kissing around as if they were lovers, he alone would stay poised and smiling, the only sign of having drunk given by his customary pallor which turned into a delicate rosiness — like that of consumption. I was not partial to drinking, yet I could not help being impressed by that boy, that angel with dark hair, with eyes of so shiny and deep a blue, with such a pale and delicate face, on whom drinking had no effect whatsoever. He was poor, yet he seemed to care so little about his poverty. Always merry, a windbag full of jokes and spicy news, though always shabby and penniless, he was a personality wanting in self-awareness, who did not have a purpose in life, nor did he care to set himself one. Not withstanding, his merry-making sounded unnatural to me, his often unnaturally unrestrained laugh no better than the sad and desperate outside pretence of a heart-rent soul.

On a frosty winter midnight I was lying with a book in hand amid my fellows snoring right and left — when I heard a knock at the door.

"Come in!" I called out.

My pale youthful friend entered, clothed in a worn-out coat no longer up to the task of fighting the wind back, yet his pallor was now deeper and bluish, his lips dry and closed tightly, his dark hair in an ungodly disorder.

"Ioan," I called, "what's wrong with you?"

I took hold of his hand and looked him straight in the eyes.

"Nothing," he said with a forced laugh, "nothing!... she's dying."

"Who's dying, for God's sake?"

"She!," he blurted out, drawing me to him, holding my head close against his chest with desperate sobs — "come," he said "come along... please!"

I struggled into a warm coat and walked out with him. It was freezing cold. Our footsteps made the frozen snow creak while we were running along the streets of the town. I had wrapped myself in my greatcoat up to my face — he exposed his face to the cold driving snow prinking like needles. A high wind was blowing. Now and then we would pass a street lamp. Staring at his deathly white face I had the feeling of pacing at the side of the shadow of a long-dead man, so I kept wondering how I, a live man, could consort with a corpse and also at the destination that pale, sceptical, tall phantom was heading for. The other-worldly look on his face, his steps barely touching the ground, his fixed stare, his long tattered coat reaching down to his heels, his speechless walk beside me gave me the shivers and I could not help imagining that I had befriended a corpse, that I was dreaming and that he was only an awesome apparition in a winter night's dream. We got out of town. A long white plain carpeted with silvery snow on which the wan moon was mirroring herself.... an expanse of white thrashing-ground.... the fantastical winter night, flooded with silvery air, in all its frosty beauty, the plain of snow — with, here and there, a snow-laden thicket, a scarecrow, a silvery phantom on a silvery plain — as far as the eye could see. We went across the plain. Far away at the farther end of the plain, among the leafless trees in the midst of a garden, I could spy a light filtering out of a window and heard the drowsy bark of a dog.

We made our strides even faster and presently, through the heavy snowfall, we caught sight of a house standing in the middle of a garden. We both jumped the fence which shook off its burden of snow and made for the lighted window. Once there he asked me to bend down for him to climb up and take hold of the transom. He jumped on my bent back then on to the high porch and glued his eyes to the window. I followed suit.

The room was scantily furnished: a few wooden chairs, an unlacquered wooden bed, and a piano in a corner. An old man was sitting on a chair — a girl was lying on the bed with her eyes half open — another girl was sitting at the piano.

The girl on the bed was incredibly beautiful. She had ash-blond hair, her face was white as rime, her eyes blacker than two blackberries beneath long blond lashes and thin arched brows. Her lips were sighing out a prayer

— her eyes half-opened from time to time — her temples were throbbing gently. A snow-white arm like the most flawless marble was hanging over the side of the bed, and her other hand lay limp against her heart.

The old man was sitting on the wooden chair. His brow, bald but for a few white hairs shining silvery against the light, was clouded over with grief — his eyes, bloodshot with old age and of a hazy color, were brimful with tears — his pale, half-dead head trembled spasmodically and his arms hung along the chair rests.

The girl beside him was a rosy-cheeked angel. She was seated in front of the piano with her unmoving hands on the keyboard, her spine rested against the back of the chair and her head was tilted backward, face up. Her glance was directed skyward, so that her tears did not trickle from her eyes, for her face was horizontal. Her complexion was wan and her pain — a sublime sorrow.

The air in the room was dead and sad — the flame of the lamp flickered as if stirred by the breath of an unseen spirit. They were all speechless as the dead — the old man's sight had grown fixed and desperate when, unawares, the hands on the keyboard moved. As if inspired by electricity, they flew swiftly over the keys and enriched the air with divine, heavenly notes; the old man cowered as if to kneel down, the eyes of the dying girl opened wide and she began to sing. The notes flew now loud, now soft and hardly audible like the sighs of the angels' harps — it was one of those superb lays of Palestrina, the divine maestro of lamentations. The dying girl sang on... and what a song it was! A voice like a silver bell... The notes of the piano were dying under the fingers of one girl — the notes on the lips of the other were dying too — the moribund who had propped her body on her right elbow let her head sink back ever so slowly into the pillows — the song died, her lips became mute and bluish, her eyes turned murky then closed for ever. Their light went out!

"Sofia!" Ioan cried out and fell backward from the window into the snow.

I jumped down.

I tucked him up in the greatcoat and, rigid with the swoon and the cold as he was, I took him up across my shoulders. He was light as a girl. I jumped over the fence with him and crossed the snow-covered plain like a thief of corpses. Without the town I set him down on the ground, rubbed him with snow and breathed out what frozen breath I had left over his face, whose pallor looked silver in the moonlight. His haggard face seemed to come to life.

"Ioan!" I said, "get up and let's go home."

Still lying down he turned his eyes toward the house we had come from. The light was out.

"Haven't we been there?" he inquired, summoning up his voice and pointing toward the house.

"Nay! We had hardly left the town when you fell unconscious on this spot".

"So it was only a dream?" he said laughing hysterically. "I knew it for a dream! It must have been.... it must!"

His voice was broken, lamenting, and benumbed with pain.

"Come on home — you'll catch a cold!"

"I say! Have you not heard that divine music, or seen that dying angel or that desperate old man?"

"For God's sake, what's this raving about old men and dying angels? What would you have me see in this plain when we stayed right here, far from any of your imaginings?"

"Right you are! I'm mad! I've been dreaming. Let's go home. There's no light on their windows... they're sleeping... fast asleep... so they're all right once they're asleep and the light's out... so, she isn't dying... nay, there's hope she'll be well again now that she's asleep."

"Your head is wet" I said "for the snow has melted on [your] hot brow."

With those words I took off my fur hat and thrust it on his head, down over his eyes, for I had noticed that the lamp had been relit. Then, with my arms under his armpits, I heaved him up, took a firm hold of his arm and ran him to the streets of the town.... so that, dizzy, blinded, and taken by force, he did not care to cast a look back in his apathy.

We got home. His eyes were troubled — yet his usual pretence of quiet had taken command over his face. The lamp had been left burning on the table and was exhaling malodorous fumes, about to go out.

"Oh, my God, how I wish I could stay awake and yet I'm sleepy... so sleepy!" [Ioan said] and let his body drop onto the bed.

Sleep overcame him, as befalls all the frost-bitten; and thinking that sleep was the only medicine that could alleviate his plight, I let him go to sleep and started pacing the room in my bare feet so that I should make the least noise so as not to disturb him. Toward daybreak sleepiness got the better of me and I turned in beside a roommate. The next day when I woke up it was high noon already. He had got up and left long before.

On the third day toward nightfall Ioan entered the room with his face sad, cold, but otherwise quite composed.

"She is dead," he said. "Come."

Out in the street he took my arm in his. The evening was cold and at a distance, crossing the unpopulated street, I saw four men carrying a black deal coffin, a fast-pacing priest following, and, on their tail — as if sorrow were in a hurry — an old man in a long grey worn-out greatcoat walking fast beside a poorly clad girl. We caught up with the pageant hurrying toward the graveyard. We walked in and past the snow-covered crosses and graves and stopped by a newly-dug yellow grave which still exuded thin vapors from the heat of the earth whereas the clogs beside it were white with frost. A burial on a winter dusk. The sexton stood with the chin of his gloomy wrinkled face propped against the handle of his large muddy spade, the moon was floating like a dream among the cold wan clouds, the priest was chanting the Memory Eternal, and the aged father had taken off his hat. The skin [on his face] was sallow, with wrinkles, some fine, others deep, imprinted by many years and sorrows, his head almost completely bald — it looked as if his sparse hoary hairs had been implanted there by an untrained hand... His dry eyes had no more tears to shed... their gaze was riveted upon the coffin so that all the expression of his grief seemed concentrated in his half-crazy head and in his lusterless unconscious eyes. Before the pallbearers had laid the body into the deep shelter of clay, the old man made an instinctive sign, the lid was raised, and on the floor of the oversized coffin could be seen a white shadow with dishevelled hair, with an off-white face rigid like a marble stone, with lips drawn in, with large eyes closed and sunken beneath a withered wide brow. The old man drew closer and, for an endless moment, pressed his cold lips against the dead girl's brow. Her sister, a live marble statue, a spirit of grief, her face laden with sorrow, stood leaning against a tree which shook its yellow, snow-covered leaves over her cold-white face. Her eyes, dry and closed, her mouth, curved down with bitterness, her face which still struggled hopelessly to shed one more tear looked as if the master Canova had carved a work of his immortal genius there and set it up among the snow-laden crosses and graves. Ioan, deathly-pale, sprang from my side in a fit of madness and pressed his lips against the dead girl's eyes. Then the lid was nailed, the black coffin started sloping along the ropes into the darkness of the grave — and only the painful memory of Sofia lingered above the earth. I closed my eyes and had a dream — of what?.... I cannot recall. On re-opening them I found myself alone in the graveyard. The moon cast a light sweet as a summer's dream over the snow-covered trees that turned shiny in their silvery garb, and the old sexton, unhurried, unconcerned, and melancholy, was still there shovelling the clods which resounded on the dry boards of the coffin... It all amounted to a dream of death and the gave.

When I got back into my garret I found Ioan stretched on my bed. His hair was spread, dark as the night, over the white pillow, his hands were joined over his head, his face was rigid and his eyes closed. There was a stack of dusty books on the table by the bed, an earthen candlestick on top of the books with a candle burning which, left untended, had grown a long-ish black wick that cast its unfeeling yellow light over the unconscious face of the youth. There was a pistol on the table. I walked on tiptoe and picked it up. Ioan did not hear me in the lethargy of his sorrow. I opened the shutters and threw the pistol out into a snowdrift. Then I let myself out of the house and loitered about to calm down dreams, my vivid impressions, the ominous uneasiness of my soul in the clear and crisp winter night.

I met Ioan the next day.

"Now Toma, that you have been a witness to the drama of my heart, you might as well come along and get a closer view of its actors... let's visit the old man and his remaining daughter. Oh, Lord, I'm not selfish, yet, how I wish it had happened to the other one..."

"Hold your tongue," I expostulated, "this is blasphemy. The other one might also bring happiness to some man, Ioan. She is beautiful and seems to be as kind-hearted.... But, all right, let's go."

We went to the old man's home and entered the familiar warm room. The old man, speechless with grief, was sitting in the ancient armchair with his head dangling down over his chest. The girl stood daydreaming by the window with her gaze on the blooming cup of a rose which shone like a fiery star beside the flowers of frost on the windowpane. An old woman was pottering about in font of the hearth. The day was so gloomy that the room was almost dark. Nobody noticed our entrance. Ioan went up to the girl, took her hand in his, and asked with brotherly love:

"Poesis, what are you doing here?"

"Me? Nothing — do not speak so loudly.... Father's sleeping, benumbed by pain and desperation... Don't wake him!... Sofia, our only mainstay.... is no more."

"Meet the gentleman," Ioan said pointing to me.

"Ah, the gentleman!"... she whispered and gave me an indifferent and distracted bow as if she had not noticed me... "Ioan, I'm grateful," she continued, holding his hand as he sat down on a chair opposite hers; "you were here that night. Poor boy! What a loss it must be to you!"

"But Poesis, I wasn't here. I'm afraid I couldn't make it — this gentleman can vouch that I fainted in the snow on the way here. He was with me."

"The gentleman?" she uttered with a sad smile. "But you were here... did I not see you at the window?"

"So I was here," he whispered feelingly, "so I witnessed her departure. Alas, Toma, you did me wrong deceiving me, letting me think I'd been dreaming. The guilt of not having come kept nagging at my soul — but now... I am pardoned before her in heaven... for she knows... I was here... Why didn't you let me know? I'd have returned from there and..."

"In that frightful state?" I rejoined. "Ioan, had you returned, your mind would have been in great peril — your life too, for that matter, and, though I'm well aware you don't make much of them yourself, I felt it my duty to care."

"Poor boy! So wretched! I should have long lost my mind myself!" she said and bowed her head to kiss Ioan's smooth brow.

His brow was still unfurrowed but a cloud of dreams spread over it.

"I'll follow her" he uttered quietly and feelingly, his eyes brimful with tears." I'll follow her soon."

"Stop that nonsense" she exclaimed, "he might overhear us!" She shifted her gaze to her father who was sitting there engulfed in his mute deep grief.

We lingered a little... far too little... then walked back home... A sea of rays had flooded my heart, an ocean of tenderness had intoxicated my soul, all from an image alone.... Poesis! loan had taken leave of me. I entered the house and kneeling beside the table stacked with books, "Poesis," I whispered carried away, "I love you!"

I dreamed... I sang, I wrote about her... my soul was filled with but one dream... my mind saw but one face, that of the marble angel: Poesis!

I looked for loan with a mind to confess to him. But he had become uncommunicative and churlish... wary of any intercourse. He railed at heaven and God and scorned men so one might think that he was a king in rags, sceptical and cruel like Satan himself. There was no talking to him. One day I inquired the circumstances of that family.

"Poverty" he said, "dire poverty, the lot of great souls, of the souls of angels... whereas the high and mighty of this world, ridiculous in their pomp, will ride about in their gilt carriages. A fig for those high and mighty! Why could they not countenance and support that aged poet who dreams his life away, who is no better than a starveling for all his genius, who is forced to let his daughters walk about the streets in their poor rags for the silk-clad prostitutes to split their sides with laughter at shabby virtue; Oh, prostitution and shame will be entombed in sepulchers of marble and coffins of lead spread over with velvet — whereas virtue sleeps her eternal sleep within four boards of deal. And what are the whys and wherefores of virtue? Banish virtue and nobility to the theatre — so the ne'er-do-wells can play the virtuous, the noble and pure souls in a world of profligates, hypocrites, and egoists. Could virtue, I wonder, vanquish vice?... Has it ever done so? When? Virtue's place is on the stageboards of the theatre — far from real life wherein one must stoop to meanness to keep body and soul together — and so is the honest man's wish to die happy and unbewailed by his off-spring... the more so when there is a fortune left behind! Oh! I was present at scenes when the widow hid the husband's will in her bosom for fear of her sons who searched high and low about the yet unburied corpse for the deceased's will with their eyes stained with crocodile tears. I was present at scenes when the wife fainted readily that lethargy and the lavish pallor might lend a becoming look to her face. Everything pertaining to man is infamous... I do not trust this malicious beast who has descended from the apes with all the evil proclivities of his forefathers".

"Enough!" I said. "Sofia was not a woman herself?..."

"Woman?" he rejoined with a bitter smile... "woman? What is that nonsense you are saying? She was an angel, an angel of God's own making that He embodies from His thoughts once only in His timeless eternity. What is woman? This creature whose end-all in life is beguiling her voice with lies, smearing her face with make-up and her eyes with deceitful tears? Oh, that sighing sphinx, how her heart is full of merriment and her eyes with tears when she deceives you. Alas, she was no woman... I defy that name!"

That was Ioan's mood following Sofia's death. Long after that he, heart-wrenched and dejected though he was, would not let his eternally serene artist's brow betray his secret feelings.

As to me, having set eyes on that daughter of this earth, on that fair-haired angel, I kept dreaming of her night and day and, when kneeling down in front of a blackened wooden icon in our church, while the psalm reader in his lectern droned away prayers in an ancient, rather Slav tongue and the priest in his altar raised his emaciated hands heavenward, I would imagine that the gloomy red icon of the Holy Virgin took on ever whiter outlines on the screen, her withered and hardly discernible visage was becoming rosy silver, her hair in its gold-embroidered head kerchief started waving its tousled long golden tresses, her eyes, blotted out by time, seemed to shine forth like two bluish flowers, and her sallow and closed saintly lips were now rosy and pursed as if about to whisper something and the red drapes of her attire turned white as lilies before my blurred sight. In church, instead of seeing the Holy Virgin, I would behold the dearly visage of Poesis through my bitter tears of love.

Who was she? And what? And what did she do for a living?

A second-class actress with a second-class company, it was her routine to act maids-in-waiting for all her carriage and poise that bespoke the tragedian.

The theatre house stood in a suburb of the town, a wooden contraption erected amid a clump of trees which, together with another cluster stretching farther on, made up a park of sorts or, rather, a grove.

Through a back door one could catch a glimpse of the disorder on the stage before the performance with makeshift thickets — an assortment of green and red tatters standing for rosebushes, upturned benches scattered about, backgrounds of painted cloth hanging in midair, and farther on the backstage littered with furniture piled up in random heaps — candelabra over chairs, tabletops on settee cushions, their legs pointing up to the ceiling, mirrors facing the wall, wrapped-up carpets, a mound of stage properties and on either side, rows of plank booths — the so-called dressing-rooms — wherein the actors and actresses put on their costumes and make-up.

I climbed onto the stage and elbowed my way through the bustling crowd of hard-swearing stage hands to the plank booth I knew was set aside for her. I peeped in through the chinks in a plank. Poor wretched girl! She had hardly had the time to get accustomed to the loss of her sister and now here she was — about to impersonate a merry girl. Her off-white face needed a little white powder, and a touch of pink lent her complexion a rosy blush like the light spread over the twilight sky. A flimsy gauze chemise covered her bosom which, far from concealing, showed to advantage the most flawlessly rounded, the whitest and smallest breasts, as if carved in silvery marble by the hand of a blind sculptor, had he had a pair of eyes gazing out of his head, he might not have been beyond smashing his own work in a fit of jealously. She was to act the part of an angel in a meaningless vaudeville *dei ex machina* whose only enjoyable and entertaining quality lay in the appeal and beauty of the histrions.

Having fixed a pair of white wings to her shoulders she completed her dressing-up and now that the orchestra struck the notes of the overture to the *Norma* prayer, Poesis let her body subside on a chair, titled her head backward and joined her hands assuming such a dreamy pose that it would have been no marvel if, abducted by the heavenly tune, she had taken wing herself.... gentle, quiet and sad like the soul of an angel floating up to heaven — gliding smoothly thither on her silver-white wings.

I stood there feasting my eyes upon her. The voluptuousness of that marble-white breast, the dreaminess of that pale face gazing toward heaven, the dainty white hands joined in supplication, the round and naked youthful arms hanging limp by her sides in a symbol of despondency, her body yearning to kneel down, the wings about to spread out and raise her clear of the ground — all were unmistakable traits of one visage, on sweet, beauteous and ideal body — Poesis!

Presently the prompter's dumb bell broke the quiet offstage and I stole away from the booth lest she should notice my prying into her beauty in its most appealing and divine guise. The next moment she emerged from her booth. Noticing me she vouchsafed me a smile and I set to racking my brains for a not-too-clumsy compliment.

"What brings you here in this unbreathable atmosphere of oil dies and lamp oil?" she asked me still smiling.

I turned red in the face and lowered my eyes like a schoolboy caught red-handed at making paper toys surreptitiously under cover of the desktop. Yet I managed to pluck up what spirits I had for, willy-nilly, I had to...

"You!" I exclaimed.

"Me? You must be poking fun at me," she said... yet I could see she had blushed crimson for all the white make-up smeared over her face.

The backcloth had been lowered and we found ourselves alone behind it.

"Ever since I saw you," I continued and possessed myself of her hand, "my eyes are dazzled by your light and my heart has shut the world out, brimful with love for you. I've forsaken my dusty books, science and poetry alike and the ideals of both since you came into my life. You wouldn't know, nor can you guess at how dearly I love you. Everything that looks worthwhile to me today is all here in yourself: flower and bird, spring and winter tale, the whiteness of the North and the flame of the South — I've rediscovered all the lost ideals in the one and only image — which is yours."

"My curtain call," she blurted out, flurried, and moved.

"Do you love me?" The question out of my bosom, I knelt down and clung to her.

"Yes," she replied flurriedly, smiling and blushing at the same time, and hurried off to whither her duty summoned her, and presently I listened to the velvety youthful timbre of her voice enriching the stage and to the audience clapping their hands at the appearance of that earthly angel.

I had been staying there, behind the backcloth on my knees with hands locked together, my soul drinking in the silvery notes of her barely audible voice, beside myself with bliss. In that ecstatic mood, with my eyes staring at the ground as if enraptured by some sweet memory, my soul longing for one more note of her voice which was now silent, I heard the rustle of a dress and uplifted my eyes... she had come back... There was infinite pity and infinite love in her eyes, as she stood there looking down at my kneeling body.

"Poesis," I whispered, struggled to my feet and reached my arms toward her.

In an instant she was a marble statue resting on my chest, her naked white arms encircling my neck. My lips set to searching for her face cuddled against my breast, but presently she disengaged an arm from about my neck... touched the back of her hand against my thirsty mouth, turned her back on me and vanished smiling. My longing arms reached in vain for her departing shadow... She was flying away.

She returned.

"My sweet child," she said with a grave mien, stroking my brow, "you may walk me home. My father plays the cello in the orchestra... there's still a long time till the fourth act... and he can come home by himself for once." She went back into her booth and called out "Bye for now" and a rosy blush spread over her face, as if she were ashamed of her words.

She emerged in no time wearing her street clothes, a becoming short fur coat wrapped about her shoulders and a velvet hat on her head.

"Here! help me with this bundle!" she said and gave me a bundle to carry.

We left the theatre by the back door and before long were at the edge of the plain whence we could see the aged musician's cottage whose window-panes were shining in the night like a pair of silver plates. The plain was so silent and white, the air so crisp and clear, my love so ardent and dark! I walked by her, the warm youthful soul of a child, whose feet were barely touching the snow-carpeted ancient plain... She meant everything to me at that moment... my ideal, my angel, my woman. My woman... on imagining that the tender-hearted sweet girl walking by my side might call me husband at some future time, an incomprehensible charm, the warmth of a room heated in wintertime, a balmy, wholesome, and familiar draught of air flooded the cold barren night of my soul. Scores of times I had to refrain from holding her tight in my arms with unrestrained childish love, scores [of times], divining the workings of my soul, she would give me a reproving sly smile flouting my intentions.

Eventually we arrived home. Graceful and frolicsome she jumped sprightly over the fence and vanished laughing among the snow-laden trees in the garden. I followed suit — and we let ourselves in by the back door and found ourselves in a dark hall wherein the only lights came through the key-hole of a door opening onto the lighted room. We entered it. The open grate of the hearth radiated reddish light and warm air and a pervading fragrance of freshly roasted coffee rendered the air and light in the room even drowsier. The only change I could notice was the piano moved alongside the wall with the keyboard facing the window on whose ledge were two pots with a blooming red rose and a silvery lily, the latter wan-faced like a maid in love. She rid herself of her fur coat and remained in a bodiced dress of grey silk.

The sight of her slender waist, her smile and her sly eyes, and the gentle drowsiness of all her slow gestures fired my eyes with a boundless and incomprehensible desire. I pulled an armchair by the fireplace which radiated an enervating heat and resorted to mild force to seat her in it. The red firelight washing her face and pale brow, her bittersweet lenient smile, her drooping lashes... bid me kneel at her feet and take both her hands in mine and feast my thirsty and yearning eyes on her countenance.

I put my hands about her neck and started rising from the floor with a mind to steal a long bewitching kiss from her lips. But that roused her from her gentle drowsy dreaminess... Her eyes opened slightly, she held me back gently at arm's length, stroked my brow and smiled:

"You, reckless boy! Let go of me!"

She freed her hands from my clasp with a graceful show of strength, seated herself snugly in the armchair by the piano and raised the lid. I followed her and knelt down again, put my arm round her waist and nestled my intoxicated head on her lap. She let me have my will, rested her hands on the keyboard and started strumming the keys with melancholy liveliness; it was a passionate, affectionate, and doleful waltz by some German maestro, the sound of which made me even dizzier and more distracted. It was not mere notes and harmony that I heard, but rather a melancholy and voluptuous hum receding ever so softly out of hearing.

I uplifted my loving eyes to her face flushèd with the heat and the clasping of my arms — it was such an arduous task to keep my intoxicated senses in check that my eyes were afire and my embrace — a mad fury.

"Poesis," — my voice was thick — "I love you!"

"Hush! There's my father!" She choked back a cry, stood up, and rested her right hand on the window sill.

I left my kneeling position at the unexpected news. She culled the lily from its pot at the window, her eyes closed so tightly and the kiss she gave the flower was so ardent, that for a split second the silvery whiteness of the lily seemed to turn red — then she proffered it to me with her left hand, her serene countenance beaming love. I kissed the lily — neither whiter nor purer than the visage of my chaste bride — a fiery kiss, an eternal kiss! Then I bolted for the door... but stopped short in the doorway and looked back in rapture at her slender tall frame watching my departure with a hand resting on the piano. One more glance over the shoulder and I walked out, for now I

could hear distinctly the old man's footsteps creaking along the frozen foot-
path in the front yard. I let myself out by the back door, crossed the garden,
jumped over the fence and swept across the plain as if I were a gust of wind,
burning with blissful love... and back in my humble cell I felt as happy as a
king strayed among my snoring roommates. Seated by the smoky lamp light
I wrote some lines of verse which I came across later, strayed among my
sundry papers. Here they are, word for word as I wrote them at the time:

When, at night, my soul ecstatic vigil kept,
My guardian angel alighted in my dream,
Enfolded in a cloak of clouds and moonlight,
Airing my head with his seraphic wings,
But as I saw you clad in that dress, pale-white,
A child in longing and mystery wrapped,
Before your sparkling eyes that angel departed.
Just as the sea sleeping, deep, calm, undisturbed,
In its endless bosom of light and affection
Divinely reflects the divine source of light,
Shedding golden days onto her watery breast,
So, too, you, my darling, you, sweet dream of love,
Can change into daylight the night in my soul
With your dark stars, with your faint smile.

My happiness knew no bounds. In my endless daydreaming I took
every flower and every star for a sister, the gentle sisters of my beloved. Oft
in my excitement would I forget the name of God and dream I was the
world with its myriads of stars and myriads of flowers, with the black
mountains and green vales, the moonlit nights and sun-scorched days, and I
bid them all bow in homage with the incense of their lives to a pale silvery
shadow that was to me the center of that world, a shadow climbing down
the sunrays as if on a golden ladder — the shadow of Poesis! The whole
Eternity often seemed too short for my worship and, clad in the shroud of
death though I was, I wrestled against the hoary time, tore off his wings,
and sentenced him to non-existence! At other times all tongues sounded
stupid and all words meaningless... any word that did not ring of her
sounded foolish and foolishness it was to puzzle over it... my mind had
ceased interpreting the meaning of words... dazed and mad, in every concept
I imagined to see the pale contours of her divine shadow.

But this love, bashful as that of silvery doves, was doomed to happen in the year of sorrow '48. Wherefore should it have been born at that of all times? Wherefore? Could that pitiful year have passed without loving? All Transylvania was seething and the virgin spring bestowed pretty flowers and golden days all over it — yet, if a careful diviner had chanced to scour the blooming plains of Transylvania, his eyes would have beheld the sunken and sightless orbs of corpses in the place of flowers. The bloodthirsty archangel of revenge seemed to hover over the bewildered and sickly air of the land. The Hungarians contemplated once more — and for the last time — razing the Romanians from the face of the earth by union and pitchforks, and deluded themselves they could Magyarize the cold stone and the virginal well along with the majestic ancient forest and instill the idea of Hungarian union into the hoary and awesome brains of the mountains — brains which were beginning to be fired — nay, had already been — with a grand, sublime idea, Liberty. They thought, and it was the last time they did, that the ancient and storm-beaten guards of the fortress of Transylvania — the rock-headed mountains — were bound to go on sleeping their eternal sleep and would not start awake at the mendacious howls of the mad hounds that fabricated empires with 16 million Hungarians which, fortunately for the world, existed only in the short-sighted phantasmagorias of their deranged brains. Yet the kingly sentries did start awake. The roar of the forests blowing off the rust on the iron wings of the Romanian eagle and stirring it from its centuries-old slumber frightened the enemies — and today the slumber of this eagle still frightens the ones unable to guess at what multiplied powers that slumber might lend to its natural strength. Oh, our enemies have always feared us, as testified their history-long conspiracies, openly or behind our backs, against our very existence, though all those conspiracies resulted only in rendering us hard as rocks and enduring as flint-stones on this land. Had they set us on the same footing, had they opened wide the gates to their own privileges and rights, there is no telling whether, enervated and pampered, we might not have become Hungarians. Countrymen, thank you for your centuries-old hatred and for making us eager for an opportunity to repay our gratitude in a way you will never forget. As for the homeland you call Hungarian, one must have the impudence of a Hungarian to call that any longer — as one must share the ignorance of a Rösler who calls us immigrants, albeit the immigrants be 10 million strong, whereas the site of the immigration has a population of only 800,000. Anyhow, on one side stands the impudence of the Hungarians, on the other the priggish German ignorance; either one necessary to foster the grand delusions of the Hungarian Empire and claim the unworthiness of the Romanians. And what have their misshapen ideas brought into Transylvania? The blind death that mowed them down in thousands as well as the ferocious hatred of the other nations against all things Hungarian! And they had the cheek to preach on behalf of the Magyar people who, no less kind and lenient than any other people, seemed destined to live in peace and brotherly love with the Romanians, but for the vainglorious drivel that fired their brains. Yet they purposely misinterpreted the leaves in the book of Fate and smeared its verses with blood. The Hungarians twisted and garbled God's peaceful sentence: "Live in peace, for you are the only heterogeneous nations amid an ocean of pan-Slavism", and so they brought about their doom. They willed it, not we!

All over the country the Romanian anti-unionist movement was seething. There had been a preparatory meeting on St. Thomas' Sunday and a great rally on the Field of Liberty where the flame of revival soared through the air with the tricolor banner. *Virtus romana rediviva!*

I and Ioan had participated in all those manifestations of the nation's life — eternally unique in their kind — then we returned to the fomenting town of our studies. Yet, whoever could apply his mind to study! Our brains were afire and Ioan's haggard face had become sickly red, for his heart was seething with the great love of the nation.

I called on Poesis. The night was clear and diaphanous, the moon's silvery and [enamoured] rays melted like snowflakes in the shadowy verdure of the trees and thickets scattered about her garden! I sat on a bench immersed in thoughts and God only knows why my thoughts should have been melancholy! I sat there in her garden with my joined hands resting lazily on my knees, with my brow down and my hair falling freely over it, thinking of matters I cannot recall under the moon who, floating slowly among the silvery clouds scattered over the blue sky, was immersed in her own train of thoughts and dreams of things past human ken. A gentle swish along the sandwalks startled me from my reverie. It was she. A negligé like a silvery mist bathed her tall, lithe, and slender frame in its fantastic and diaphanous whiteness, giving her the look of a sea elf. She came up to me: when our eyes met she seated herself tenderly across my knees and kissed my eyes which closed in a deep dreaminess — for I could not bring myself to believe it was she, the fantastic fairy of my long-spun dreams. I took her blond head in the cup of my hands and gazed at it. How sad that head was — how pale that face, how sunken those blue eyes!

"Poesis," I said, "are you unhappy? How pale you look, my child! Are you suffering? You are weeping!"

"Oh, that I were the only weeping soul... But let that pass. Toma, this may be the last time we are together!"

"The last time, you say? Poesis, you must be raving! The last time?"

"Alas, my child, if you knew how wretched I feel," she blurted out, her eyes brimful with tears, and brushed aside the black hairs over my brow with her white hands and scorched my clouded brow with her lips sucked in with crying. "I'm so wretched yet I can't tell you why. If there is one thing I dare entreat you in the name of your mother, of that pure angel, it is to forget me! Forget me, at least until the day I die... When I'm dead..."

"For God's sake, Poesis, what's all this? What's wrong with you?"

"What's wrong? That I can't tell you. But let's forget it... forget it all. How handsome you look this night... as if your hair were made of ebony and your eyes of two black diamonds! How handsome my beloved is... my beloved? not mine any more..."

"Not yours, Poesis? Are you not mine, my own blond angel? There, there, this comes from having cried your eyes out while I was away — which is no reason to think I'm not yours any longer. Poesis, this will be my home-land as well as the homeland of our enemies; you'll be my wife then, my beautiful wife, the fairy of my little garden, the housewife of my parental home, the mother of my children! Oh, how beautiful you are... how dearly we'll love you... both I and my aged father, the stonecutter! You'll brush the dust off my books, the books of the brain worker, your soft white hand will smooth out the wrinkles on my brow, your kisses will enliven it! And I'll love you, I'll love you as dearly as I love my homeland and as I love God! Poesis!..."

The night butterflies were swarming over the flowerbeds... the bloom-ing trees reached their boughs laden with white and pink blossoms down over our brows... the spring's intoxicating perfume instilled its bracing vir-ginal breath into our breasts, we were drinking it in with our lips pressed in a long kiss, and she kept her eyelids half closed and did not spurn my melan-

choly caresses... the moon alone was watching, like a sweet silvery sun, over
our unquenchable love.

On the morrow I got happily out of my straw-stuffed pallet, wrapped
my shoulders in my greatcoat, and set to loitering about the streets of the
town, a Romanian tricolor badge in a buttonhole, the wide-rimmed hat a lit-
tle sideways, my pale face betraying recent exertion yet still smiling — and
I let my walking-stick trail on the fine gravel of the streets and whistled an
air under my breath, no matter which.

Suddenly I heard the monotonous notes of a funeral music behind me.
I turned my head, arrested my gait, took off my hat and due compassion
clouded, my countenance. A carriage followed the bier and I saw a long silk
dress and a pale face framed with golden hair — a face so well known to me
that I could hardly mistake it for any other — it was she... Poesis! yet that
could not be. The deathly pallor, the fair hair, the visage, all belonged to
her... yet in such pomp?... She, who was so poor?...

What about the second carriage? I could not believe my eyes! Two of
the profligates of the town were laughing aloud in the funeral procession,
clad in tight riding breeches, red-braided, bluish waistcoats, yellow jackets,
wide-rimmed hats and a couple of watch chains across their chests. Their
shallow apish faces were distorted in the cynical laughter of sceptical lech-
ers in a procession that had nothing to invite merry-making.

Dazed and no longer master of my thoughts and feelings, I followed
the procession to church. There was a crowd of people outside and inside it.
I elbowed my way inside ruthlessly. There must have been something
strange in my unfocused eyes, in my not having taken off my hat on entering
the church, in my doubled fists, in my teeth grinning in savage laughter,
which made me the centre of attention.

"A madman!" someone whispered in such a carrying voice that I over-
heard him yet, in the gloom of my affliction, that voice sounded unreal, for I
was not aware of the world of humans... I felt all by myself in the spasm of a
nightmarish vision, for all I could discern were a coffin floating in the air and
my aggrieved beloved who followed the coffin leaning for support on the arm
of a man. The fiery eyes of the wax candles started dancing in the gloom of
the church like as many dingy red stars... the body in the lidless coffin
seemed to grimace at me and on the cold black walls of the church appeared
unsightly contours of faces with black eyes and heads distorted with mad
fury!

"Who's that man?" I roared in spite of the demon clutching my throat in the vise of his wooden fingers... I rushed for him... but a sexton crushed his fist against my brow so forcefully that I saw stars and fell on my back in a stupor.

I cannot recall how long my stupor lasted but, when I came to my senses, I was lying on a stone bench in a corner of the church and Ioan stood watching over me.

"Who's that man?" were the first words I could utter.

"Who! Guess who... her rich lover... a count or some such thing! Leave her to her devices... she's a woman... did you expect her to be different? Let's go!"

He lent me an arm and helped me gain my feet. Leaning on his arm, I walked out the door where the old deacon lingered in the company of two or three ragged beggars. We walked up the streets to Ioan's place. His chamber was small and dark, the darkness made deeper by a narrow wall hung over with a black woolen curtain with a white cross painted in its centre. Yet, all in all, his chamber smacked of a fine and artful elegance at variance with his rather soiled and ragged clothes. His gilt bound books were arrayed in orderly rows on a red tablecloth alongside a litter of pencils, brushes, palettes and colors in large boxes or smeared on seashells. I slumped on a chair and cast a cold glance at all those which would have struck me as strange, had I been in a different mood. To one side of the black curtain hung a white tassel on a white cord...

Ioan drew a chair close to mine, sat on it with his chest touching my right shoulder, then put an arm round my neck and the other round my chest, rested his brow against my right shoulder and whispered in my ear:

"As from now I break all ties with life, my friendship with you, my love with the shadow, the memory of Sofia. Toma, as from now I do not belong to myself any longer. I go away and leave you here... but before leaving I will confess to you the folly of my life, for you never knew I painted."

He stood up, pulled the white cord on the black curtain and there on the wall I saw a creature I thought to be alive. Indeed, it seemed fully alive to my dimmed sight. It was Sofia. The ash-blond hair dressed in a stately crown over her brow, the deep-set shiny black eyes, the finely-drawn pale face, the bluish thin lips... it was Sofia all over... in all her unique beauty... fair as only the South can breed... Ioan joined his hands and gazed in ecstasy at the life-like portrait... His eyes were flashing fire, his lips aquiver, and I sat there frightened, astonished, and let my benumbed sense take in that unbelievable scene wherein the portrait looked alive and real — whereas Ioan seemed a mere dead with only his fiery eyes burning alive in his head.

"Poor live shape, poor work of my imagination! I strived to bring you to life out of the chaos of my pain and desperation, and how painful to crush you now against the cold rock of my awakening! But crush you I must... for you are the only link that chains me to life and to my past."

He produced a small sharp dagger from his breast pocket, knifed the portrait with a diagonal cross, and the torn canvas folded over the gilt wooden framework to all four sides, leaving bare the white wall behind it. His eye was lusterless and his smile bitter in the aftermath of the cruel struggle.

"Toma," he said, "I am leaving, yet I will not bid you follow me. Stay here in my home — you'll live here snugly and free of intrusions, as I have lived, totally addicted to painting, my hobby and my madness. A cab has long been waiting for me... farewell! Consider you've never had my friendship and be of good cheer! Farewell!"

He shook my hand once more and whipped down the stairs. I slammed the door on his back, subsided onto the bed, sank my face into the pillows and let my soul prey to the cruellest pain. How long I lay unconscious like that I cannot recall... though, when waking up, it was the dead of night and the clock was chiming one of the small hours. I lit the candle, rushed to Sofia's torn portrait and set to patching up the canvas... but all my endeavours were to no avail. There was an armful of firewood scattered by the hearth. I thrust it into the stove, started a roaring fire and drew a small red sofa by the fire with the firm intention to cover up the outlet before the fire was out so as to put an end to my life with carbon. I put out the candle and lay before the flames licking the mouth of the hearth with their dragon's tongues. Staring at the flames with my legs sprawled and my head against my chest, it dawned on me that my whole life had been no better than a fantastic madman's dream without sense or purpose, and in the tongues of flame I envisaged all my thoughts, my days, and my dreams of happiness burning to ashes. When nothing remained of the fire but a large heap of coals and a few bluish flames I covered the vent hole, lay back in front of the ashes, closed my eyes and waited for the sleep of death. Outside the wind gave blood-curdling howls and the old drizzle kept pattering on the window-panes... as if wind, clouds, thunder, and rain were celebrating a savage wedding-feast in the dark demesnes of the cloudy night sky. Despite the dull yet piercing whistle of the wind I fell asleep and felt my brains slowly growing numb with the carbon. I had died! All at once I found myself in an emerald-green forest with rocks of myrrh and virginal saintly wells. Angel-voiced nightingales were carolling on the trees, diaphanous blissful shadows were wandering along the walks receding into the dark verdure of saintly groves. In the far distance I spied a golden grove whose rustle of leaves was chanting a soothing and gentle tune like the swish of slumberous waves on the sea. Among those saintly white shadows I alone had a body... I kept wandering through the forest until I reached a river with silvery ripples. The waters in midstream encircled an island with woods and gardens amid which a tall church raised its spherical domes skyward — all embossed in gold and so glittery that the sun in the clear sky mirrored himself into its main dome. A golden boat was rocking by the bank... I stepped into it and, tearing the silvery ripples of the river with the oars, I reached the beach of the island. All was silent there, no birds were warbling, only from inside the church there wafted out a soft sorrowful and mournful dirge like the choked wailing at the bedside of a dying man. I entered the church by its gold portals. Its floor was of milk-white marble, its tall arcades all of gold, as were its columns, the screen with tall wan icons of saints and angels of other-worldly beauty looked like gold leaves on silver canvases; in the altar — a marble table with the last sacraments... There was no one on the church floor, only the nuns chanting funeral dirges up in the choir... By a side door, holding white wax candles in their hands, emerged a pageant of haggard figures with long, white veils drawn up so to cover their heads — so wan they were that one could hardly tell their faces from the white of their garb, but only the lusterless glassy eyes swimming sadly in their sockets. They paced ever so slowly to the center of the nave... I took cover behind a gold column, in fright. I singled out one of the shadows... a white-haired old man with a haggard face, wild eyes and sucked-in lips, his stare focused on the flame of the candle burning away in his hand... I could tell I had seen him before. A pale girl with a bluish marble face stood leaning against a column... right in front of me; she smiled sadly and beckoned to me... It was Poesis... Poesis! I cried out... and opened my eyes. The fire was not out yet... but the window was open and the high wind was howling in through it. I thought the wind

had opened it and I went there to close it back. But when I turned my eyes...
I saw.

• • •

Sooner or later the body would have healed but the real illness, the all-consuming illness, lay at my heart. I threw into the fire all things reminiscent of that traitress and they were burnt as my heart, nay, my very life, had been burnt out. Pale as a ghost I would drag my feet along the city walls, more dead than alive. My jaws had drawn in, the whites of my eyes had turned sallow and their blacks were murky and lusterless. I let my hair fall untidily over the unbrushed slimy collar of my jacket — and I wandered in that guise among an alien world wherein I did not belong and, if I chanced to stray into a public garden with flushed merry faces giggling around and taking cover behind the trees, I tended to take them for malicious ephemeral spectres jeering at my pain. At other times I imagined I saw grinning corpses around them whose sallow faces were smeared with red, the more appalling and ghastlier by the contrast between the truth of death and the smeared likelihood of life. Occasionally I found myself gaping in a mirror and making faces and when I came to my senses from such a vacant mood I was terrified at the certainty of having gone mad and scared by my own self. Uppermost in my mind was the fear of madness; I was afraid lest I should go mad. I often stared vacantly at the sun with my naked eye for a whole hour, until blinded by its scorching light I could only discern a bluish-red chaos which seemed to daze and twist me about until I found myself sprawled on the grass in some field. I was stultified, absurd, senseless. I often lay like that, buried in the fragrant grasses, a swarm of tiny blue summer butterflies fluttering over the flowers, the hot sun beating down on my bare head, all things beauteous as only summer days can make them... with me alone without a single sane thought in my head. For whole days I would scour the plains until I came across the river. Once there, I stood on the wooden bridge gazing at the yellow waves floating by and gurgling swiftly, murky waves like my barren soul, murky and gloomy like my dead heart. I could not bear the sight of the crystal-clear water in the wells and, chancing near one, I would set to stirring it up with my stick until, muddied by the dun earth, it turned into a live icon of my thoughts.

Yet things could not go on like that indefinitely. One more month of such a life and I was aware I should be dead. Not that I cared if I died... I might even be happier down there in the earth... but I had an aged father to think of and my death would have meant the end of him.

One fine summer day I packed my belongings in a bundle, hung it on the end of my stick and went straight for the imperial high road. I walked between cornfields... The fragrant corn was ripening in the blistering sunshine. I had cocked my hat on the crown of my head so as to leave my brow free and uncovered and set to whistling a carefree and soothing tune while shiny large beads of sweat kept trickling down my brow and along my cheeks.

Happy as the day was long I walked at a steady pace with never a moment for rest. The sun was skirting the horizon, the air grew cooler, the fields seemed to fall asleep from their indefatigable rustle — along the country road people were returning from their toil balancing their scythes on their shoulders, the girls carried pots and pails in both hands, braces of oxen pulled slowly at their yokes, the carts creaked and the peasants walking by their sides smacked their whips and shouted their eternal hoy, ho!... The Mures was asleep between its banks, the boat-bridge grunted under the weight of the carts... In the far distance I caught sight of my native mountains, ancient giants with rocky brows soaring up through the clouds and shining above them, surly, hoary, and gaunt.

One by one stars lit and twinkled in the blue boundlessness of the sky, some higher, some lower, and the moon, their fair queen, pale as a bride, floated like a silver sickle among the thin whitish clouds. The cartloads of timber coming down from the mountains creaked and grunted; the peasants lay on their bellies atop the loads or walked beside the carts whistling, and their doinas sounded ancient and sad like reminiscences of the times of yore. All the charms of a summer night were there — the white moon and the golden stars, the melancholy pipe and the slumberous fields and straight ahead the rocky old giants — the mountains that now looked as if crowned with stars a-twinkle over their brows.

I followed my way steadily along the white paths crisscrossing the cornfields — some of them still green — and I gained the cool of the mountainside. There I followed a rocky mountain footpath. On several hilltops I could see blazing campfires and men seated round them, or hear an occasional alpenhorn booming its brassy pain from the thick of the forests that wrapped the mountain shoulders in their dark green mantle; beside some other fires I saw girls and lads dancing, and here and there in the forests the braves would whistle or play heartfelt and homesick doinas on tree leaves. On and on I walked along an upsloping narrow path winding along the rocky bluffs. The path had crumbled in some places and was blocked in others by boulders tumbled down from the peaks and stuck right there in its middle. I would jump over the gaps and the boulders and continue my way heedless of the moon that had set, the fires that were dying out, the songs that had ceased, until the rising sun spread a faint blush over the east. The crisp morning air filled my lungs and I felt my throat benumbed with the chill... and eventually I saw my village with its small thatched cottages scattered over the stony heart of the mountains as if it were a village of eagles' nests. I walked through its centre, past the small wooden church, and at the far end of the village I stopped by my father's poor hut. The little window pane was lighted. I drew back the wooden bolt on the cracked door and let myself in. A few brushwood embers were still glowing in the hearth and I saw father sleeping on a bed of planks raised as high as the hearth. Behind the oven there still was mother's bed, now covered with a strip of carpet, above it hung a smoked old icon of the Holy Virgin, and a small oil lamp was flickering below the icon. I could not bring myself to wake father so I lay down on mother's bed and fell sound asleep with exhaustion. At break of dawn, when the day was still young, the cock crowed on the roof and in my sleep I heard father getting out of bed, dipping his hands into the tub of water to wash his face, making the sign of the cross while mumbling a prayer under his breath, then picking up his hammers from under the bed and letting himself out without a look back, so he did not see me sleeping behind the oven.

It was high noon when I woke up from my deep dreamless sleep. Somebody was fidgeting about the house and beside the hearth. It was a cousin who was feeding brushwood into the fire and cooking.

"Is it you, Finitza?" I called out, got out of bed, took her head into my hands and kissed her.

"Oh, Goodness me!" she exclaimed smiling, covered her lips with her fingers and took me in from head to foot. "You're a reg'lar man now... Look at you... with a beard and mustache!... I say, cousin, you're yellow like a corpse... is it the pangs of love?"

"You have no inkling," I said looking her in her shiny innocent eyes, "nor can you have any into how I have suffered."

My, how pretty my cousin looked! Her face was white and her cheeks rosy, her thick chestnut hair was plaited into two pigtails falling down her back — smooth hair parted in the middle —, large hazel eyes that gazed at me in wonder, arched knitted eyebrows, a fine ladylike nose, a well-rounded flawless chin and, when laughing, two dainty dimples appeared on her cheeks. Her white peasant's blouse was embroidered and wide-sleeved, her skirt was new and clean, and her feet bare. The more I gazed the prettier she looked to me, so I kissed her again.

"Naughty!" she said with a merry laugh, "look at the master taking his fill as if from his own. Have you no other business?"

"There, there," I said, "don't take it amiss... Besides, I won't fall for your eyes... though they *are* pretty."

"Hear, hear! Here comes the cousin and the first thing he says is I've a squint in my eyes! That's a nice thing to say!"

"Oh, you see..."

"Course I see... the gentleman's lived in the city and thinks ladies's eyes are prettier than mine, poor me!" she said laughing with her arms akimbo, Eve's garrulous daughter, her teeth shiny as pearls.

"Finitza, should you know," I said with a strained laugh "about my love..."

"Love" she said in a flurry, "love, you say?" and arched her eyebrows with curiosity, "What love?... tell me... please! Please, cousin!" she added with pursed lips and lowered her eyes so winsomely that they could hardly be seen under her eyelashes.

"Sit here on the bed," I said, took her in my arms and seated her as if she were a naughty child. I sat beside her, placed my arm around her neck, and gave her the story of my love misfortune.

She sat listening with childish earnestness and attention — and when she lifted her eyes to look at me, they were stained with tears.

"My poor cousin," she exclaimed and her kiss was ever so gentle and fresh.

The pots on the stove started boiling.

"My," she said remembering, "I must take the victuals to your father! Be seeing you again in this evening, or tomorrow morning" she added, then flavoured the food, chose a couple of full pots, smiled to me with all her face, walked out of the door, and started across the village.

By and by father came home, having heard from her of my return. He hugged me to [his] heart. His hair was white, the wrinkles on his brow and the furrows on his face deeper — so much change I noticed in him though it was enough to bring tears to my eyes.

I languished home for a long time in a dull lackadaisical dejection. I had found a book on a beam with moth-eaten leather binding and red margins — with tales handwritten in an antiquated script and initials illumined in red ink... doubtless, an heirloom from the aged priest who had died long before. For days on end I would lie in the shade of the porch, book in hand, puzzling mechanically over the old text or just staring up at the smoked beams of the eaves, until I felt my head lifted up and sheltered into someone's lap. I would raise my eyes as far backward as I could and see Finitza who, having secured my head in her lap, started telling me riddles or fairy tales, or sing away in a low voice some hora, or extemporize a tune on lyrics invented by herself. Long evenings would I lie like that with my head in her lap, while the cattle were lowing by us coming back from the mountains with udderfuls of milk and the bells round their necks enriched the dusk's sweet air with their drowsy and melancholy tinkle.

The revolution had flared up all over the plain of Transylvania — yet little did I care. I had been reduced to idle indifference, idleness of thought, idleness of feeling, to the most complete and idiotic sluggishness, by my love for a woman. Her very name, Poesis, could no longer rouse any feeling in my breast. She was long dead and I had forgotten her — with hardly a spark of recollection; for it did not dawn on me that my heart had been killed and my intelligence slain though I was languishing precisely in that vacant mood.

Autumn had set in and the forests on the shoulders of the old mountains turned rusty, the mists about their peaks were thicker — eventually one day the first snowflakes spread their silvery down over the misty cold air uphill. The news in the villages that the Romanians had risen in arms against the Hungarians and the king of the old forests and of the barren hoary mountains had called up the eagles from their rocky aeries around the Romanian colors. The tricolor was flying in the rocky heart of the mountains and in their cold air, heralding Transylvania's liberation.

One night I watched a magnificent scene. Big fires were flaring up higher and higher on the mountain tops, on their rocky brows — it looked as if the mountains themselves had caught fire. Bands of men were seated

round the fires, the lances propped on their shoulders sparkled in the air...
scythes turned into lances that were to spread terror among the enemies.
From up there on the peaks, the Romanians let go lighted straw-wreathed
cartwheels which turned demonic somersaults and fell roaring into the deep
precipices, heading for the core of the earth. The alpenhorns bulged on the
peaks so heartily that the brass souls of the mountains seemed to have
woken to trumpet the Last Judgement. Every peak was afire, with so many
huge red eyes, one on every mountain brow. The ancient forests stirred into
life from their winter hibernation, the stars and the moon looked paler
against the sky, the sky itself was grizzlier. It was one of those grandiose
sights that only God Himself can paint on the world's vast canvas for our
amazed eyes and overwhelmed hearts.

The revolution had reached our mountains. As our village lay at the
foothills, the Honveds would scout it at regular intervals in search of young
men, but they had thoughtfully joined Iancu long before. The more elderly
would have had me for their tribune but, owing to my mood, I stayed insen-
sitive and unresponsive to their grand cause. Braving all perils, Iancu's tri-
bunes often visited the village, while bands of rebels stayed the night with
us and vanished before dawn lest the Honveds should get wind of their
whereabouts and fall on them by surprise. One night I heard the noise of
shooting in the neighborhood. Worried, I flung the bedclothes aside, ran out,
climbed the fence and held myself onto the poles so as to gain a command-
ing view over a cluster of houses in the neighborhood. A house had been sur-
rounded by the Honveds who were now pounding on the door with the butts
of their rifles to ram it in. In that instant a volley of shots flashed through
the window and I [heard] the groans of the attackers — the door was broken
in no time, letting out a bare-headed [youth] with his sword in his teeth and
the guns in his hands levelled at the men on the doorstep, at whom he fired.
On his tail a handful of men set to thrusting their lances right and left and,
making headway, ran for their lives toward a cluster of rocks where they
took cover, so that the moonlight only shone on the steel of their levelled
barrels and on the shots fired at the men now ransacking the house.

I thought I had recognized the pale bare-headed youth. Though I had
only glimpsed him in the light of the rifle shots, I felt he could be no other
than Ioan. I returned home and went to bed again, but a whirl of thoughts
would not allow me to catch a wink of sleep. What if it had been Ioan... the

thought kept nagging at me... for, if it was he, I was left no choice... I had to follow him.

Tossing about in my bed I felt a horde of demons taking command over my fretful soul, like as many embodied dreams... dreams with iron talons. I would turn my face to the wall... but the wall seemed smeared with red faces like those on the wooden icons in old churches... or turn over toward the oven but the bluish coals on the grate were demons' red eyes dancing a savage jig and the green smoke curling up looked like the waving of the unplaited grizzly hair of a bloodthirsty fury. I would close my eyes tightly to chase the dreams away, but if sleep it was what I acquired, it only gave me headaches and heart-throbs. I felt a wooden talon wring out my brains, a heavy rock lying on my breast, someone on top of me stifled my breath, clasped me in his grisly long arms, and dropped me into a gloomy chasm wherein I fell... The ragged top of a rock loomed in sight halfway between heaven and hell and I was bound to crash against it. I screamed out my lungs in fright and tried to wriggle out of the course my body had taken downward, but at that moment I reached the rock and an excruciating pain... My insides had been broken... I woke up. I had really fallen... but only out of bed. The fire was still glowing and the tiny lamp flickered before the Mother of All Sorrows, lighting up her saintly visage. I made the sign of the cross and gained my feet.

It was impossible to go back to sleep, or even remain there any longer. I decided to let my first intention get the better of me and go into the wide world wherever my nose might lead me. I fed some brushwood into the fire and it started crackling gaily and scattering fiery sparks. I drew a low stool near the fire, picked father's scythe from a corner of the hut, sat on the stool in the light of the brushwood fire, unsheathed a knife, and set with a will to fashioning a lance out of the scythe. I tapered the handle to fit into the blade hole, then I sharpened the blade, especially its top, on a whetstone, making it razor sharp so that, had I touched a hair against it, the hair would have been cut in two. Fortunately father was so sound asleep that he did not hear me sharpening the scythe or fumbling under the bed for a brace of rusty long-barrelled pistols, which I loaded with gunpowder from an ox horn and slipped under my belt. I covered my shoulders with an old coarse woollen coat and my head with a sheepskin hat, balanced the lance over one shoulder, and let myself out. It was cold outside, but a gorgeous moon was floating over the blue airy plains. In the house next door, where the skirmish had been fought, the door was wide open and a big fire was burning on the dirt floor, started by the soldiers that were now sprawled over the hay puffing at their pipes, with their rifles within reach; a capacious pot was boiling on the stove and the soldiers killed their time spitting into the fire, sometimes missing. Their faces were savage and beastly. The saddled horses were tethered to the fence poles — I singled out a grey horse standing aside without a bit in his muzzle, munching away at a truss of hay. I walked round the house to the back and reached the grey skirting the open door. I produced my knife from the belt, made fast work of cutting the straps that tied him to the fence, gathered his mane in a firm grip, bounced on him, and stabbed my heels into his ribs. Mad with fury he kicked the air with his hoofs, neighed, yet broke into a fast gallop and I darted off into the night with never a look back, as if mounted on a spirit of wrath. I heard the report of a rifle behind me, a bullet whizzed past my ear, but I let go of the rein and kicked [the horse] in the ribs and he kept up his gallop tearing through the night's cold air with his hot body steaming beads of sweat. The galloping horse jolted me terribly, making every fiber in my body vibrate. The moonbeams flashed on the lance on my shoulder and were cast back to pierce the darkness, and the flint-stones sparkled and cracked under the horse's iron shoes, their shrieks rousing the slumberous echo of the mountains. Thus the horse ran on and the ride was rather like a flight in midair between heaven and earth, taken on and on by a bodiless genius, or carried off by a dragon of yore or by an evil spirit roaring through the air. How long our flight went on I do not recall, but this I do remember, that suddenly my horse floundered and gasped for breath, slowed down to a clumsy canter and foamed at the muzzle and nostrils. Unawares I had left the highlands and was now in a plain.

So far I had been no saner than a sleepwalker. Everything I had done was done unconsciously, in the grip of some unexplainable desire or on a dark senseless impulse. I stopped where I was, rubbed my eyes, and started taking in the lay of the land. The mountains were behind me, the Mures flowed straight ahead in the far distance, and to one side I noticed a townlet which, set fire to at all four corners, was beginning to burn. It was at about a two hour ride. The horse was exhausted and could hardly raise his hoofs clear of the ground. I urged him toward the town. Before long the limpid breath of the night became chillier and brisker. Though the sky was clear, tiny flecks of snow began to prick my face and brow, so I spurred the horse who changed into an easy trot. The wind was growing stronger and stronger

until, swifter than my horse's trot, it began to blow its chill through all the
seams of my old clothes. The fire was spreading wider over the town and,
when I approached it, my ears could discern distant faint moans. The horse
turned into a canter, the wind started to howl and whistle and, spurred by it,
the flames took wings and soared sky-high. As I drew nearer I noticed the
savage cold wind storming the sea of fire and spreading it to all quarters
while drowning in it the thousands and thousands of swift, snowy souls.
The concert of moans and groans was appalling to the ear and the cobble-
stones themselves would have splintered with compassion harking to such
sounds; the town beridden with fire and wind had become one with the sky,
for I could not tell the sky from the earth. The blaze soared slantwise carried
by the wind... the air and the smoke alike were afire, the sky was aglow and
its blue dome menaced to burn out and cave in. Trembling, shy gold-eyed
stars were entangled in the red clouds of smoke. Earth, air, and the sky
above — all fell prey to one ruthless fire... my horse, without rein or spur,
continued his advance by leaps and starts. Outside the town I dis-
mounted... hid the lance in the gutter by the high road, adorned my hat with
a red feather, mounted back, and entered the streets ablaze at both ends. In
the savage hubbub of the enemy's drums, the houses crumbling down with
the fire, the dark-red flames, and the black smoke rushing out through the
broken window-panes... the rows of houses looked like arrayed for battle
with their tops burning and their eyes filled with flames and smoke. People
scurried about and shouted, the black streets were bustling like as many
anthills, some were carrying trunks with scared faces and eyes glaring at the
soldiers who were in two minds as to the object of a proper chase... the loot
being spirited away, or the half-naked women running in the streets dishev-
elled and pale as ghosts. Their husbands, run over by cartwheels or brained
against the burning walls were lying on the cobblestones, some dead, some
half-dead, and some still managing to give a faint moan... the children were
crying their eyes out, their lips whimpering their mothers' names. A cocked
pistol in either hand, I spurred the horse and he trotted along the streets
over corpses, over carts broken into pieces, over shattered boxes overflowing
clothes and tools onto the road, over broken furniture, over slain animals —
I rode with gritted teeth through that savage scene, through that terrible
heart-rending drama highlighted by the all-consuming fire. On either side
the rows of burning houses — the small white cobbles of the pavement
strewn with corpses and splashed with black blood, all the townspeople

moaning... murder and night down on the earth, clouds and smoke up in the sky! Such was the long and the short of that blood-curdling scene.

A priest of my acquaintance lived in the town and I felt I had to look for him. I gave a sigh of relief when, out in the unlit greenery of the outskirts, I saw no house burning! Large gardens hedged with a thick tangle of thickets lined the streets and behind the thickets, left leafless in the autumn, stood the homesteads surrounded by clusters of trees. I stopped by the front gate of the priest's courtyard. The gate wings were wide open. The windows were also open and through them I could hear a woman's faint moans. Entering the house without precautions would have meant taking great chances, so I sneaked nearer to the window to cast a glimpse inside. But what a scene, my Goodness!

The room was teeming with soldiers outdoing each other in savagery and drunkenness, who crouched laughing and yelling beside a broached sizeable cask. There was a nook in the wall on the right of my window with a wooden icon of the Mother of the Lord and a small lamp, filled half with oil, half with water, burning in front of it. There were sheaves of dried self-heal and yellow flowers in the nook and above it, hung on hooks. Under the nook was the desk with the priest's old, leather-bound religious books, now in disarray and some scattered on the floor. The icon nook was in a wall between this room and a smaller one. The priest was dangling on a strong iron hook above the door... His eyes eerily showed only their whites, the bluish foam of death trickled from the corners of his mouth down into his beard, his hands were tied in front. His daughter was leaning against a wall, pale as wax, her large black eyes sunken and lined with large bluish rings, unfocused like the eyes of a lunatic. Her thin bluish lips, her unplaited jet-black hair streaming down her neck which had turned white like an insensitive block of marble, her long black silk gown, everything about her gave her the look of a Fury of sorrow, of a Fury carved in marble. Her dried-up eyes glared in demonic and lunatic desperation at the men flushed with drink who, sprawled on the floor, were ogling her with lecherous glittery eyes and savage subhuman desire.

"Haw, haw!"... yelled a narrow-browed one with flushed fat cheeks, small green eyes, and fiery-red hair. "Haw! my beauty... what's that look on your face... We've hanged your old man... the god-damned priest! So what! Might as well laugh at the old fool... What's that to you... you're going to live with us... you'll be my woman, my chick! Hehehe!" he laughed on his tottering legs... "How d'you like me, girlie?... handsome, ain't I? ...such a handsome lad... my own ma's fine lad.... red-faced to boot... and more... hehehe! and the white-skinned girlie's fallen for the red-faced lad... or hasn't she?"

With that he drew nearer to the girl who was trembling like a leaf with her lips opened in fright... He was going to lay his hands on her... but she dropped onto her knees... Grieved and beautiful, she lifted her large eyes that would have moved a heart of stone...

"I entreat you," she said, "kill me! kill me as you have killed my father and I will be grateful."

"Hehehe! What a thing to say!... How come? Indeed! D'you hear, Istvan, she would rather die! No, no, no!" he added with a stupid grin "you're not to die."

"She's not to die!" echoed the others in the room, all jeering, "she's our woman... she's not to die!"

"The lot fell on me," said the cannibal, "so leave me alone with her!..."

The others struggled to their feet and tottered out of the door...

With terrible determination the wretched girl lowered her head and hit its crown against the wall, but she only fainted and recoiled into the arms of the cannibal who, in his unbuttoned shirt leaving bare the red furry hair on his chest, grabbed her in his filthy arms and fumbled with his sparsely-mustached filthy mouth for her lips, now bluish like two sloes... She divined his intention, mustered her strength and wriggled out of his arms. I had levelled the pistol the moment she opened her eyes... She was rushing for the door but, on noticing the weapon... she stopped short, a marble statue of sublime distress, the pride of a lioness writ all over her face and a savage virginal sparkle in her eyes. With a firm hand I fired straight at her bosom... I had taken good aim for, she smiled the angelic smile of a martyr and subsided onto the floor. At the crack of my weapon the Hungarian dropped the earthern candlestick with its tall tallow candle. Presently all his mates rushed in, relit the candle, and staggered, with eyes bulging out with shock, nearer to the body of the dead girl now lying rigid on the floor with her hands joined on her bosom. I could ill afford to linger by that window, so I walked round the house and jumped over a window ledge into the room adjoining the one wherein the tragedy had befallen, separated by a door [fortunately a locked one] from the scene of that barbarous cruelty. It did not take me long to find the nook with the icon of the Mother of the Lord. There was a window which opened to my side and I swiftly removed the icon propped against the pane and snuffed out the lamp. As in every country house there was a small glass partition through which I could see all that was going in the other room. I was not afraid for I have never laid much stock on life; besides, I was determined to sell my life dearly if it came to fighting for it.

"Haw, haw," said the repulsive red-haired man, "you're dead as a door nail, damn you and your piety!" and he kicked her.

She was dead indeed... The hem of her black gown was spread on the floor... the large eyes were closed and, for all her sorrows, a bitter yet sublime smile had lighted up her bloodless dead face, white as a shroud. Her hands, joined on the heart I had stopped beating with my bullet, concealed the wound, yet a trickle of blood dripped onto her black gown. She was beautiful lying like that... a saintly white virgin martyr lying on the floor amid those Satanic brutish figures.

One of the party pushed the priest's legs swinging him to and fro, another raised a candle to his white beard which caught fire and the flame rose to his cheeks... The bluish skin on the old man's face started to split, his whitish long eyelashes were aflame, the burning skin on eyeballs rose up and the still shiny whites of his eyes savagely at those dull-witted men. It was a terrible, blood-curdling sight indeed! The burnt beard, the singed blackish face, the sunken eyeballs turned inside out, the gaping mouth with froth sizzling in the heat of the fire... in a word, the mutilated head of a corpse with eyes eloquent of the cruelty of their wrong-doing glaring at the laughing brutes who did not get the meaning of the dead man's wordless grin.

"He, he!" said Ianos, "while you're having fun with the priest, I'll have fun with his daughter. D'you think she's rid of me now that she's dead?... no, no! girlie, get up and give Ianos a nice kiss."

As good as his word, he grabbed her by an arm and dragged her out of the room through the dust on the floor that soiled and bleached her black gown. Though I was not sure I made sense of the cannibal's intentions, a horrendous idea struck me. Could those men be that sacrilegious as to rape the corpse of a virgin? Yet, along with that apprehension the idea of a dreadful revenge took possession of my mind.

It hardly took me a minute to take off my shoes, to fetch several armfuls of dry straw from the backyard up into the loft, to strew it about the loft, and to light it. I climbed down the ladder in no time and, finding the key in the door of the entrance hall, I fixed the latch and turned the key in the lock without letting the drunks inside notice a thing. The open window was now the only escape. In superhuman fury I fetched a whole haystack under the window, then heaved the big yard-gate clear of its hinges, propped it against the window and lighted the straw which caught fire readily, being dry and helped by the wind. At that moment the men inside seemed to sober up and they started pounding on the door in mad fury. But the deal double door was reinforced with steadfast iron rivets. They stampeded to the window, but the gate propped there had caught fire and I had added another gate and haystack on top of it. Presently the roof was ablaze, the beams started crackling, the wind joined forces with the smouldering flames lending them redoubled strength, and the savage yells of the cannibals buried in the flames grew as loud as the groans of the sinners doomed to hellfire.

Still barefoot I bounced onto the horse, kicked him in the ribs, and retraced my course across the town. The fire had relented, the streets were deserted and in some places the corpses had been stacked in disorderly heaps. I rode swiftly out of the town, retrieved my lance from the gutter by the high road, took off the red feather from my hat, blew it into the wind, and rode back toward the mountains, though not toward my village.

I came across a mountain trail and urged my steed along it. He took it at a slow pace, floundering and panting, his hoofs stumbling against the bigger boulders at the bends in the trail winding up among the rocks. The farther I rode into the highlands the fresher and colder the air grew under a clearer sky, and the moon showed her yellow visage through the clouds' silvery veil. My mind was as void of ideas as the meaningless motley of discordant colors — red, black, green, yellow — all smeared on the same spot of a canvas — anyhow, a preposterous chaos like the thoughts of an idiot was whirling inside it. I could not make head or tail of the recent events like a person who, having gone without sleep for days on end, his brain a-jumble with sleeplessness, walks among people and cannot tell reality from dreams and lets his mind imagine deep traits, threatening grimaces, and ominous projects on the countenance of every acquaintance, who sees the shadows growing taller and taking on human contours on the walls or, gazing at a clear water, imagines his very gaze stirs up the mud therein — in a word, a mood wherein no concept perceived by the senses is apt to be passed on unmuddled to his inner consciousness. It seemed to me I had lived out a tale with dragons and bloodshed wherein, in other places and on other shores, lovers would still roam about the shady verdure of the groves, their faces washed silvery by the light of a pale moon smiling through the clouds, faces beautified with the melancholy of love's tender dreams. That night was a meaningless courtly romance of the Middle Ages wherein there was no room for scenes smeared with blood, fire, and the bluish-red darkness of smoke, though such a procession of hideous masks of corpses and Satanic, red and grimacing faces had seemingly passed before my eyes. They mixed in my troubled soul and resulted in such a torpor of the organs of thought and feeling that uppermost in my wearied mind was an overwhelming wish to sleep. Hardy natures will sleep soundly before a catastrophe — and I think they will sleep as soundly after it, for there is nothing so apt to render a man completely insensitive and dull-witted as such terrible scenes. Reaching the crest of a hill with an outcrop of rocks scattered about like as many sleepy white sheep, the white moonlight caressing their silvery fleece, I dismounted and tethered the horse to the twisted and gnarled branches of a bush with frost-bitten yellow leaves. All by myself there and prey to the deepest torpor, I pulled my fur hat over my eyes and ears, laid my head on a slab and my body on a heap of dry leaves, and went to sleep. The dream — to me an untroubled world suffused with adamantine clear rays, studded with stars pure as gold, fragrant with the shady verdure of laurel groves — the dream unbarred its golden gates and let me enter its poetical and forever youthful gardens. The mountain top whereon I lay sleeping turned into one of Semiramis' hanging gardens, its highest terrace joining the sky, into a wondrous garden of Eden bathed in an eternally untroubled sunlight, with wide palm alleyways, walks strewn with white sand, and fountains overflowing long adamantine rays which gurgled and trickled along the grooves of a cluster of jagged rocks, crystal-clear yet heavy with the sweet scent of amber: the sleep-inducing nectar of the East. And all that wonderland was above the clouds! The sky was clear and emerald-green and its firm dome reached down in both East and West into the undulating green mirrors of the seas... in one place only the sky looked scorched and burnt with a large gap wherefrom blazing stones and rubble of broken walls were falling onto the earth. The stones thus falling to the earth piece by piece built up a wild lifeless city by the bank of the Mures, a burnt-out city with gloomy paneless windows, easy prey to savage roar of the chilly winds.

Presently the scene brightened, the gap in the sky grew deeper and wider, the blue dome embracing the earth drew aside, uncovering another dome beyond it, one far higher and wider, of a limpid pure gold like the yellow light of the sun, so that the whole of it looked like a huge sun embracing its own world, the world beyond the sky. Golden light soaked the air, everything about was golden light enriched with the gentle innocent moan of silver harps played by a silver-clad flight of angels floating on glittery long white wings across that golden kingdom. Like ethereal genii were they floating, transparent shadows, their skin bluish as soft marble, their large eyes blue, their long black curls enframing their marble white faces and necks and streaming down the long folds of their silver raiments that embraced their sublime bodies in their soft whiteness.

Among those blue-eyed angels I singled out one with large black eyes, likewise snowy but thin of face, clad in glossy long black attire, with hands joined on her breast; she was floating in the golden air with her tears-stained large eyes directed upward. I knew her... I had seen that dishevelled black hair. I had seen that deep sublime sorrow; a boundless desperation, whose only guiding star is Gold Himself, had engraved its deep traits over the visage before me and I had seen it before. All the sky was clear and blithesome, one angel only was sad... It was Maria, the daughter of the aged priest, now beatified and transfigured... yet to me she stood for the genius of the martyred Romanian nation, a tear-stained pale genius whose only hope was God, whose only support was heaven.

The night's icy hoarfrost had deposited two silver-grey gums on my long black eyelashes. Eventually my eyes felt the chill and opened. The moon had set long before, the sky was bleak... and far in the east a sleepy and dingy dawn appeared, which hardly splashed a little red color over the bluish-grey sky. I shook the cold off my body... lifted my hat over the eyes and stirred the horse who was sleeping on the ground with bent legs to let them share in the warmth of the body, and had closed his obedient large eyes. He jumped onto his legs. I mounted into the saddle and resumed the ride across the mountains. As we advanced the horse sped his trot, for the ride was a godsend to him also, allowing him to warm his blood. By and by the sun was up and the higher it rose the warmer its autumn rays grew and before long I felt their heat on my back. I dismounted — the lance on my shoulder sparkled in the sun — and walked barefoot beside the horse on the fine gravel of the mountain trails.

I spied a Romanian outpost sentry perched on a rock and sunning himself, a pipe in his mouth and the spike of his lance thrust into the ground. I went up to him.

"Good day to you, my lad," I said stroking the horse's smooth neck, "is there with you someone by the name of so-and-so?" (I gave him Ioan's surname).

"I should think so. You'll find him all right, for he's our tribune," answered the lad and set to shaking the ashes off his earthen pipe.

"I wonder if you would take me to him," I added.

"Me? Not likely!" he replied and took out a pinch of green-black tobacco from a pleated white pouch which he stuffed into his pipe with his little finger. "Not allowed to leave my post, have to stand watch here, but the trail to yonder hill will take you right to the camp."

On his last words he produced a thin awl from his belt pouch, made a hole in the tobacco, and lit it with a white-handled tinderbox. When he set to puffing at his pipe, the tips of his mustache drooped around the corners of his mouth and his eyes focused naively on the pipe mouth, apparently awaiting in great concentration to soon see it glow like a hot lump of coal. His frizzy sheepskin hat had lowered over his eyes.

I took the trail uphill and saw there, round the big bonfires burning in broad daylight — the flames licking the crisp, clear air with their forked yellow tongues — bands of peasants roasting rams and ewes on the spit, shouting, singing, or playing their flutes — to one side some bouncing on the ground with their light sandals to the tune of an elder flute played by a lad seated on a boulder. The merry shouts, the smoke curling up from the ring of fires, the pairs of eyes outdoing each other in size and inquisitiveness — all bore the stamp of the genuine Romanian peasant, his face sunburnt yet well-drawn, with lively hazel eyes, glossy long curly hair falling freely about his smooth wide brow, black moustaches, aquiline nose and protruding chin — like an effigy of the warriors of yore. The brown sheepskin coat hanging down from his shoulders, the unlaced white shirt leaving bare his sunburnt chest throbbing from the beats of his free heart, the white homespun tight trousers, the sandals turned up at the tops and laced with black woollen cords round the legs, the green belt, the red pouch under it holding a sheathed knife, a timberbox, and spare flint, and, finally, the pointed fur hat shading the piercing eyes — the same type of character over and over again in various guises about all those children of the mountains.

I inquired after Ioan and a peasant pointed to a tall fire built at some distance from the others... and told me that was the tribune's place and that he was ailing. I walked to that fire whereon a rotten hollow tree-trunk was firmly bent on showing that where there is a smoke there is a fire. Ioan was lying on a makeshift bed of dry leaves, his bare feet stretched toward the fire and his sheepskin coat pulled over his head, to expose no part of his face to the cold. The spike of his lance was thrust into the ground. I tethered my horse to the lance, knelt down by his bedside, and raised his coat clear of his face. His large eyes were closed and a network of fine blue veins showed through the white thin eyeskin; the former large deep rings round his eyes had turned their bluish hue into copper, only his face was as pale as ever. I sat at his head and took an eyeful of him. Eventually I shook him by the arm and made him open his eyes. He looked up at me with sleepy eyes and, in the melancholy idleness that sleep is wont to spread over a visage, he reached his arm round my neck and said with a drowsy smile:

"You here?"

His untroubled smile bespoke a man without a passion in the world, his countenance was saintly, as it were — it was obvious that all things mundane had been stifled in his heart.

"So I am," I blurted out and took his hand in a firm grip. "So I am."

"I thought you'd stopped caring for your people, so insensitive your love for an unworthy woman had made you", he said wrapping his feet in two white woolen cloths and putting on his russet calfskin sandals.

"Not caring for my people," I rejoined with a bitter smile, "I might never have cared if it were not for that terrible night that taught me once and for all to care."

And I gave him the long and the short of what I had seen with my bodily and inner eyes. With each word I uttered his large blue eyes turned more worried and flashed an unnatural demonic fire and deep terrible traits furrowed his pale delicate visage.

"The cannibals!" he whispered through clenched teeth.

"Well, here I am," I concluded, "because there's nowhere else my steps would take me. What do I have at stake? Life?... There's naught uglier, bleaker, more tedious than life... I've had enough of this absurd dream, anyway. The soul perhaps?... Could anyone think of his in times like these?"

"Calm down, my friend" he soothed me." True enough, it doesn't pay to live unless one has a goal in life... and on my soul, we'll set ourselves a great goal indeed!..."

His shiny eyes flared up in their sockets and a show of pride spread over his countenance.

It did not take me long to feel at home among the peasants. Before long I changed my city clothes for long tight trousers, plaited round the shins, and light calfskin sandals. Clad like that I would often take turns at keeping night watch on some mountain top, bathed by the moonbeams, like a Roman sentry of yore who, while guarding the iron crests of the Carpathians, would rivet his watchful gaze southward thinking of his mother, the beloved snowy queen bathing her alluring body in her skyblue warm seas, her brow crowned with dreams of love and her blooming white breasts caressed by the transparent blue waves; the uncaring mother who, engulfed in her own dreams, had abandoned her eagle-eyed princely son on the barren time-old crests of the Carpathians. Italy has forgotten the Romanians... yet the Romanians still love Italy.

We saw the winter out in skirmishes and hardships. Bringing to life those hardships would mean unearthing the history of those lancer legions which, even after the imperial army withdrew from Transylvania, continued to abide by their oath to the throne, relying only on their scant numbers, their brave hearts, and on the blades tied to the handles of their scythes.

One night while I was keeping watch in an outpost together with a score of men, Ioan included, a scout came and broached the news that two or three companies of Honveds had quartered with a Magyar count in his castle and were now having the time of their lives. The night was so freezing cold that we blew the frostbite off our fingers with our breath.

Ioan's eyes flared up.

"Friends, make ready for battle!" he ordered in a compelling voice.

It was like bringing grist to their mill, for in a split second the lads stood erect from their sitting or lying positions and gripped the lances from the grass in their sinewy hands. In another moment we were downhill, then crossed the fields of soft grass, and headed for the castle standing in the centre of a well-tended large park. All its windows showed lights against the night's dense darkness as if they were beacons luring us to draw nearer. Soon we reached the railing of the park. A bulldog started to bark and his throaty bark stirred the night air, yet it did not interrupt the clinking of glasses and the drinking bout inside and, before long, we heard him lying down on his straw bed, grumbling with disappointment and shaking his chain. Wary of his light sleep we skirted the park and jumped over the fence at a convenient place. It was a two-storied castle with a balcony overlooking the garden on the upper floor, below which was a causeway of rough flagstones. In all the rooms downstairs the tables were laid... the men had propped their rifles against the walls and were enjoying themselves drinking, laughing, and singing. I picked out the lads with rifles, deployed them by the window and, at my sharp command, they fired.

The bullets whizzed through the large halls and everybody jumped to his feet in fright; some were shot and their mouths distorted in the grin of death... most of the party dropped their glasses, forgot about the weapons, and stampeded headlong for the door.

"Death to them!" I shouted, hoisted a window clear of its hinges, and was the first to jump into the hall. The others followed suit. Everyone still in the hall was slain. We took possession of their loaded guns, rushed through the lighted large rooms of the castle, and smashed everything to pieces. An alarm bell was tolling in the turret. Inside the castle the reports of rifles and the drunken beastly yells of the dying mixed with the happy shouts of our lads. I and Ioan climbed the grand stair to the upper floor. I forced the big door open with my shoulder and entered a large drawing room with a door opening onto the balcony, actually a French window, its panes letting in the white light of the moon, now clear of the clouds. The moonlight shone on a wall hung with weapons. All at once two frightened eyes sparkled in the dark... a tall man in a corner seemed ready to attack us. I held out my arm and pulled the trigger and, in that faint light I caught a glimpse of a bluish face I had seen before.

"It's he!" I cried out in a rage. It was Poesis' lover.

Instantly Ioan caught hold of his lapels yet disregarding the grip, the count opened the door to the balcony with one hand and made an effort with the other to throw Ioan over the rail onto the flagstones. In a split second my sword cut off the arm gripping Ioan's chest... and Ioan fell down with the severed arm. The count raised his other arm, pistol in hand, which he levelled at my brow... Ioan, back on his feet, stabbed his dagger into the count's elbow throwing his arm out of balance, so the shot went and whizzed through my hair. Yet he managed to put his arm round Ioan's throat. The Magyar had intended to bite the crown of Ioan's head and his teeth might have broken his skull bones, had not Ioan raised his shiny dagger and thrust it at the count's nape, deep into the brain. A horrible yell ensued and the battle was over. The door opened and our lads entered with torches in their hands. Ioan had fallen over the Magyar and I drew nearer them with a torch. The corpse was a terrifying sight; his mouth half-open, his teeth bared for biting... the frightened and distorted bluish face betraying the madness of his shattered brain... his teeth had apparently ground the poisonous bluish foam trickling at the corners of his mouth.

I stood staring in unutterable hatred at the man who had robbed me of all I had who was now only a wretched corpse. The lads made merry, took the weapons down from the wall, and shared them out. We climbed down the grand staircase, entered a room with laid tables, opened all the windows and disposed of the corpses, then sat round the table as if nothing had happened, and we were wedding guests. Some might consider such things unbelievable yet should they know how revolution and uncertainty as to one's life are apt to render one insensitive and to turn bloodshed into man's natural way of life, they would get an inkling not only into our behavior, but also into the centuries wherein the peoples' main occupation was fighting and looting.

That was one of the many events of the year. Yet I shall recount another, one that cost me so dearly. There was a Saxon who owned a mill moored on the Mures, from whom we used to buy our supplies of flour, which made the Saxon hold his tongue in front of the Magyar posses scouring the country. The mill rocked quietly on the Mures bathing its skeleton of rotten timber in the white foamy water of the river, its deafening wheels turned like two black dragons, and the ruddy, fat and moon-faced Saxon, his head covered with a hat as big as a roof, strutted with his hands in the pockets of his white apron amid the crowd, who came here with sacks of grain for grinding and with treasures of stories, tales, and news, making the loft look like a fair rather than an ordinary attic. Often, without disclosing my name or trade, I would sit on a sack of flour with the rim of my hat over my eyes, puffing at my pipe and listening to the giggle of the girls, the tales of the elderly, the curses of the men, or to the drowsy yet sweet squeak of an old fiddle on which an aged Gypsy would play sometimes merry and sometimes sad tunes. The expressive swarthy face, the snow-white beard, the almost blind eyes dimmed with old age, the hairy bare chest, only half-covered by a black shirt, the battered brown sheepskin hat letting out the white hair through its gaps [made a sight of] the old man who would sit on a heap of diffused millstones stacked in a corner of the mill and tell his tales not by word of mouth but by the tunes of his strings. It was a warm day and our party, who were to make a sortie down the valley, had decided to spend the night in the Saxon's mill so as to be on our way at break of day.

The queue had thinned out, the sun was setting behind the hills for his due sleep, the old Gypsy had laid his head on a millstone and gone to sleep with the pipe still burning in his mouth, like a king in his soft gold-tasselled bed... the men had loaded their sacks on their carts and yoked their white, fat, long-horned oxen and were now setting out on their sundry ways, with a spate of whiplashing and shouting, toward the highlands or the plains. Dusk had closed in, the millstones had been stopped, only the huge mill continued its lazy rocking on the Mureş, pulling at the long linden basts that tethered it to the banks. The Saxon sat on a flat slab at the wide door of his mill, lit his pipe, and watched in melancholy the rise of the evening star. I sat beside him in the dusk that was growing darker and suddenly I heard the woeful moan of an alpenhorn.

"My men!" I said, jumped to my feet and hurried off toward the plain; but when I was about forty feet away I looked back and, in the dim twilight I through I spied a Honved sitting beside the Saxon and casting impatient glances about him. The import of that scene did not dawn on me. I met my lads in the plain and Ioan was with them. How handsome he was that night... the scene is so well imprinted on my mind as if it had happened a minute ago. His coarse woollen coat was unbuttoned, leaving free his throat and front, so his white chest showed through his linen shirt, his face was pale yet sweet and full of kindness, the gaze of his blue eyes melancholy, his long fair hair fell freely on his shoulders from under a wide-rimmed black hat... In truth, he was handsome as a woman in a fair-haired, pale, appealing way.

"You look like a girl!" I exclaimed and hugged him to my heart.

"And you like a boy," he retorted with a reckless laugh.

Yet his cold firm handshake evinced his delicate long and white fingers through which ran a lion's strength.

We reached the mill and greeted the Saxon who opened the door. It was the Gypsy who sat beside him telling him how, back in his youth, he used to outwit his neighbors stealing their chickens, hanging them by the

legs on the hooks under his coat, and then walked whistling about the vil-
lage with the coat dangling on one shoulder and it did not cross their mind
what he had hidden there. The Saxon roared with laughter, though his
laughter sounded strained to me. Yet I might have been wrong for, as you
know, deceived by the distance, I had suspected it was a Honved he was
talking to.

As all men were tired, we lay down right and left about the mill — the
miller pottered for a while about his sacks and tubs, put out the fire in the
stone hearth and lay down downstairs, where the millstones were. Everyone
set to driving his pigs to market outdoing each other in snoring and moaning
on the sack where he was lying. I had spread my coat on the floor and went
to sleep there beside Ioan who had reached his arm about my neck before
falling asleep. For whatever reason, I could not sleep. Yet I overheard the
Saxon getting up and pacing the floor-boards downstairs. He climbed the
stairs cautiously on tiptoe with a rushlight in his hand. He had hardly
reached the top steps when I fancied I saw the bluish barrel of a rifle shining
at the window taking aim at the sleeping men. I kept silent and closed my
eyes so that, through the slits under my eyelids, I could watch the Saxon
drawing nearer and leaning over us to see whether we were sleeping. There
was a frightening look on his face. But just when he had retreated to the
door, also on tiptoe, and intended to put up the strong wooden bolt, I jumped
to my feet.

"Get up, friends," I shouted at the top of my voice. "We're done for!"

In a split second all the men, though sleepy and scared, were on their
feet. The Saxon, taken unawares, dropped his rushlight — he would have
been killed that instant if the extinction of the only light had not plunged
the room into darkness. A rifle went off through the window, but no moan
was heard... which meant that no one had been hit. The hubbub outside
redoubled.

"In battle line!" Ioan's silvery voice called out loudly and, in the moon-
beams sifting in through the slits in the wooden shutter, I saw the lancers
arrayed in the front line and, in the second line shone the short-barrelled
mountain rifles levelled on the shoulders of the first-liners. It had taken no
longer than a minute. At that moment the big door cracked on its hinges and
fell in.

"Fire!" Ioan ordered and the enemies rushing in by the doorway started to groan, some to death, others only wounded, accompanied by the incessant cracks and barks of our rifles.

"Forward!" ordered Ioan and the lancers swooped down with a will on their numerous enemies.

I had caught hold of a battle axe and, using its spike and edges, played havoc with everyone within range.

They fired a volley and our ranks thinned.

"Forward!" called Ioan in mad rage.

With one more savage attack we broke through their ranks and rushed out into the moonlight.

Hardly had we left the room when some pistol took aim at Ioan's naked chest. It cracked and a fiery snake rushed out of its muzzle, but in the same instant I crashed my axe onto the head of the shooter and split it in two, as if it were firewood.

"My God, I'm dying!" said Ioan in a low voice.

I took him in the crook of my arms and set to running like a phantom, swiftly and mad with rage, leading my men who stampeded after me followed by shots and mounted men. Straight ahead we ran, for the shelter of the mountains. The poor boy's chest was bleeding fearfully, the moon in the sky had caught fire and was scorching the crown of my head, the men looked like mad phantoms flying and whizzing past me. Before long we came across a trail leading up to the mountains.

The run was more difficult, the climb more strenuous, yet we managed to reach a hilltop with a rich outcrop of scattered boulders.

"Halt!" called out one of the oldest of the mountain-folk. "Friends, array these boulders in line!"

No sooner said than the boulders were arranged in two lines, in battle array, like a fortified wall. As soon as the enemies started coming uphill, the first line of boulders was sent rolling and, after much cracking, splitting, and crashing against the rocky ridges jutting out through the grass and thickets, they eventually broke the lines of men downhill or tumbled from the rocks with their full weight straight onto the heads of the more daring. The rifles had been levelled behind the second line of boulders and they fired at every enemy in sight.

"Toma" said the man who had taken over the command fidgeting with the old sword at his hip, "Toma! Run away with Ioan, run straight ahead as far from here as your legs will take you... we'll follow suit later... but run we must, for it looks to me that there are many soldiers downhill and, when we are short of large boulders and bullets, we'll have to run for our lives."

I took off my woolen coat and wrapped it around Ioan's seemingly dead body, I ran uphill through shrubberies, on craggy slopes, plodded across the gravel left by the autumn torrents, forded bridgeless brooks and, at long last, high on a summit in the middle of a coppice of thornbrake, I spied a fire wherein a few embers were still glowing amid the grey ashes. I laid Ioan by the fire which I kindled with all the brushwood and dry leaves near at hand, and I started a big fire with tall flames and much smoke. I gathered several armfuls of dry leaves, contrived a bed for Ioan, and bared his chest to examine the wound.

It was only a dark-red tiny hole below the ribs and no blood dripped from it, which was the very cause of his lethargy. I put my mouth to the wound and sucked forcefully a mouthful of blood. Clogged black blood gushed out of the wound, the pulse started to beat ever so faintly, and Ioan opened his filmy eyes. His face had turned haggard as if it were mere skin and bones and there was a network of thin red veins over the whites of his eyeballs.

"Ioan," I said, "how are you feeling, my friend?"

"Feeling?" he said with a bitter smile. "How should I feel? I'm dying, that's all. Aren't you going to put up with it, my friend? Why? Oh, that you knew how happy I'll be when I'm dead... I'll be reunited with Sofia."

"You're raving, Ioan," I said soothingly.

"That's childish! Raving, you say?... I feel death running along my veins so cool and sweet, and he says I'm raving. Believe me I'm happy, as happy as can be."

His alabaster-white face, chiselled with long lineaments of pain, was serene and sweet... A new fainting fit was coming. His head sank back into the dry leaves... his pulse stopped and once again he appeared to have expired.

I stared at his face confused and helpless; he showed no signs of life and there was nothing I could do about it. The deathly silence was broken only by the distant shots of our fighters, and each crack made me start, that cowardly had that misfortune turned me. I knelt by him and took his head in the palm of my hand, but when I lifted it, his head hung limp — I kept looking at him and, words failing me, I only kissed his alabaster-like face with my mouth gory with the blood of his heart. His face stayed unmoving and unresponsive, its whiteness in eerie contrast with the smears of my bloody kisses. A shrill whistle on a leaf roused me from my stupor; the shooting had ceased and I heard the sound of footsteps coming nearer — it must have been my lads who, no longer able to continue the fight, were now retreating. Before long I saw the old tribune sweating and panting and the shooting resumed, this time nearer us.

"How's he?" he asked in a tired voice and cast a frightened glance at Ioan.

"He's dying" I replied curtly and apathetically.

"They're after us. My lads will be putting up a fight as long as they can... yet, in the end, they'll have to run for it."

He knelt by Ioan who, because of the proximity of the fire with its tall flames that gave a rosy hue to his pallor, had begun to show signs of life.

"What are we to do? We can't take him with us — and we can't leave him here, either."

"Chieftain, they'll be here in a moment" cried a lad scurrying toward us from the battlefield. "Our lads can't hold out any longer!"

We gained or feet in shock.

"One moment!" said the old man motioning me aside and looking at Ioan whose large dying eyes had a vacant gaze, like the eyes of a lunatic!

"Step aside, Toma," said the old man, "there's something I must say to brother Ioan."

He had unsheathed his sword and stood glaring at it through the large tears welling down his old eyes.

"Brother Ioan," he urged in a quiet, hardly audible voice, "cross yourself."

Slowly and painstakingly Ioan made the sign of the cross. The sword swished through the air and Ioan's head rolled on the dry leaves.

"You, lunatic!" I shouted and levelled my pistol at the old man's brow, "you've done wrong."

"Wrong?" said the old man falling in my arms and bursting out in tears on my chest, like a child, "Wrong? What else was I to do?"

The fit of trembling, the convulsive moans, the tears emerging strenuously out of his breast like a demonic power bespoke the intensity of his grief. The noise of the retreating men was nearer and we expected the shots to whizz past our ears.

"Come on!" cried the lad standing by us, "come on, wake up: let's run for it!"

He had covered Ioan's body with leaves and stones and thrown his head into a well nearby. Like frightened panting buck deer, the lads came from all sides.

"Run for it! Run for it!" all were crying, and took us by force in their disorderly retreat.

Dazed and troubled I ran wherever my legs would take me, until the pursuers lost our traces and we thought it was safe enough to stop to catch our breath.

On a mountaintop we struck our flints, started several huge fires and sat round them. All men dog-tired, yet one of us had to stand sentry. Some were nursing their wounds — most of them skin-deep — others lay on the bare ground. I volunteered for night watch and they consented only too gladly. The old man sat wrapt in thought and staring at the fire's innards which would burst and scatter sparks. The lads went to sleep with their hearts in their mouths and the old man set to whittling a piece of wood. I alone stood up, reached for my lance, and went off to take the air among the rocky skeletons.

The night was cold and dark, my painfully rambling thoughts gave me a splitting headache, and I felt my skull was about to burst under the pressure of my rebellious and sinister brains. One more thought would have been the last straw. Thus I watched all that night in a burning fever and if I do recall it now, it is because there is naught to recall except that, dazed and insensitive, I had succumbed again to the torpor that always went hand in hand with my griefs.

On the morrow when the golden sun shone high in the sky and when the lads who, long up and about, kept watch over the plain like as many eagles in their aeries were sure our pursuers had ceased their chase, I put a spade on my shoulder and walked downhill to where Ioan had died. The enemies had searched the place, but failed to come across the body under the heap of leaves and stones. I set to digging his grave in the blistering heat of the day. My brow and chest were afire, yet no bead of sweat trickled down my body. I kept digging in a rage as if I had a treasure to hide. When the grave was sufficiently deep, I uncovered the beheaded body from under the stones and leaves and laid it slowly and carefully — as if his senses were still alive — into his cool eternal abode. Then I went to the well wherein his head had been thrown. The sun mirrored his face in the shiny crystal-clear water shimmering like an undulating silver mirror wherein at the bottom of the well lay the youth's finely-shaped head. The running water had cleansed and removed the smears of blood and his pale blond head showed up its silver-white face with his lips bluish as two sloes, his large eyes closed and the silky hair floating freely down the current. A smile seemed to brighten his thin pale face. I took a handful of water and washed my feverish face, then more water which I let flow down my burning chest. The water turned muddy and red with blood, but I bent over its surface and swallowed large mouthfuls of the water mixed with his blood, then dipped both hands into the well, took out Ioan's head and lifted it in the sunlight for a long and painful last look. I laid it in the grave above the body, covered it with my coarse woollen coat fearing that the clogs might harm him, and filled the grave with earth. Every now and then I had a mind to lie at his side and wait for a rock to tumble on me over the brim of the grave, or to shoot myself and thus to put an end to the misery we call life. A peasant was standing sentry on a distant rock, his firelock shining in the sunlight and his gaze scanning the clouds. An eagle gripping a white dove in its brass talons flew over my head with much croaking and flapping of wings, and scared by my presence he circled up toward the clouds. The peasant took aim at the black speck sailing in the air and fired — and the eagle whirled down into the precipice with the dove in its talons.

"Revenge!" I gasped out. "Why should I die before avenging him? After that there'll be time enough to die or even to live, if I so choose."

I filled the grave with earth, tore a green branch from a tree, and laid it across the grave — and, whistling through my teeth with a sinister carelessness, I retraced my way uphill.

When I arrived at our Roman-style camp I saw the old man sitting by the fire, sad and wistful, with his legs stretched out and his brow propped on his hand. I drew nearer and sat by him.

"What shall we do?" I enquired in a low hoarse voice.

"I've been scheming and now I'm mighty glad to let you know that it'd take the devil and his damned to outfox my plans. I killed a child — but it wasn't me who really killed him, as you well know. I chose to cut his life short rather than to leave him in their hands, easy prey to torture and laughter. Don't you know, Toma, that torture will stir up man's soul and the cruellest pains only spark up the life in the dying... but what a life! And d'you think I could forgive them all that... or that I could forgive the Saxon who sold us as Judas sold our Lord Jesus? I've sent Florea's boy Nitza a-scouting, for he knows the Gypsies' tongue. He smeared his face with soot and put on rags and went sneaking about the mill to see whether they're still thereabouts. If they're gone we'll call on my good friend, the Saxon, and drink a jug of wine to his health, as soon as it gets dark."

A hubbub of voices came from the lads. They were laughing while carrying Nitza shoulder-high who, barefoot, with his hat titled over one ear, the hair jutting out through its holes, as his elbows were jutting out through his coat sleeves and his knees through his tight trousers, black-faced and thin like a devil, the eyes two pinpoints in his head, was boasting in a throaty mock-Gypsy voice on how cleverly he had duped his beloved godfather, the Saxon. But when he was nearer his eyes glinted warfare, only for us to see. His was the mocking merry mask of a soul incensed with hatred and revenge, the countenance at variance with the heart, the alternately shy or stupid smile at variance with his mood. The lads stepped back and left him with us to tell us all he had learnt. The old man advised the lads to snatch as much sleep as they could in the day-time, for we had some urgent business to attend to that night. Nitza culled lettuce from a grass plot and squeezed their sap into large balls of cornmush which he stowed in his knapsack.

The day had declined, the lads had gone to sleep — and I alone was roaming in silence, my head prey to an indescribable restlessness, my heart brimful with a terrible dejection, never experienced before. What was there left for me this side of earth? He had been my last link to life and now he too was gone. I do not know if the loss of a brother, if I had chanced to have one, would have aggrieved me more bitterly. Pleated fidgety grey clouds had crowded the sky; they flew to and fro in the night's warm air and the ruddy-faced moon was out of place among the clouds' glossy ashes. The lads began to wake up and shake the sleepiness off; their bluish lances shone against the moonlight, their pointed fur hats lent them a heroic, sinister look.

"Make ready, friends!" said the old tribune, "we'll have a dinner you're going to relish tonight. A Saxon roasted whole!"

A chill crept up my spine at his words and for all that, I could not help feeling elated.

Nitza led us along the pitch-black mountain trails. His stealthy panther-like footsteps stirred no sound on the pebbles and fine gravel of the trails, so easy to upset. Twin mountains cast their shadows across each other, the gloomy sky begot more clouds, and the wind whistled among the rocks — misshapen stone skeletons. Now and then a boulder set rolling downslope, a block would split off a rock and tumble roaringly down toward the valley. We climbed down the mountain and took a path leading to the mill. The mill was locked and shuttered, only the unchained dog was baying in distress at the moon. His sleepy foreboding bark carried far across the darkness. Nitza signalled and we lay down on the ground. He stepped cautiously toward the dog and, from a safe distance, threw the cornmush balls which the dog caught in midair and swallowed greedily. Before long the lettuce juice took effect and he started to writhe in the sand by the riverbank. Nitza beckoned and we moved on. The dog's belly had swollen tight as a drumhead and he was writhing in great pain. A lad took pity on him and stabbed his lance into his heart. We edged closer to the mill, tapped at the door and heard the miller's frightened voice:

"Who's there?"

"Me, godfather." answered Nitza impersonating a Gypsy.

"What's it you want now in the dead of night?" the miller asked.

"I've got bad news for you, godfather; the shepherds are coming this way... I saw them from here and I've come to tell you to run away while the running's good."

We heard the Saxon climbing up the steps, unwieldy and coughing, and stopping behind the door. As soon as he opened up Nitza caught him by the throat, so the Saxon, losing his presence of mind, dropped the lantern and the key, his eyes set to whirling in their sockets and he turned blue in the face. He would surely have strangled him if the old man had not called on him to let go. He had him gagged and bound fast. The Saxon was given no chance to break the silence with a yell. The old tribune's eyes were flashing fire and whirling ominously in their sockets. He looked like the pale old herald of death. The mill hands and the miller's wife were roused from sleep and bound tightly.

"Set the wheels moving," roared the old man.

The wheels started turning and set the millstones in motion, which revolved grinding each other with much uproar. The deafening uproar of the stones turning to no purpose, the mill that had started reeling and groaning at all its joints smothered the faint choked cries of the gagged and tied men. A handful of lads climbed onto the roof of the mill and set to breaking it apart with their axes and throwing the shingles into the water, wherein they sank and, coming up, floated downstream black as the souls of the drowned. They found a hogshead of black oil and spilled it all over the loft. The bound men were brought and fastened to the thick beams from the devastated roof, that had remained unbroken. Then their gags were taken out.

"Why did you sell us?" the old man shouted coldly and terribly, his face the face of a marble Fury, staring the miller in the eyes.

The Saxon was struck dumb with fright. No words, whether of mercy or hatred, would come to him, his jaws were glued and trembling, his eyes glassy like a madman's, his tongue stammered inarticulate sounds. Fright had rendered him speechless. The woman was shedding bitter tears, the servants were casting earnest imploring glances at the awesome demon of revenge.

"Unbind the servants and the woman and take them to the river bank. The miller's to stay here".

In a moment they were escorted to the bank.

We climbed down the loft and went to the bank. A big fire was started quickly.

"Who sold us?" the old man asked the woman.

"He did," she blurted out through her lamentations... "my husband. I advised him in vain not to meddle in anything, whether right or wrong. But to no avail... he wouldn't listen. The Hungarians paid him two hundred gold zloties and he sold you at that price."

"Woman," the old man said, "we hold no grudge against you; nor against you, my lads" he spoke to the servants. "Unbind the woman and let her take the money and everything she can from the mill."

"Hey you, lads, load your rifles! Let's finish them off!" Nitza said laughing.

"No bullets," they whispered to one another.

The servants were unbound.

"Let's see the last of you!" Nitza ordered them. "Fire, friends!" he urged our men.

The Saxons took to their heels — the rifles cracked but, being unloaded, they only threw the running men into a greater scare. The woman came out of the mill with the money and the valuables and departed wailing. The miller started keening on the beam to which he had been fastened.

The old man wove a rope of straw, soaked it in oil, lit it and threw it up onto the roof. In a minute the oiled loft caught fire and the miller's howls rose above the roar of the wheels and the din of the unfettered stones. The old tribune gave a savage laugh — his Satanic idea was coming to life. He raised his axe and cut the ropes tethering the mill downstream.

The blazing mill jerked and started floating downstream.

"Both fire and drowning!" the old man exclaimed terribly on the stone where he was standing and shook his fist at the sky; "If I've done wrong, may his blood fall on my head!"

A blood-curdling scene. The wheels howling kept howling, the stones droning, the mill was crackling with fire, the miller was screaming his lungs out in his fiery tomb. The mill had the shape of a crippled old fiery dragon who howled and furrowed with his disabled wings, while the water turned red with his flames. It swam rapidly carried by the turning wheels and the swift current. The groves lining the banks reddened when the burning palace passed by any let the spectator have a glimpse into the recesses of their paths... The clouds in the sky changed from grey to red and the heavy thick smoke trailing in the wake of the departing mill choked our breaths.

"The show's over, boys!" said the old man heaving a deep sigh and stepping down from his stone. "Back to our mountain!"

I shall never forget that unique scene.

In the meantime the Hungarians had become unbearable. Mere suspicion, or less than that, was conclusive proof to them to hang or shoot to death. Death had become man's natural, life his unnatural state. They plundered the Romanian villages most barbarously, killed women and children ruthlessly, outdid each other in cruelty and savagery. It was but natural that the Romanians, driven to revenge as they were, should reciprocate with tooth for tooth and like for like. The Hungarians had staged a brigandage rather than a revolution, a privileged plunder as it were — the more pardonable as it was perpetrated on a nation of underdogs — the Romanians. Yet they had met their match." Tooth for tooth, like for like!" was the lancers' watchword — and they paid back in kind. The Romanians did not plunder — they killed. People were not appraised according to their social rank, the curly black head of the magnate and the hound-headed Honved were all the same — just as many heads to cut off — to the impartial scythe. These people could be terrible when shaking of their iron chains — as terrible as the scourge of God. Are not all peoples like that? Gentle and peaceful while peace lasts, with genial physiognomies and sincere eyes — the shoulders bent under life's heavy burden. But meet them again in revolution! Look at the depth of the terrible soul concealed under the mask of geniality, see how they unearth the past offences on conjectural evidence, behold how they throw the chains from round their wrists in the face of the soulless rulers. And the soulless rulers are frightened and would gladly barter all their riches for their lives. Yet the common people will have no riches, no use luring them with gold, no use clothing them in silk. You would fain weigh in gold the bread you have robbed from their babies' mouths, you would repay their bitter tears and their bloody sweat with all hoary pearls of the East; yet they will not have your gold and pearls — they are after your life! And are they to blame for their conduct? Is there any law in nature that would not extenuate their deeds? Is there such a law in nature as to deprive you of the right to kill the ones who, throughout the centuries, have flogged your parents, have burnt your forebears at the stake, have strewn the wells and rivers with the children of your soul? The very laws standing at the basis of ethics entitle you to demand full compensation for what you have been robbed of, to pay back in kind, which is the only way to restore balance and justice in the world. Yet virtue would have you stop short of murder. No one can be obliged to be virtuous, everyone is to be just — and when the sentence passed by that justice will not appoint an executioner, you had better turn into the executioner yourself. A man to kill — an unread letter; a town to burn to the ground — a leaf to turn — that is the lawbook of revolutions, of God's own justice!

. . .

(At this point several pages in Toma's manuscript are torn off. He might have considered it advisable to tear them, or else an alien hand having read them might have committed the indiscretion of finding them interesting enough as to appropriate them for safekeeping in that manner. Whatever the case, we regret we are not in a position to give the reader an account of those missing pages; yet we shall continue the story as it stands.)

...that he had seen him at home. What else was he to replay? On the other hand my mind had been made up long before I was in possession of that piece of news. Old Terente droned away that I ought to settle in their village, for they would have me as their parishioner. They would get a licence from their bishop and ordain me, never fear. The revolution had come to an end and nothing stood in the way of my becoming a priest — but for my nature that would not bear the sight of the cloth.

Before long peace was declared, though we, sentries of the Carpathians, had not dispersed yet. One day Terente handed me a pail and asked me to fetch water from a well nearby. The day was warm and sunny, the forests green with new leafage. An itching wanderlust seized my soul. I reached the well, stood staring at the water at its bottom for some time, then dropped the pail inside and took the path toward the distant mountains.

Most of our village [was] burnt and deserted, only the dogs were in the lanes, baying with hunger or gnawing at the carcass of a cow. I entered the hut. I threw myself into the arms of my aged father who had taken me for dead. Reunited father and son, we hugged each other for a long time — father's eyes were brimful with tears and no words would come to him, so he only kept stroking my hair and brow, kissing me and shedding tears of joy. I told him all that I could remember for a whole day and night, yet he would hear more... I inquired about his doings during the rebellion and, with a sly smile, he pointed to an old lance hung on a hook.

"I daresay I've done my bit according to my powers. No juice left in the old bones, I'm afraid!" he said cheerfully — "oh, that I'd been your age... but I'm old, and that's that."

And his happy gaze took me in front head to foot as if to make sure I was not an apparition.

By and by Finitza came round. She was engaged to be married to a tall handsome lad. I inquired about the wedding date and she blushed crimson up to the tips of her ears. Yet... I could see she could hardly wait.

The country was at peace. Finitza got married and I gave her away — anyhow, I stayed home doing nothing until one day I found myself fatherless. He had fallen asleep with old age — to sleep for ever. I laid him in his grave beside mother's and put up a wooden cross hung with a wreath of basil at his head. Poor Finitza, wiping her tears with her apron, gave me her word she would lay flowers on their graves and light a candle now and then, on a holy day, unto their memory. Despondency was gnawing at my heart, despondency and solitude.

Poesis

I repaired to Cluj. I waited for the nightfall to sneak to her house and see what had become of her. I had a mind to forget and forgive her betrayal and, if I could sense one spark of love left in her bosom, to take her with me and make her my wedded wife. My heart was yearning for love and, like a drowning man, I was eager to catch at a straw.

The night was rainy with black clouds flying across the sky and occasional snatches of moonlight sifting down through their deep rifts. I took a small lantern with me and paced the streets under the humming patter of the drizzle and, without the town, I walked on across the oozy fields with yellow runnels crisscrossing the green grass, my feet treading the ripples which flooded the plain. It was pitch dark and I could hardly see beyond arm's length. I stopped at the front door of her house, took out the lantern and lit it, but when I nerved myself to knock, I noticed the lock had been sealed by the authorities. What could have happened? Like all women addicted to a life of vice, she must have fallen in debt and now they intended to auction her only property: the little house. I did not care — I had to enter the house to recall the only moments of happiness in my life. I tore off the seal on the lock and then broke the lock itself.

I entered the house — and her room. All the furniture was where it had stood on the first day of my love. The lid on the piano was drawn up, the chair was still in front of the keyboard. The old man's straight-back chair stood facing the hearth. Her tidy white bed was alongside the left wall. I set the lamp on the table — and my glance fell on an epistle sealed with black wax. I picked it up. It was addressed to me in her neat hand... I tore it open and read it. The handwriting was trembling and the ink was smeared with the tears dripped onto the sheet. I shall reproduce it word for word:

My love, my own sweet love!

You took me for a traitress, for an abandoned woman, and went into the wide world. Aye, my sweetheart, I was a criminal, as Mary Magdalene was a criminal. Toma, I shall not ask you to love me again for, when you read these lines, there will be naught to love but the buried skull and the sightless orbs of a mad girl — mad with love for you and destroyed by the love that nature had urged on her, the love for her aged father. Father was ailing — and I could not turn an honest penny. What was I to do? The thought of begging made me blush. So, I sold myself. And I made a great deal of money, far too much for the good it did me — for father died. Shall I describe my feelings after I buried him? Time and again I contemplated going to you and throwing my arms about your feet — to beg, to beseech for your forgiveness. I would have fain become your slave for I loved you, nay, I love you still! I went to Ioan. I entreated him to look after you and gave him all the money I had, but I pledged him to swear he would not as much as utter my name within your hearing. Before leaving he came here and apprised me of your predicament and I sent him back to you, for I knew what your first thought would be: suicide — and I also knew your love was no less ardent than mine. One day you vanished. What good was the sacrifice to me now with Father dead, with you away?... I wrote my will and bequeathed you this little house... then I started a fire in the hearth, locked the door and shuttered the window — for the idea was luring, of dying your kind of death. In that stifling air I committed to paper the lines now before your eyes. Then I sat at the piano and played again the soothing sweet waltz I had once played with your black-haired genius-inspired head resting in my lap. To caress that marble brow once more — was hoping against hope. Yet I do hope for your forgiveness. If the world had been made of only you and I... how we would have loved each other then. We would have roamed about the green forests until we died in each other's arms, only to become two angles in the next world and keep on roaming arm in arm among the stars in heaven. Farewell, my child! I love you! Remember me — if I can, I will think of you and of you only. Do not spurn me, my child — let me be yours...

Yours, Poesis

I read her letter over and over again pressing the tear-stained lines to my burning bluish lips in an uncontrollable fit of sobbing.

"Poesis!" I kept calling and hugged the air of the room to my heart, "Poesis, forgive me!"

I subsided in the armchair by the piano wherein she had passed away and strummed the keys that had been so submissive under her tender dainty fingers — and my pain grew sweeter from sheer desperation and melancholy. Perhaps her innocent soul was hovering gently about my brow. Perhaps her ethereal entity was stroking my hair and kissing my brow. I paced the room haunted by sweet and bitter thoughts in turn. Finally I took off my clothes and went to sleep in her white bed. I dreamed she was lying by my side — her sweet blond head on my chest — my burning lips on her snowy brow — wooing a shadow! Hugging the darkness, making love to the air — wooing a shadow! My nails kept clutching at the infamous pillow until sleep took pity on me and benumbed my weary mind.

I could have stayed in her little house, which was now mine — I could have idled my whole life away re-reading her tear-stained epistle in a sweet madness — I could have dreamed a life-long dream — of her walking about my home, smiling at the flowers at the window, watching, while darning or knitting, over my baby. I could have invented a make-believe happiness, a make-believe family, an ideal woman — I could have gone mad. But to what end? Besides, however long-lasting that madness, the time is bound to come when one goes through spells of awakening wherein one's uppermost thought is suicide — spells of weariness, scepticism, disappointment. Therefore I went into the wide world... That epistle epitomized all the history of my life.

Translated by Joan Giurgea
Revised by Kurt W. Treptow

FINIS

Caesara

A summer morning. The sea spread out its boundless blue beneath the sun rising languidly in the limpid azure depths of the sky, the flowers were rearing their heads refreshed after the night's restful slumber, the rocks, sable with dew, were exhaling steam and turning hoary and, here and there, enervated by the heat, grains of sand and fragments of stone tumbled lazily into the water.

An ancient monastery surrounded by citadel-like walls stood among the crags in the west and the green crowns of a clump of poplars and chestnuts rose behind the walls. The moldy tiles on the pointed roofs, the blackened dome of the church, the decaying walls invaded by a horde of lush weeds, by ants setting up their kingdoms, and by long processions of red insects basking in the sun with voluptuous laziness, the stone steps well-worn and corroded by many a footstep — all combined would have made the spectator think it was a ruin preserved as an old curiosity rather than a dwelling place.

To the right side of the monastery rose hills carpeted with woods, gardens, and vineyards and hamlets with whitewashed houses were scattered along their narrow valleys; to the left the ribbon of a road twisted and wound amid a vast expanse of cornfields stretching as far as the eye could reach; facing it was the sea with its watertable broken by an occasional cliff rearing its head out of the depths.

Footpaths littered with molehills ran along the hillside and the surrounding walls. An old monk is walking along a path leading to the monastery gate with his hands locked at his back. He is wearing a sackcloth surplice gathered with a white band round his waist, his woolen rosary dangles out of his bosom, his wooden shoes shuffle and clank with every step he takes forward. His beard is rather scant-haired, his watery eyes inexpressive and rather idiotic; no mark of resignation or austerity about him.

Without the gate he pulls the cord, a monk lets him in, he steps into the seemingly deserted courtyard paved with square flagstones overgrown with blades of tall grasses and with a pond in its centre whose sides are a wilderness of weeds of every description: tall burdocks, mulleins, melitots, and vetches which entwined their flowery network over the whole vegetation stifling it amid the tangle of their stalks. The old man walks toward a shadowy long and multi-pillared verandah with a flight of stairs leading to the courtyard. He opens the door and disappears inside the building.

In the long high walls of the monastery there are windows encased in black bars, like the windows of disused cells; one only is enmeshed with ivy and a few potted white roses wriggle their heads through that net of shady foliage into the sunlight. The window opened into a cell the walls of which were daubed with all manner of strange sketches, all of them in pencil — a saint here, a puppy gambolling in the grass there, in another corner the exquisitely drawn icon of a Gypsy girl, flowers, bushes, female heads, bonnets, slippers, in short, a sketchbook scattered all over the wall. A case of religious books, a straight-back chair, a few surplices hung on a hook, a chest painted with flowers of every description, an unpretentious bedstead under which a pair of slippers and a black tomcat showed up their noses — that was all the furniture. The sunlight creeping into the cell through the trembling live net at the window pierced the semidarkness and thousands of moving specks were disporting themselves in its rays vanishing from sight along with them.

A youthful monk is sitting on the chair. He is indulging in a moment of snug idleness such as a hound is wont to enjoy when basking in the sun, lazy, sleepy, and happy-go-lucky. A flawless wide brow enframed with glossy black hair rises above his sunken eyes and finely-built nose. A thin-lipped mouth, a well-rounded chin, eyes self-satisfied as it were, gazing with a self-consciousness which might become daring — a singular blend of dreaminess and dispassionate reasoning in their look.

He went to the window and cast a glance at the garden below, overgrown with soft herbs sheltered in the virginal shade of the trees, at the oranges barely showing through the leafage, then pencilled an orange on the wall. He picked up a slipper, put it on the table, scanned it, then opened a

religious book and pencilled the slipper in a corner of a page. What a dese-
cration of sacred books! All their margins were scrawled with profiles of
women, priests, knights, beggars, histrions... in short, life as he saw it,
daubed in every available corner.

Presently the old man entered.

"Bless me, father."

"God be with you. I say, Ieronim," continued the merry old man in a
bantering voice, "what're you working on, you naughty boy?"

"Me working? But when on earth have I ever worked? The mere pre-
sumption is a smear on my good character, father... Do you call this work? I
only enjoy myself drawing all kinds of everything on these walls; work
indeed! I'm wiser than I look."

"You do wrong you won't study painting."

"I do neither wrong nor right, for I do nothing. It's only a pastime."

"You're withering your talent, my son, withering your talent."

"Whitering the devil, father."

"Apage Satanas!" exclaimed the old man hopping on one leg and fall-
ing on Ieronim's neck. Ieronim burst out laughing.

"God only knows where so much mirth comes from, father. I do have
my spells of sadness, but you... not you."

"Me sad, Ieronim? May the devil take me, my son, if I've ever been
sad. Sadness will keep clear of me as my friend the devil of the holy incense.
But let it drop... come to town with me. I met your abbot today and pulled a
long face... this long... and asked him for your assistance in collecting some
money for a funeral... I lied as ever — anyway, he deigned to entrust you my
mournful company. You and I, Ieronim, are going to paint the town red...
there's such good wine in a pub I know that you'll smack your lips over it
and ask for more... we'll play cards with our pious brethren, puff away at
pipes longer than your arm, and glut our eyes on the damsels passing by the
windows! But mind you, we'll stop short of..."

"Of course. Short of..."

"I wonder who the devil made a monk of you Ieronim, you heathen?"

"As I wonder who the devil made a monk of you, father."

"Whoever but the devil?"

It would be deceitful to take the monks' levities at face value. Their apparent sacrileges were no worse than childish pranks, for all the licentiousness of their words. An occasional glass of wine, a game of cards, a pipe of tobacco, a furtive glance at the profile of a smiling girl — that was the sum total of their famous debaucheries. All the charm lay in the mock aura of mystery with which they flavoured their sins against the properties.

Ieronim struggled into his surplice, put on a sinister mien to match the funny old man's distraught one — both for the benefit of the dismayed gate-keeper — and they hurried out of the monastery and did not slacken their pace before they were on the high road leading toward the city.

II

"Countess, I have means to persuading your father to make you mine."

"No doubt you can do it and no doubt you will take advantage of your position. My father owes you money and you will have his daughter to cancel his debt. It is only natural. The twain of you will agree on a price in your own gentlemanly way... yet, until I become your woman it is within my rights to beg you to leave me alone... Thenceforth you will have plenty of time to impose your presence on me."

The beautiful woman turned her back on him and gazed out of the window into the street. She burst out laughing on seeing a funny old man endeavouring to put on pious faces in order to cut a good figure with the passers-by. Ieronim and Onufrei were standing in the street, the latter counting the beads with his hands resting on his belly, the former's face recollected in deep and noble gravity.

The Marquis Castelmare glowered fiercely at the girl who dared spurn his love, then strutted out and slammed the door.

"What a good-looking monk," the countess whispered with a smile. "And that funny old man... like a paiazzo in a villain's role... what noble lineaments on the youth's face... like a demon... handsome, grave, indifferent. The very model Francesco seeks for his demon in "The Fall of the Angels..." if only we could cozen him into sitting for it..."

"Maestro," she called out at the top of her voice and drew two chairs to the window.

An elderly man in a velvet shirt entered. He was wide-browed, grey-bearded, and serene of countenance. He walked up to the girl, his lips shaping a question.

"Come nearer... sit here... have a look at that young monk. He would make a handsome demon in your 'Fall of the Angels,' wouldn't he?"

"He would make an equally handsome Adonis in 'Venus and Adonis,' rejoined the painter with a smile, "with you as Venus."

"Come, come! You're stretching things too far."

Francesco took her hand into his and touched her beautiful brow with his lips.

"You're green behind the ears," he whispered, "wherefore not? You need love... all your heartstrings quiver at the very word... Will you sooner yield to a man you do not love, that Castelmare, and be his wife?... You know how rich I am... and you also know that I care for you as I would love my own daughter if I had one... and you are well aware that your impoverished rake and gambler of a father would gladly sell you to the highest bidder... and that there is naught you can do to avoid your misery except to flee from this home. Will you have a father?... Here I am... Will you have a home? My house is yours. Will you have a lover, Caesara?... There he is. I loved once myself. The taste of that sweet madness has stayed with me since my halcyon days of youth... You thirst for it... yet in the teeth of that you would let go of the most handsome model of a painting... an angel of genius, for demons are genius-inspired angels... the ones still in heaven being rather silly."

"Come now, father, will you have me run after him?"

"Shall I do the running?"

"Nay..."

"Which means yes... My regards, young lady," said Francesco and dashed toward the door. She would have stopped him... yet she did not have the heart for it... not to let him have his way... would not do, either. She did neither, which was more thoughtful in the case in hand. The painter walked out with a mischievous smile, delighted at the faces Caesara was pulling... of contrariness, vacillation, despair...

She could not collect her thoughts. She stood gazing at Ieronim. How handsome he was... her heart was pounding in her bosom... she could have smothered him if he had been hers... That crazy she felt.

But how beautiful, how exquisitely curved, how lovable she was! The amber-white of her face was toned down by a violet-blue shade, the transparence of a fine network of veins focusing the ideals of art on the domed brow and the dark blue eyes, their glitter turned sweeter, darker, and more demonic by the shade of the long lashes. Her hair — blond like gilt rime, her sweet mouth with a fuller underlip inviting kisses, her fine nose and sweet rounded chin gave her the look of one of Giaccomo Palma's women. She was of exceeding nobility and beauty as she raised her head in childlike pride like an Arab thoroughbred and her tall marble-white neck assumed the yearning vigor of an Antinous.

She rested her head on the palm of one hand and gazed at the youthful monk with an undefinable, hopeless desire. She considered Francesco's harangue as a mere quip though she would have liked it to come true. What mysterious joys her heart presumed in that gaze... how she would have liked... liked what?... Alas! what mortal has ever rendered, what mortal can ever render, nay, which language can boast on having the suitable words to render that ocean of feelings which overcrowd not love itself but rather the thirst for love? She stands dreaming at the window... let her dream away... any analysis of her feelings would be a callous intrusion...

III

Onufrei and Ieronim walked along the streets taking no notice of the man tailing them. It was the painter. Ieronim dropped in at the post-office where a letter was awaiting him from an uncle of his, an old hermit. Here it is:

My beloved nephew, may the Lord bestow His bountiful mercy on you.

I am writing these lines on such a glorious day, my soul is so brimful with its fresh sweetness, with the fragrance of the fields, with the myriad whispers of nature, that I feel inclined to take nature into my counsel and unbosom all my thoughts and feelings, everything that comes to pass within my soul. My world is a vale girt all around by unscalable rocks soaring up like a wall secluding it from the sea so that no living soul is ever likely to descry this earthly paradise which is my dwelling. There is only one entrance — a movable rock perfectly covers the mouth of a cave leading into the island. Thus, the world with denied ingress in the cave will take this island for a cluster of barren rocks rising from the sea, with neither vegetation nor life. You ought to see its center... All around are gigantic granite rocks looking like black sentries and the deep vale, doubtless below sea level, is carpeted with tufts of flowers, wild vines, and fragrant tall herbs forever free of the intrusion of the scythe. And this soft blanket of verdure is teeming with a world of wild life. Thousands of honeybees scour the flowers hovering nigh to their mouths, velvety bumblebees and blue butterflies crowd an airy realm beneath the quivering sunlight. The towering rocks narrow my horizon. One patch of sky I own, but what a patch! A dark, clear, transparent azure dotted with an occasional white cloudlet as if a pail of milk were spilled across the sky. There is a lake in the middle of the vale into which flow four springs that keep pattering and bickering and murmuring and upsetting the pebbles night and day. They suffuse the summery quiet of the vale with eternal music; you can descry their limpid and frolicsome liquid silver twisting and wind-ing through the green grass, down the distant gravelly sides, thrusting their waters into the grip of the whirlpools, twirling madly therein, then darting forward and subsiding into the lake with a moan of con-tentment. In the heart of this lake shaded by a bonanza of reeds, grasses, and willows mirroring themselves into its water stands another island adorned with an orange grove. Amid that grove is the cave I have converted into a home and also my apiary. All this islet within the larger island is a flower garden I have planted specially for my bees. I keep myself busy from dawn to dusk. You may remember my apprenticeship to a sculptor in my youth. Thus it comes that I have smoothed out the granite walls of my cave and embossed their surface with ornaments and bas-reliefs, in much the same way as you fill your walls with sketches; with the difference that sculpture being naked, so are the figures I have carved. On a wall are Adam and Eve... I endeav-oured to embody primitive innocence within their forms... Neither is alive to the meaning of love yet... they love each other unconsciously... the forms are virginal and unripe... I chose to render affection rather than passion on their countenances — a quite candid idyll between two beings unconscious of their beauty or nakedness. They stroll in a long embrace in the shade of a row of trees and a flock of lambs keep romping at their feet.

Of a different mould are Venus and Adonis. Venus is all love. She leans her infatuated head on the shoulder of the girlishly-handsome youth who, bashful and self-enamoured, casts surreptitious side-glances at the rapturous curves of the doting goddess, for he is too diffident to take an eyeful of her. He plays the role of an artless maid caught off-guard by her lover.

I take a liking in rendering the aggressive woman. It is man's inborn trait to be aggressive, which is to say nature does no more than repeat itself in each and every copy, whereas its exceptions lie in aggressive women. There is an undefinable gentleness in the way in which a woman in love has to overcome her innocence and bashfulness in order to lure a man sulky for some reason or chaster and more childish than herself. As you may perceive, I do not mean the courtesans — the women whose experience lies in urging men toward love — but the aggressiveness at the heart of female innocence. With that in mind I am carving now Aurora and Orion on the whitest of my walls. As you may know, the youthful Aurora abducted Orion from the island of Delos whereon he had been secreted away by the cruel, virginal, and love-smitten Diana. In Orion I render that essential trait of ignorance and pride to be seen on most youthful countenances and in Aurora the unquenchable cheerfulness of young maids — how arduous a task to depict aggressiveness on such a face... One thing puzzles me though. After those hours that in love are called pastoral there stays with man an overwhelming discouragement and sadness — I take it that at such moments man is more apt to commit suicide and more indifferent to death than at any other time. On the other hand I gather that a chaste youth is harder to seduce than a maid and that poor Venus must have belabored her brains over Adonis. There is some deep mystery in the reluctance before and the sadness after pleasure. Yet I do not grasp it.

I go to school. You know where: to my honeybees. I am of the opinion that all ideas rippling the surface of men's lives are no better than the folds which a cloak tends to shape on a moving body. They have no share in the movement itself albeit they arise from it. Firstly consider the bees' state: what order, craftsmanship, and harmony in that work! Should they have books, magazines, and universities you would behold a plethora of scholars puzzling over that order as if it were a brilliant work of intelligence though it is not intelligence but something deeper that arrays all things in their proper place with a confident, flawless insight. Secondly, look at their colonies. Every summer two or three generations will forsake their native village to set up their own colonies and what strikes the eye pleasantly is the absence of the verbiage and argumentation in which men are wont to word the emigration of redundant people. Then take the revolutions. Hardly a year passes by without some revolution against the aristocracy, the queen's favorites — to say nothing of the social contract, the speeches in parliaments, the controversies on divine right versus natural right. *Cinis et umbra sumus.*

But you might retort: "Father, you transfer ideas and reasons to nature by analogy with human circumstances, in other words you envisage the state organizations of beasts solely by what they have in common with the human ones and thus level our world to theirs." Far be it from me. The humans themselves lead a life based on instincts. Subjective religions, wicked and deplorable deeds sponge on customs and institutions originally founded on nature, purposefully and fittingly adjusted to the narrow-mindedness of most men. And that has been going on for a long time. You are born, get married, beget children, and die, and likewise do the beasts with the only difference that in place of the village lane wherein the four-legged Don Juans strut to and fro, men have invented the ball-room with dance and music wherein the monocled young jackanapes can sniff the females at their convenience. Days and years pass like that, you are gulled by or undeceived with the arguments in favour of the excellencies of this world up to the day you die and no one bothers to inquire any longer after that fly who may have amassed knowledge, committed scholarly wastepaper or, according to circumstances, sermonized, carried on republican propaganda, and so on and so forth. You might experience occasional spells of lucidity wherein, as if roused from sleep, you look around in wonder at realizing you have lived in a rigidly organized state of things, neither being aware of nor having wished it. And can this mind, this puny clog of nonsense for all its occasional flashes of lucidity ever have its own say in the troublesome and futile bustle and strife of human history, in the history of that elementary what-is-it? Could it have any impact, could it mean anything, could it leave its stamp on nature when itself is nothing more than a meagre stamp of that self-same nature? Not the ghost of a chance.

Thus it comes that in the great migrations of peoples wherein the redundant sons forsook the homeland on behalf of the maternal bee-hive we perceive an analogy with the swarming of bees. Search for the truth in the actual facts rather than in the explanations they are pro-vided.

All positive doctrines whether religious, philosophical, of jurispru-dence, or state policies are in the long run as many cleverly-contrived pleas of the mind, that *advocatus diaboli*, forced by will to exonerate everything. That wretched advocate is hired to set all things in favor-able light and, as existence is miserable in itself, he will embellish its squalor with flowers and a front of profound wisdom for the benefit of school and church, both eager to deceive the brats, hardly entered into the limelight, as to the value of real life. Honour for civil servants, glory for soldiers, glamour for princes, fame for scholars, the heaven for fools — that is how one generation deceives the next one by the agency of this inherited *advocatus diaboli*, this slave compelled to resort to cunning and sophistry who, in turn, will keen as priest, pull grave faces as professor, or likewise parley as barrister or bewail his wretchedness as beggar. This one performs his part for a glass of wine he intends *in petto*, that one for a title, another for money, another one for a crown, albeit the driving force within every one is the same: a moment of intoxication.

This is what I learn from my masters, the honeybees — my school-ing makes me realize that we are will-less shadows, automata that do no more and no less than what they are bid to do and that, so as we should not take a loathing to the game, we are given this handful of brains which will have us believe we actually do as we wish, the choice being up to us... It is a self-delusion wherein the multitude of probabil-ities is taken for what we are compelled to do.

History's inner life is instinctive: its external life — the kings, priests, scholars are sheer lustre and verbiage and, as the silk cloth over a corpse will not give away its real state, likewise these menda-cious raiments will not allow us an inkling into the sorry plight of his-tory itself.

Thanks to nature's guidance I have cast away the cloth of vanity. I take it you are still a novice. Do not take orders, my son... Be sensible and do not barter your nature for a surplice and a black hat. I have been a hermit, not a monk. I should like someone to take my place in this hermitage, for I am old and my hour of salvation is drawing near. Come hither, but not before I am dead... while I am still alive you might spare me your presence. I am jealous of my solitude. Old age is a slow extinction — how slowly my heart is beating now and how recklessly it kept throbbing before I turned threescore... This is the way of all flesh! One day it will beat more and more slowly, then its beats will cease altogether, for the oil in the lamp will be burnt out. I know I shall not be aware that I die. It will be a quiet and natural extinction which I do not fear. I shall fall asleep... only that I would not wake any more... I kiss your brow, beloved soul,

Euthanasius.

IV

Francesco noticed Ieronim and Onufrei coming out of an old building and struck up a conversation with the youth asking him for a few sittings. He consented, seeing nothing amiss with the elderly maestro, and the three of them directed their steps toward the painter's home. On the way, Father Onufrei contrived to touch the painter's hand, found a few gold coins therein and, loath to quit certainty for hope, shook that hand amicably with acquisitive fingers, remembered some loose ends of business he wanted to clear up, the more so as the pub tables were beckoning to him lovingly, so he muttered some thin excuses and betook himself off.

In the meanwhile the inquisitive and reckless Caesara was rummaging about the painter's studio. She approached the picture, raised the cloth cover and examined the progress of the work "The Fall of the Angels". The serenely grave Archangel Michael was stabbing the air with his fiery sword. His blond curls enframed his marble-white face and domed brow and his blue eyes flashed force and energy. His sword arm reached out toward the chaos... his long white wings were hoisted above his shoulders into an ellipse and a swarm of blue stars studded the semicircle above his brow. The background was chaos, the upper side streaked with an occasional dying star, the lower side dark and cold. But the angel's sword was directed toward a grey stripe left vacant for the figure of the chased demon.

She heard the thud of footsteps across the verandah. There was a screen partitioning off the artist's bed from the studio... she took cover behind it... sank onto the bed... and started peeping... Enter Francesco and the young monk. Her heart was thumping savagely against her ribs on the brink of failing her. The artist showed Ieronim the picture and pointed to the place his face was to occupy on the canvas. Then both withdrew to a cabinet. Caesara sat motionless where she was... keeping a still tongue in her head.

Francesco reappeared, looked for his palette and brushes, spread a blue silk curtain over the window frame turning the air in the room violet blue... drew a black wooden dais to a convenient place, the cabinet door opened and... Caesara had to stifle a cry... a dainty hand stopped her mouth, another one covered her eyes. Let us keep our voices low... I entreat my readers to imagine I am whispering in their ears... but first let us see if Caesara's hand has remained over her eyes. Her breasts had swollen so savagely from her heartthrobs that a button burst free of the tight corset of black velvet... serve her right that she had buttoned it up. But how was she to know that her heart would play ill turns on her? She unbuttoned the corset, her snowy breasts wriggled free of their velvet prison, and she heaved a deep yet inaudible sigh. Then she returned her hand to her eyes to quiet the tumult within her soul... then lifted a finger.... the little one, above her eyes and peeped through the other fingers... She beheld a handsome head on a pair of white broad shoulders on a bust seemingly carved in marble... It was the turn of the necklace to give her a warning... so she undid its clasps and, breathing with more composure, started to feast her eyes on that handsome model whose muscles and forms exuded pride and nobility... She let her hands drop to her sides, for her soul was exhausted with emotion though her eyes were far from satiated. Yet she was still trembling like a leaf and one would have heard her teeth chatter if she had not been careful to keep her mouth closed tight.

The painter's brush swept swiftly along the vacant space on the canvas with downward stroke and Ieronim's forms gained contours under the movements of his hand, curve by curve down to his shoulders on which the painter sketched two long and glossy black wings... The sitting prolonged. Ieronim had been sitting up on the dais straight and proud like an ancient Apollo in the bluish semidarkness of the room which the painter had created purposefully to capture the basic tone of the figure.

"Ieronim!" Francesco broke the silence reigning in the room.

Caesara started at the sound. A discomfiting idea flashed through her mind that the painter was going to draw the screen aside... and she would be found out... with untidy dress, dishevelled hair, her eyes blazing in her head, her face scarlet... But the painter had other things on his mind.

He said:

"I've come to the head. You must have been visited by doubts at least once in your life. Oblige me and recall that moment that I may notice the expression on your face."

Ieronim recalled to mind old Euthanasius's letter and his lips parted slightly in a cold sceptical smile. Oh, that he were turned to marble like that! The proud pain writ all over his face brought a tear into poor Caesara's eyes.

"Right, that's it! Just what I need!" exclaimed Francesco in a fit of inspiration. His eyes sparkled with exhilaration and his brush hurried to catch the traits of painful bitterness on the face of his dark infernal genius.

"How wretched he must have been if the mere memory is apt to change his expression so deeply," thought Caesara and a tender quiet affection suffused her soul... She was not her old self any longer. Her former trembling fit had subsided — she was in love with him now. She gathered that handsome white marble statue, that stone-still Adonis must have a soul... She felt like crying now... her lips parted in a sweet expression of grief and love, she sank her head into the pillows and closed her eyes. She left her long-stifled tears welling freely from her eyes.

"I could do with a few more sittings" said Francesco.

Caesara opened her eyes but... Francesco had draw the curtain and she beheld her Adonis, this time in the clear sunlight. She covered her eyes again and listened to the painter and Ieronim repairing to the inner cabinet. She jumped out of the bed and, noiselessly and stealthily stole out of the studio, ran to her boudoir, threw herself on the bed, hid her face into the pillows and started rumpling them in her hands. When Francesco entered her room she fell on his neck, hugged him spasmodically, caressed, and kissed him...

"What's the matter, my child?"

"Nothing."

"You like him?"

She blurted out a few inarticulate words, her eyes shiny with tears and desire.

V

Caesara to Ieronim:

Bear with a woman confessing her love for you. A pretty young woman, for I dare say I am pretty. Yet, I also know... you look so proud and there is such a cool aloofness in your gaze... Oh! that my mouth could melt the ice on your eyes... my beloved! Wherefore should I conceal my love beneath the veil of prudery... when I love you so deeply that I would fain lower myself to become your servant, if you only would suffer my presence in a corner of your dwelling and suffer me to cover with kisses the pillow whereon you lay your head for your nightly rest. Do you see what a submissive and humble child love can be? You might consider me now an impudent, wicked, and debased woman; yet rest assured that if you would deign to return my love I should behave like a lamb and be as silent as the grave while gazing at you in speechless bliss. However could I sound the depths of your heart? How? Come and tell me... what comes to pass in that nook wherein I should like to dwell... I only. And do you know my name? It is...

Caesara

. . .

Ieronim to Caesara.

That you are pretty, I believe; that you love me, I am thankful; your offering me everything you think that might bring me happiness urges me to lay down my life to your service. I humbly kiss your hand for your willingness to make me happy albeit it is a delusion on your part that any woman's love could accomplish that. Love is a mishap and all the happiness you offer is sheer poison. You being unaware of it makes you the more adorable. If you were to look through my eyes for one moment, how different this world would seem — the world wherein you are seeking and hoping to find the one thing it cannot offer — happiness. You entreat me to return your love. If I could love you as I love a star in the sky, the answer would be — aye! But if you expect me to start sighing and wishing... do I not hear all around the same vulgar sighs, the same yearnings... vulgar, too, for what is their object? Sheer beastly pleasure, the reproduction within the earth's anthill of new generations of worms nursing the same filthy lusts in their breasts, which they are wont to clad in the light of the moon and the shimmer of the lakes, and the same loathsome kisses which they liken to the murmur of the zephyr and the delirium of the beech trees. Aye or nay?

Behold the youths of your world unbosoming their womanish feelings in trite smiles and equivocal whispers — behold those women reciprocating with alluring winks and biting of lips — behold! All human life turns round and round this instinct. Nourishment and reproduction, reproduction and nourishment! And would you have me fall so low?... To beg for a kiss?... to be at your beck and call, to start trembling at the sight of your naked bosom... the bosom that will be a corpse tomorrow, nay, that is essentially a corpse even today? Do you expect me to smarten myself up to your liking, to tell lies so as to divert your wayward mind, to turn into a puppet so as to... whoever could be sure to what end? Nay? I will not be the fool of that plague that rides the world; I take pity on you, on me, as I take pity on the whole world. I would sooner quell the fire in my heart and let it squander its sparks about rather than allow it to kindle a feeling that I consider not only culpable but also vulgar... Let them take delight in their feelings, let them love, let their deaths be as sordid as their lives; I intend to keep myself like an exile, like a pariah, like a madam... indifferent to their ways and wiles! The kernel of life is egotism and its rind is falsehood. I am neither an egotist nor a liar. Oft when standing on a high cliff with the folds of my cloak thrown back over my shoulders I feel I have turned into a bronze statue and that people pass by me well aware that the bronze and themselves share no feelings... Leave me to my pride and indifference. If the world were to be extinguished and it were up to me to save it with a lie, I would sooner let it die than let that lie pass my lips. Wherefore would you have me climb down my pedestal and mix with people? I am only looking skyward, as is Apollo's statue... be my heavenly star, cold and bright! and I shall let my eyes feast on you forever.

I.

• • •

Ieronim had left the monastery on Enthanasius's advice and lived by himself in the city in a little room which he had adorned with flowers and sketches by his own hand. In that hermitage he was often visited by Francesco. One day he showed him Caesara's letter.

"Well, are you going to answer no?"

"This is my answer," he rejoined showing his.

"That's up to you, but come to my studio today, for the picture is finished."

They left and arrived at... Caesara's home.

"The lady Caesara," Francesco introduced her when they were inside.

"Caesara?" murmured Ieronim taken aback and his gaze focused searchingly on the poor girl's shy and blushing face. Ieronim sat in a corner of an ottoman in a bad humour... Francesco walked out; Caesara... knelt at the youth's feet with supplicating hands, her body trembling and her eyes on the verge of tears.

"Oh!" she whispered as if afraid of her words, took his hand in hers and lifted it to her lips — "will you suffer my love? just that, suffer it... for I will not presume on you to return it; just to suffer yourself to be loved... as a child will... I have heard you hate women and you cherish your solitude, but my love for you has driven me to despair..."

He reached an arm round her waist, raised her gently, and sat her by his side, then cradled her nape in the palm of his hand and looked her straight in the eyes for an endless moment... It was so strange... he could hardly believe his eyes.

"Was that straight from your heart?" he asked.

She bowed her head. She had seen him smile which was enough to put a chill on her hopes... "Alas!" she said to herself, "what pleasure could such a man take in a shallow puppet, in a mask of wax? Though... Any other man would feel flattered, but not he... he is not even flattered... he knows it is his due to be loved and he is questioning me as a tutor would question his ward: Straight from your heart?"

A woman of a disposition, prouder of her beauty, would have stalked out of the room blue in the face with anger and deadly offended. No woman offers her love to be spurned. Yet she... she was only sad. She would have cried... would have cried her eyes out but could not bring herself to show the slightest anger.

In his turn, the more he gazed at her, the more beautiful he found her. He felt pity on her yet did not wish to rouse idle hopes in her breast as any other man would have done.

"Far from me to say that you are not beautiful, Caesara. Let us keep our voices low... I shall call you *thou*, for you have become dear to me, though I do not love you in the way I wish I could. Bear with me. I have never fallen in love and perhaps I am not made for love. Yet there is one thing I want you to believe: I do not love any woman, but, if I did, I know that you would be my beloved. I feel some kind of adoration deep in my heart which might turn into love... if... well, if only you did not love me. I do not know how to put into words the strange feeling that cools my heart, I mean that makes it drowsy rather than cool. I have nursed no wishes and you have taught me to do... You might think that strange... yet so do I. I might kiss you... if I were not afraid you would return my kiss; I might love you... when you sulk at me."

"I cannot be... cannot feign... to be any other" she said. "And that is a pity" she added in a calm, lower voice, "for the happiness of my whole life depends on your love... This gives Castelmare a free hand... I have no excuse to oppose the wedding now that you will not have me. I have no wish to leave my father for I can only try to forget my present misfortune by running into a greater misfortune... I am a woman. I deluded myself I was beautiful... I think so no more... I thought I had a right to spurn the love of a man who loved me... and now I am severely chastised with scorn for scorn."

"Caesara" he said in a low, compassionate voice... "will you let me reflect upon this all? My heart and my mind are strange bedfellows; nothing comes to them directly. An idea will linger on the surface of my mind for days on end; it will neither impress nor interest me in the least. It takes many a long day for it to creep into the back of my mind and all of a sudden it grows deep roots among whatever other ideas it might find therein! Caesara... my feelings are no more responsive. Suppose I see a man dropping dead in the street: in that instant it cuts no ice with me... it takes hours for his image to loom large into my mind and only then I will burst out sobbing... and keep on sobbing for a long time as the mishap stays imprinted in my heart. You are begging for my mercy? It is I who needs your mercy... for, if love were to seize my heart, I could die with love. You do not know what to make of me, but this I feel that once love takes hold of me death will follow suit. The one available feeling I have is compassion — and it is all yours. Love me if you will, if — suffer me to utter this sweet word — if you are so merciful as to will it. Do you imagine I am beyond loving you? You are mistaken... Grant me time enough... so that your icon can reach the recesses of my heart, so that I might come to terms with the idea, for up to now I have never known what loving or being loved mean... and I believe there may come a time when I shall go mad with love for you."

He kissed her brow and walked out... She smiled. She picked up a pack of cards, shuffled them to find out if he would come again on the morrow, and whispered quietly while she was aligning them:

"Should he come tomorrow, I will love him; should he not, then... well, then I will love him no less."

· · ·

Ieronim to Euthanasius.

My fancy plays with a maid's visage in its own peculiar way... which is to say I scrawl in an album the various expressions of one visage. It is strange that my eyes for all their limpidity if I may say so, should not be able to perceive any phenomenon at the moment it occurs. I keep scrawling the walls. I have made the acquaintance of a maid who loves me, though I do not love her myself. I saw her face scarlet, bashful, excited... I have rendered that expression in my sketchbook. She knelt at my feet... and begged me to suffer her love... I cannot put into words the look of innocence, candor, and love on her face... but I have sketched it... My sketch is worth kissing. It may be one of the best I have done yet. I have put it by my beside. Discomfiture and sweet resignation. An angelic profile. I vouchsafed her a few kind words. A gleam of hope in the maid's amorous sorrow. An adorable sketch. Yet I can tell my sketches are taking a heavier toll on my heart. I love her not. Nay. Farewell, father.

· · ·

Euthanasius to Ieronim.

You are in love with her, my son, though you know it not. *Cinis et umbra sumus.*

Euthanasius

VI

There are people whom quick-witted men and all women can size up at a glance — men of little wit yet of a hardy, resolute, unyielding character. Such was Castelmare. Should a woman hear him pulling the bellcord, her face would assume the proper expression of welcome; should a good actor hear his stern footsteps resounding steadily and severely along the galleries and corridors of the Bianchi palace, it would be an easy task for him to imagine the man's character by mere hindsight: a nature common, unyielding, and firm.

Having set his mind on prevailing over Caesara by hook or by crook, all means seemed welcome to him, though the means he could devise were scanty, due to the scantiness of his own wits. Yet he had enough brains to try to find out whether the wily girl had a lover.

Albeit Ieronim could not define his feelings for Caesara, he enjoyed obeying her, as a child would obey an elder sister and, if truth be told, she took an unpardonable advantage of her power over him. In her presence he felt an unexplainable tenderness creeping into his heart, an incomprehensible thrill of pleasure, the memory of which would stay with him for days on end. It could not have been love — for, though her presence made him happy, he was even happier when thinking of her in her absence. During such spells of retrospection in which he would toy with her image, her bodily presence was cumbersome to say the least. He would feel nervous in her company — no chance to give free rein to his dreams, an occupation which was the essence of his life and the only happiness a self-contained character, keeping himself beyond love and hate, could relish. "If she would leave me alone," he said to himself, "things would not be half so bad. I would hold her dainty hand in mine and we both would gaze at the moon — the virginal moon; I would gaze at her then as if she were a marble statue or a portrait painted in a book of icons against a luminous background... Her hair is as soft as a spume of gold... and a singular luminescence lights up her face. But she would not allow me a moment's rest... always strangling me... and kissing me — and letting me know I love her. Love her indeed! Otherwise... she is outright beautiful — that much I must concede. Her chin rounds off like a golden apple... at time her mouth takes the shape of a cherry... and the eyes, oh, her eyes! I wish she would not draw them so nigh to mine... when her lashes touch mine my body is all pins and needles down to my toes. For all her beauty... a mist blurs my sight... and I would fain kill her at such moments... She turns my life into an ordeal! Yet the poor girl... in all fairness... little does she know she torments me!"

Now he was strolling about the garden of the Bianchi palace. His dry black hair enframed his tried handsome face of Paros marble like the wings of a wild eagle. His half-closed eyelids showed off the largeness of his demonic, weary, dark blue eyes; his half-opened lips betrayed vivid pain, only his curving neck was actuated with the pride seemingly left intact by life's burden. The night was translucent and the air snowed over with moonbeams creeping through the benighted leafage of the trees. He sat on a bench, his locked hands resting on his knees and his hair streaming down over his bent brow, immersed in a train of disconnected ideas while the moon sailing among the clouds was turning the night into a dreamland. He heard a quiet swish and started awake... It was she. How she had changed! Her face was no longer haggard but rounded off, her breasts were plumper, the blush over her cheeks had vanished in favour of a pallor that lent her an air of undefinable tenderness. There was no trace left about her eyes of the former savage tenebrous lustre beneath which had flashed her dark love and equally dark desire... now they were so limpid and unfathomably deep that they invited the gaze to feast on them for whole days. Quiet and melancholy peace reigned over their depth... And in that rounded yet sad pale face, her purple mouth curved in a dreamy smile... a rose of Jericho of unfading beauty. She was approaching along the walks bathed in the night's clear air, along the white paths dappled with the shadows of the leafy meshes. She noticed him but her pace would not quicken. Had she divined his character? Possibly. He sat still with watchful eyes while she was drawing nearer at a slow pace, like a lunatic or a sleep-walker.

He... rested an elbow against the back of the bench, buried his chin into his palm, his fingers gently stroking his cheek, and let his bright eyes gaze in wonder at her approaching glowing visage. She sat by his side, between him and the moon. She did not as much as touch his hand... just sat still. The moon rendered her contours even more graceful and she was wily enough to contrive her whole body be bathed by the sweet voluptuous light. He kept gazing at her. Then he slowly reached for her cold dainty hand. "Oh!" he thought and an unknown thrill ran through his heart... "Oh! I really like her now." And, with a gentle movement he pressed his cheek

against hers, his mouth fumbling for her ear and whispered in a soft yet
ardent voice:

"Behold the moon, this midnight moon — beauteous like a fortnight
old baby and — so cold. Feel you not that all life's sorrow, every wish and
every aspiration have ceased while gazing at this resplendent picture which
you enrich... My mind's my eye, and it beholds an angel now, beauteous as
you have never looked to me before... and sweet... Do not you see that I am
in love with you...?"

A thrill ran through her body yet she gave no answer.

"And gaze at the whole city, this rich blend of palaces and domes, and
see how the spires in the city and the ship sails along the river glitter in the
moonlight above the benighted dwellings. Withal the centre of the picture is
you... you! you! There is no sound in the air... except a nightingale trilling in
that remote garden and the far-off muffled rumble of a millwheel. And you
are gazing down in silence and innocence upon this world... Roses bloom on
your face... You, queen over all souls — are you not chaste like the spring
water? willowy like the cypress? sweet-voiced like the nightingale herself?
youthful like the full moon, childish like a canary, worshipped like a god-
dess? Behold," he continued in an even lower voice, "that dark narrow
street; in one corner only does a streak of light pierce its shadow, yet the
spot looks like covered with snow... come with me... come to my home... We
will draw aside the curtain at the window and gaze at the sky all night
long... Oh! I love you!"... he exclaimed with finality... "I love you!... the film
over my eyes has vanished and I can see I love you!"

He hugged her so ardently that their bodies were entwined in a long
vigorous embrace. Then, exhausted by his newly-born feeling, he leaned his
body against the back of the bench, closed his eyes, and titled his head back-
ward. Caesara stood over his moonbathed face, put her supporting hands on
the bench, bent over him, half-closed her eyes, and covered his face with
countless kisses. He was past feeling anything... like a child overcome with
sleep abandoning himself to his mother's caresses.

She heard a rustle among the leaves of a thicket. "Goodness me!" she
thought in fright, "what if someone has been spying on me? it might have
been Castelmare himself. Poor child! However is he to return home safely?
That man *could* lie in wait for him!"

She allowed him a minute to sober up... then asked him gently, loath to
intrude on his thoughts and his lifelike dreams:

"Are you any good with a sword?"

"Aye!" said.

"I'll fetch you a blade — shall I?"

"Aye."

"For a kiss."

"Aye."

She hurried off into the palace and was back in a couple of minutes with a sword; she girded the belt round his waist not missing the opportunity of another embrace.

"My sweet ice floe — you, block of marble! you stone, you!"

"Leave me alone, Caesara. I feel like dying."

"Nay, my angel... go home... Take good care nothing befalls you on the way... think of your Caesara... my own gem." She could not forbear taking his head in her hands and giving him one more kiss... a passionate and noisy one.

"Go now, go! I beg you."

"Why beg me?"

"I could kill you if you lingered here."

"How?"

"Don't I know how?" she said, wily as a child.

She walked him to a thicket and pushed him out of the garden. Then she turned back, threw her arms round a tree trunk, and unbosomed her thwarted desires.

"Ieronim! I'll bite you now!"

She smote her fists against the trunk; then repaired to her room, tore off her velvet corset, tousled her golden hair in a frenzy, and looked in a mirror at her tear-stained eyes and quivering lips. Then she threw herself onto the bed in a sobbing fit and started whispering in an almost inaudible voice sweet words, exceedingly sweet and endearing. One name came out loud and clear through her moans... Ieronim.

It was not so easy for Ieronim. He was approaching a narrow street, the night's bracing air had sobered him and, being of a less sensual disposition than his sweetheart, only a theoretical conviction that he was in love with her had remained in his mind. He walked on along the dark street, his springy step bespeaking, as it were, an elastic weight, his gait resembling the canter of a thoroughbred, and he heard the thuds of soldierly rigid and regular footsteps following him. He recognized them as belonging to Castelmare. He stopped short and turned toward the noise... Castelmare caught up with him... A hushed silence. Ieronim struck his blade point against a granite wall and the sparks enabled the rivals to recognize each other. Without wasting words they crossed swords, then a groan was heard... a heavy thud on the rough pavement; one of the two shadows vanished into a house close by... the other lay there speechless.

VII

Ieronim had drawn aside the curtain and was now lying on his bed looking out of the window at the setting moon sinking into the river and turning its surface into a luminescent smooth road, when he heard the sound of cautious rapping at the door. He got out of bed and answered it. It was the painter.

"Young man," the latter urged, "you will have to flee this city post-haste."

"Why?"

"You have killed Castelmare."

"I know as much."

"You know as much. But what you do not seem to know is that he is the grandson and sole heir of this city's podestà and also that duelling is outlawed and that you may hang for it."

"So what?"

"So what? Ieronim, my son, however have you come into this manner of speaking?" the old man added placatingly. "It would be a pity to lose such a good-looking head. Besides, there is one more thing to consider... here it is."

He handed him a sheet of paper scrawled with slanting lines. The youth unfolded it.

Caesara to Ieronim

Run away, please. You have not killed Castelmare. Choking with blood he ordered his men to carry him here. He has divulged the whole story, including the man to whom he owes his wound. Run away... please! They might come for you before the night is out. What is worse: the count will affiance me regardless of his plight and I am powerless to refuse!... Yet I love you. Rest assured I shall not outlive my misfortune. Your lingering here, far from saving me, would only make me die with worry... my hawk! Run away and perhaps... woe me! Where is the straw I could catch at?... I am in two minds about what to write... How I would write: come to me, but my heart will not let me. Consider: should I destroy you only to behold you once more? Nay. Run away, Ieronim; some chance event might still make me yours... the count might die... How I wish he would... I love you! Nay, nay! I will not have you think I love you so much as to bid you stay... Farewell... my beloved!

Caesara

Ieronim threw a cloak over his shoulders and they walked to the river-bank where Francesco let him have his own boat. He embraced his aged friend, unfastened the boat, stepped into it, and sailed downstream to the shiny expanse of the sea and once beyond the waterfront, he threw the helm and oars into the water, lay back on the bottom of the boat, his face upturned toward the star-studded grandeur of the sky and — a mere speck adrift across the boundless water — he felt fast asleep.

On the morrow when he opened his eyes the sun was high in the sky... and his boat had been stranded among a rocky outcrop... The sun, the heavenly lord, caressed the bosom of the sea with fingers of light. On the shore of the mainland he saw an old convent rising from among the wooded rocks, with a cloister lined with colonnades of grey stone along which the nuns were taking the air at a slow and regular pace. A garden rolled down from beneath the walls to the shore of the undulating sea which reached its waves toward a grove of cypresses and rosebushes sheltered among the rocks in a declivity sloping down to a secluded bathing place.

He took off his shoes and set to exploring his rocky kingdom leaping from boulder to boulder. He came across a swift brook running noisily from the inside of a cave. He entered the cave... a bracing coolness welcomed him after his sun-scorched sleep... on and on he went... but the cave was longer and darker than he had expected. Presently he spied a speck of blue light but he brushed the thought aside for one of his imaginings. Yet the light did not vanish and he went down deeper and discovered a hole no larger than his hand. It must lead somewhere... he peeped through it... and saw large thickets and smelt a sleep-inducing fragrance of herbs. He strove to enlarge the hole with his bare hands, but it was a granite wall and his exertions were of no avail; yet it seemed to him a big boulder had given in a little. He pushed it hard — the boulder turned as if set on hinges and disclosed a narrow passage which he could negotiate by crawling on all fours. He squeezed through quickly, pushed it back into place, covered the hole with stones and dirt and, on turning his head to take a look at the place he had entered, he was stunned with the beauty of the landscape.

Gigantic grey rocks were piled up sky high on all sides and a vale sloped down in their midst, a garden-vale furrowed by springs subsiding into a lake crowned with an islet on which he saw an apiary with long rows of beehives.

"Euthanasius's island!" he thought in amazement and each step he put forward held a new wonder in store for him. The insects themselves were tame in this garden of Eden. Inquisitive blue, gold-speckled, or red-winged butterflies alighted on his long black hair so his head looked like strewn with flowers. The island air was suffused with the festive buzz of honeybees, bumblebees, and butterflies; the grass grew chest high and the vetch trapped his legs in loops of flowers... a voluptuous warmth and fragrance pervaded the garden. He walked to the lake and waded its water to the islet. Buzzing bees kept hovering over the youthful new emperor of their paradise. He looked around for the cave he knew had to be there on that islet; he found it true to fact carved into a wall of rock, saw the chisel and other sculpting tools, the bedstead, a jug of water; yet there was no trace of the old man. A written sheet of paper lay on a low table.

I feel my marrow turning to dust, my slow-moving blood is thin as water and cold as ice, my dimmed eyes can but painstakingly discern the world without. I am passing away. And of me only the earthen brazier will remain wherein the light of a rich life has burnt. I shall cuddle beneath a brook's waterfall so that creepers and waterflowers might gird my body in their verdure and entwine my hair and beard with their stalks... and in my palms, turned up toward that eternal fountainhead of life which you call "the Sun," may a swarm of wasps build their honey combs, their waxen citadel. May the running brook dissolve my body into its eternally fresh water and merge me with the bosom of nature and may it save me from putrefaction. Thus my dead body will stay for long years beneath the swift-running torrent like an old fairy tale king, in a centuries-long slumber in a bewitched island.

Ieronim swept his glance along the walls embossed with love scenes, noticed the old books and the stacks of sundry writings on the shelves of a case lining one of the walls, then smelled the water in the pitcher and, seeing it was flat and foul, concluded the old man must have passed away.

Thus he, the heir apparent to this peaceful shrine, to this garden walled-in like a cell, felt at liberty to thumb the books whose pages were worth their weight in gold and promising of many an hour of spiritual delectation; then he passed on to the old man's writings wherein each and every reflection was a stamp of that profound and blissful mind, their impact so powerful that every sentence roused an endless trait of thoughts and analogies in the youth's brain. Before long he familiarized himself with his tiny kingdom and felt at home in it, and made busy tending the garden beds and the beehives, stalking like a buck-deer among the islet's thickets and grasses. Oft of a warm night he would lie naked on the lakeside tucked in a flimsy sheet of linen cloth and the sweet sounds of nature — the gurgling of the white-foamed springs, the rumble of the sea, the grandeur of the night — all concurred in lulling him into a blissful sound sleep wherein he went on living like a plant beyond suffering, beyond dreams, beyond desires.

VIII

On the day when the wedding of Caesara and Castelmare was to be celebrated, her father, the Marquis Bianchi, died of an apoplectic fit in the company of his boon companions and amid clinking of glasses. When she beheld him lying in state, the lids still open above his glassy eyes, foam still trickling down the corners of his mouth, she leaned against the architrave of a window and cast a look of disgust at the corpse who had known no goal in life other than the gratification of his own desires and who, in order to continue giving free rein to his passions, had contemplated selling his daughter, an icon of the Madonna, to the man she hated most bitterly in the world.

Castelmare put it an appearance and started consoling her:

"Countess," he said, "now that your sire has passed away, you will find comfort and support in me, your pledged husband."

"That's a cold consolation" she rejoined, "for you have ceased to be any pledged husband — at least my year of mourning has procrastinated that blessed prospect. Will you kindly spare me your presence before the year is up?"

Castelmare stalked out disgruntled, turning a wolfish glare upon her. Francesco advised her to leave the city where she would be importuned with the tempers of her cruel admirer, to retire to a nunnery at a few hours' distance — advice she followed readily after her father's obsequies.

The poor child had grown thin with grief... the only news she had of Ieronim was that Francesco's boat, which he had sailed out to sea, had been found shattered to pieces on the seafront, so she thought he had drowned and been dead for a long time.

Within the quiet monastery walls she regained her composure. The window of the cell assigned to her overlooked the garden and the seafront; and oft she would bolt the door to be free of intrusion and stare for long hours at the myriads of waves vanishing in the offing, at the blooming wilderness of the rolling garden which reached its tangle of thickets and trees to the shoreline — or, at other times she would lose herself along the shadowy walks weeding the grasses that invaded the footpaths, or would take shelter beneath some thicket by the shore heedless of the hours passing by, prey to her hopeless yearning.

On a warm day she would take off her clothes, leave them beneath some thicket, and walk down to the shore. An exquisite figure, a snowy apparition whereon the youthful delicacy and softness of girlhood enhanced the noble, ripe, suave, and well-curved beauty of the woman. The violet-blue veins showed through the general transparency of her smooth skin and, as her feet waded through the water abandoning her body to its mellowing embrace, her smile regained the wayward unruliness of childhood; struggling against the time-old ocean she felt even younger than her years, the smile of her closed lips exuded vitality, and her body yielded to the boisterous embrace of the ocean, her white arms slicing the blue waves, swimming on her side or with backstrokes, or just lounging voluptuously on the bed of waves.

The light merged into dusk and she resumed her love affair with the sea, smiling at the approaching waves with intense and sweet voluptuousness; she had bared her snowy throat and let her hair stream down over her round shoulders and her love-swollen breasts and stood naked and beauteous like an ancient statue, yet surpassing it in beauty for she was endowed with life and a warm, sweet, and smooth skin whereon the mere touch would have left the marks of bruises. She dived into the sea and set her mind on reaching a group of cliffs about a quarter of an hour's swimming distance.

The submissive waves carried her and before long she reached the cliffs. She walked carefully along the bluff leaning her hands against the rocky wall and came across a cave wherefrom a glittery spring was flowing out along a rocky bed; she entered the cave keeping to the brook and all of a sudden a heavenly panorama opened wide before her eyes...

"By God, what a paradise!" she thought, "I will rest here for a little while." She walked on through the warm sweet-smelling grasses which tickled her skin, dived into the crystal-clear lake whose water made her slumberous, then ran through the orange grove chased by a swarm of butterflies and bees... She was frolicsome like a child wandering about a bewitched fairyland. At long last, noticing the sun had skirted the horizon, she tried to retrace her steps, but to her consternation she could see no way out.

What was she to do? Thinking she had lost her way she swept her glance all about her... still no way out...

"Oh!" she thought, "what if I spent one night in this earthly paradise? Not a soul around to pry or chide me for it."

. . .

Night had closed in. Large white stars were twinkling and the moon's silver shield was sailing across the sky, tearing through the waves of translucent rolling clouds. Sheaves of blooming flowers intoxicated the warm night air, the hills shimmered beneath a veil of mist, the quiet water girding the grove was glazed white and every now and then it washed the slumberous lakeside with trembling waves. And in the midst of this benighted fairyland encircled by the sea Caesara sauntered like a snowy apparition, her long fair hair streaming down to her heels... She walked at a slow pace... All the dreams and charms of the fragrant summer night suffused her virginal soul... she could have cried! The figure of her beloved loomed large in her mind's eye and she felt as Eve must have felt in Paradise, alone with her sorrow. She drew nigh to the lake and descried a footpath beneath the water. She set to pacing it and the water whirled round her ankles... She held her gaze on the charming grove... a yearning for happiness took possession of her bosom... she thirsted for love like an unripe youthful girl, her lips were parched with pining for a kiss, her thoughts impassioned like a bed of flowers drooping in the drought. When she reached the grove the scented shadow of the tall trees flooded her skin with their blue reflection and she looked like a marble statue against the violet-blue light... She started at descrying the figure of a man among the trees... she thought it must be one of her imaginings taking shape against the leafy meshes... yet the figure took on sharper outlines... it was *he*.

"Alas!" she thought with a smile, "how foolish of me... I see him wherever I may turn my eyes, in the beauty of the night, in the hush of the groves..." He came nearer... He likewise thought an embodied imagining was standing before his eyes... He stared at her, they stared at each other.

He took her hand in his... and she unbosomed a stifled cry.

"Caesara," he cried, enfolding her in his arms..." Caesara! are you an apparition, a dream, a shadow the night has painted with the moonlight snow? Or is it you? Really you?"

She was sobbing... and no word of answer would pass her lips. She thought she had gone mad, she thought it was all a dream and how she wished her dream would last for ever and ever!

"Is it you? Really you?" she asked in a strangled voice, for her mind was sober again and all resplendent dreams were crowding it, eager to come true... She could nor would tear her gaze off him... heedless of her nakedness.

Translated by Ioan Giurgea
Revised by Kurt W. Treptow

Printed by R.A. MONITORUL OFICIAL